Richard Rayner is the author of eight previous books, including *The Blue Suit, Drake's Fortune,* and *The Associates: Four Capitalists Who Created California.* His work appears in *The New Yorker,* the *Los Angeles Times,* and other publications. He lives with his family in Los Angeles.

"Los Angeles—a bright and guilty place."
—Orson Welles

A BRIGHT and GUILTY PLACE

Richard Rayner

Constable • London

For Paivi and Harry and Charlie

Constable & Robinson Ltd
3 The Lanchesters
162 Fulham Palace Road
London W6 9ER
www.constablerobinson.com

First published in the US by Doubleday, 2009
This edition published in the UK by Constable,
an imprint of Constable & Robinson Ltd, 2010

A copy of the British Library Cataloguing in
Publication data is available from the British Library

ISBN: 978-1-84901-205-8

Printed and bound in the EU

1 3 5 7 9 10 8 6 4 2

Contents

Acknowledgments vii
Cast of Characters ix
Photo Credits xiii

1 The Mystery Is Announced 1
2 Dam Disaster 9
3 A Hero Named Clark 21
4 Angel City 32
5 The Gangster Goes Down 45
6 Oil, Law, and Scandal 54
7 Our Detective Learns the Ropes 65
8 Shots in the Night 72
9 Beverly Hills C.S.I. 79
10 Cover-Up 89
11 Good Time Charlie 100
12 Systems Under Siege 116
13 Reach for a Typewriter 129

Contents

14 Raymond Chandler – Oil Man! 135

15 Entrapment of a News Hound 144

16 Running with the Foxes.....................................151

17 Zig-Zags of Graft 158

18 Red Hot Bow 171

19 The Gutting of Clara 180

20 Hard Times in Lotus-Land 192

21 Double Death on Sunset 200

22 The Ballad of Dave Clark 211

23 They Can Hang You...227

24 Telling It All 238

25 Verdicts 251

26 A Hooker's Tale...261

27 Music of the City...268

28 Black Mask Merry-Go-Round 276

29 Sad Song...285

30 Lives Go On...291

31 A Personal Note 298

     Sources 305

     Bibliography..316

Acknowledgments

So many people lent a hand during the writing of *A Bright and Guilty Place* that it's tough to know where to begin. My particular thanks go to "Skip" and Kathy White, the children of Leslie White, for their help and encouragement.

Vicki Steele and Simon Elliott and everybody else at UCLA Special Collections were unfailingly diligent and generous. Likewise Fernando Sauceda and Carolyn Cole at the magnificent Los Angeles Public Library's photo collection. Charles Johnson, historian, perched in his timbered aerie in the lovely building that formerly housed the Ventura County Museum, was brilliant. Archivist J. C. Johnson was my guide to the Leslie T. White Collection in the Howard Gottlieb Center at Boston University. John Wilkman, in the process of completing a documentary film about the St. Francis Dam disaster, gave me invaluable pointers. Russell Johnson, lecturer at the University of Otago in New Zealand, graciously let me see his research on Clara Bow. Thanks to Michael Parrish for sharing his insights and knowledge concerning the L.A. County District Attorney's office, where Sandy Gibbons, in the press office, always returned my calls and helped me find the Dave Clark trial documents. My friends at the Santa Monica Library Used Book Store helped me track down many books of local history.

This subject has haunted me for years. During that time I've had useful, inspiring, suggestive conversations with many friends and colleagues: David Ulin, Nick Owchar, D. J. Waldie, Carolyn See, Ric Burns, Paul Greengrass, Cressida Leyshon, Dave Smith, Jonas Goodman, Dan Conaway, Norman Klein, Tom Curwen, Bruce Hentshall, Judith Freeman, Peter Loewenberg, Tom Tomlinson, Matthew Snyder, Pete Micelli, Taylor Hackford, and Pico Iyer. Thanks to all.

Bill Thomas commissioned the book at Doubleday. Kris Puopolo edited it and made it about a hundred times better. Her careful readings and suggestions were always on the money and inspirational. Many thanks also to editor Kate Henderson and to Stephanie Bowen. My agent, Jeff Posternak at the Wylie Agency, was as always a sounding board, a support, and a great friend.

Cast of Characters

Leslie White: An eager and bespectacled young photographer turned investigator whose experiences in Los Angeles later inspire his career as a pulp-fiction writer.

Dave Clark: A suave war hero and crusading prosecutor, drawn into the darkness of the rackets.

Nancy Clark: A petite blonde, daughter of a famed New York judge and Dave Clark's volatile yet adoring wife.

Albert Marco, aka Marco Albori: A plug-ugly gangster brought down by Clark.

Gene Coughlin: A top reporter for many L.A. papers, notably the tabloid *Illustrated Daily News*, who comes to know Clark only too well.

Buron Fitts: A decorated WWI marine and longtime District Attorney for Los Angeles, he becomes an immensely controversial and influential figure in the city's history.

Cast of Characters

Asa "Ace" Keyes: Fitts's predecessor as D.A., indicted for bribery.

Lucien Wheeler: A graduate of Notre Dame, secret service bodyguard to presidents, FBI bureau chief, and private eye—a man of power and subtlety, carving a high-profile career in law enforcement.

Blayney Matthews: An investigator for Buron Fitts and another former FBI man, he was also White's colleague and pal.

C. C. Julian: A breezy oil speculator and Ponzi-scheme operator whose company, Julian Petroleum (the Julian Pete), seizes the imagination of L.A.—and much of the city's cash.

Jake Berman, aka Jack Bennett: A slick and handsome con artist, milking millions from the house of cards that Julian built.

E. L. Doheny: An aging oil magnate—the richest man in L.A. in the 1920s, and one of the richest in America—embroiled in the nationwide scandal known as "Teapot Dome."

Ned Doheny, Jr.: His only son, found dead with a bullet in his brain one night in 1929.

Hugh Plunkett: Ned's personal secretary, chauffeur, friend, and possibly more; he is also found shot through the head.

Charlie Crawford, aka The Gray Wolf: A one-time saloon keeper who runs the Los Angeles "System," the discreet yet all-powerful and money-spinning network of graft and racketeering; he meets his end with a slug from a Colt pistol.

Kent Parrot: A USC football hero, law school graduate, and political force; he is also Crawford's enabler who has the mayor in his pocket.

Morris Lavine: A famed newsman for the *Los Angeles Examiner* with a finger in too many corrupt pies; he later becomes a top attorney.

Erle Stanley Gardner: An attorney in Ventura County who works at his law firm all day and writes 4,000 words of fiction every night; he becomes a close friend of Leslie White's.

Raymond Chandler: The future noir laureate of L.A., who worked through the 1920s as an oil executive; he sees and remembers it all.

Dashiell Hammett: The former Pinkerton detective and leading light of hardboiled writing; he plays an unwitting part in the demise of a Hollywood star.

The Reverend Robert "Fighting Bob" Shuler: A radio evangelist whose down-home appeal and attacks on Hollywood depravity make him a political player.

The Reverend Gustav Briegleb: Shuler's onetime lieutenant and later his rival; friend to Charlie Crawford.

Motley Flint: A banker to Hollywood and brother to a U.S. senator; gunned down in court.

Clara Bow: The biggest movie star of her era, a reckless redheaded bombshell who beds Gary Cooper, John Gilbert, John Wayne, et al., et al.

Cast of Characters

Daisy DeVoe: Clara Bow's tough and smart-mouthed assistant, herself no slouch in the vixen department.

Herbert Spencer: Another reporter working all the angles; also killed by a bullet.

Guy McAfee: Nicknamed "Slats" and "Beanpole" due to his height; onetime LAPD vice cop turned racketeer; plotting to seize control of The System.

June Taylor: Albert Marco's trusted confidante and a knockout brothel keeper; instrumental in Clark's downfall.

W. I. Gilbert: A canny defense attorney and friend to the stars, celebrated for his courtroom stunts.

Joseph Ford: A veteran prosecutor and founder of the law school at Loyola Marymount University.

Lincoln Steffens: Author of *The Shame of the Cities*, classic muckraking account of urban American graft, and a mentor to Leslie White.

With supporting appearances from:

William Mulholland, Roscoe "Fatty" Arbuckle, Earl Rogers, F. Scott Fitzgerald, Edmund Wilson, Louis Adamic, Carey McWilliams, Al Capone, Budd Schulberg, B. P. Schulberg, Alexander Pantages, Jerry Giesler, David O. Selznick, Charlie Chaplin, Albert Einstein, Myron Brinnig, John Fante, Horace McCoy, James M. Cain . . . and others.

Photo Credits

1

The Mystery
Is Announced

"CHARLIE CRAWFORD AND EDITOR SLAIN!" screamed the headline in the *Los Angeles Illustrated Daily News*. The date was Thursday, March 20, 1931. At about 4:30 P.M. the previous afternoon the fifty-four-year-old Crawford, nicknamed "The Gray Wolf" because of the silvery-gray hair that waved and curled across his head, had been gunned down in his office on Sunset Boulevard. Also killed was Herbert Spencer, a veteran journalist who'd been with Crawford in the room. "EX-BOSS FALLS TO LONG-FEARED GUNMAN BULLET," the *News* went on. "Crawford, kingpin politician, lived until 8:32 P.M. last night, a little more than four hours after the shooting. He died without revealing the identity of his assailant, according to detectives . . ."

Crawford had been, and many believed he still was, a "boss," a key player in what was known as "The System," a low-profile but all-powerful syndicate that ran the gambling,

1

prostitution, and bootlegging rackets in Los Angeles. "He was the most feared and dictatorial power in the city, its behind-the-scenes czar," wrote Beverly Davis, who ran an upscale brothel for Crawford. "You could get away with murder under his wing." This was L.A.'s brand of gangsterism: Crawford used officers of the Los Angeles Police Department to collect the take from the underworld captains. He worked behind the scenes with Kent Kane Parrot, a fixer who'd had George Cryer, the mayor of Los Angeles from 1921–29, pretty much in his pocket. It was a discreet yet effective arrangement that had been in place since Crawford and Parrot contrived to get Cryer elected. As far as the rackets were concerned, L.A. had been a closed town ever since, locked down by Crawford and The System. "It was the most lucrative, the most efficient, and the best-entrenched graft operation in the country," *News* city editor Matt Weinstock wrote later. Now somebody was monkeying with that operation, trying to destroy it perhaps, or take it over.

"Racketeer bullets declared open warfare in the Los Angeles underworld yesterday," said the *L.A. Examiner*. "MAN HUNT ON!" An announcement went out over the newly perfected LAPD radio system: "Wanted for murder—an American, about six feet tall, weighing between 150 and 175 pounds, and between 35 and 40 years of age. Hair, brown. A small black moustache. Dressed in neat blue suit and wearing sailor straw hat."

Was this the killer? It seemed so.

"The political structure rocked precariously while everybody tried to imagine who could have fired the fatal shots," wrote Leslie White, a young detective working in the investigative unit of the District Attorney's office. For

White, the case had a particular significance, a poignancy almost. He'd met Charlie Crawford several times and had liked him. "Despite the unanimous opinion that the murder of Crawford was a piece of civic betterment, I felt a pang," White wrote. "Would his death improve the city in any way? I doubted it. A new boss might be less efficiently corrupt. The King was dead—but who would seek the throne?"

White worked downtown, in the Hall of Justice, a new building opposite the even newer white tower of City Hall. On that morning after the shootings, White was in his small cubbyhole of an office, talking with colleagues, trying to figure out who could have pulled the trigger when his boss, Blayney Matthews, the burly and genial head of the D.A.'s investigative unit, came in with the news.

"We're looking for Dave Clark," Matthews said.

Leslie White blinked—unable, for a moment, to believe his ears. *"Our* Dave Clark," he said.

"That's right," Matthews said, and White rocked back in his chair. Dave Clark—known to the press as "Debonair Dave" or "Handsome Dave"—was a crusading litigator and former assistant district attorney who was now running for judge. He was a war hero with matinee-idol looks. He was, moreover, Leslie White's friend.

"Had the chief suddenly accused *me* of the crime, I couldn't have been more astounded," White wrote.

Sorry to see Dave Clark's name in any way connected with this sensational crime, White hoped for the best, believing that at any moment Clark would arrive at the Hall of Justice and clear his name. But hours went by and nothing happened, and White himself became involved in the unavailing search for the suspect. Dave Clark had vanished, nowhere to be found.

A great crime saga had been set in motion, with toothsome details that Raymond Chandler—who, at the time, was an executive in L.A.'s oil business—would soon feed directly into one of his very first works of fiction, the short story "Spanish Blood." Chandler, when he turned to writing, wrote what he knew, and he knew Los Angeles—not just its map and climates, but its history of corruption and violence. Like James M. Cain, Horace McCoy, and others who wrote in and about L.A. during the years of the Great Depression, Chandler drew material from the headlines and bullet-prose of the tabloids. True crime tells the story of how L.A. got hardboiled and noir.

Flash back to 1910, when the population of Los Angeles was 310,000 or thereabouts, many of them Spanish-speaking. "There were more cows than people," says the writer and historian D. J. Waldie, and he might not have been joking. Ten years later, in 1920, the population was 576,000. By 1930 the figure would rise to 1,250,000, and L.A. County—which gathers together various unincorporated cities, including Santa Monica, Beverly Hills, Venice, and Culver City, as well as the city of L.A. itself—would be home to almost 2.5 million souls.

Throughout this astonishing period, L.A. was the fastest-growing city in the world. In America only San Francisco had ever grown so fast, during the years of the Gold Rush following 1849. But by the 1920s, San Francisco's boom was long done. New York, Boston, and even Chicago had never known an explosion like the one that was happening in L.A. Every working day throughout the 1920s, builders started more than fifty new homes. Each week a new hotel went up. The year 1923 alone saw the construction of 800 office buildings, 400 industrial buildings, 150 schools, 130 warehouses, 700 apartment buildings, and more than 25,000 single dwellings. Property prices doubled, tripled, quadrupled, eventually rising sixfold through the decade. The city began to spread, amoeba-like, in search of its suburbs, although in those days L.A. still meant downtown, thriving with business and residences. In 1923 a *Saturday Evening Post* article about the boom ran a photo showing the district, chockablock with office buildings, all about twelve to fifteen stories tall, as high as the earthquake regulations would then allow. "Most of these buildings are less than a year old," said the caption.

L.A. was "a civilization that will not need to hang its head when the Athens of Pericles is mentioned," wrote the *New Republic* in 1927—when L.A. seemed like a strapping youth, foolish and violent at times, bursting out of its skin with exuberance. Within a few years the *New Republic*'s pronouncement would seem bizarre and deluded. By 1931 the depression gripped California. Capitalism was in crisis and people no longer spoke of L.A. as a utopia with the added luxury of a voluptuous climate. Rather, for a while the whole social fabric was stretched and tattered and in danger of being torn in two. L.A. still had the sunshine, but it could be a lonely and hellish place—rife with crime, riddled by corruption, and drained of civic and moral purpose. Banks failed, thousands of businesses went to the wall, foreclosures hit epidemic proportions, and empty lots awaited the rush of investment that had until recently seemed so certain. People blew their brains out, gassed themselves, hanged themselves, took pills and poison, slit their wrists, or walked into the ocean. Southern California became America's suicide capital, an amazing phenomenon on which Edmund Wilson would report for the *New Republic*, driven to revise its previous optimism. In 1931 alone there were over 750 suicides in L.A.; so many threw themselves from the handsome Colorado Street Bridge crossing the Arroyo Seco Canyon in Pasadena that the city first appointed a special police detail to guard the bridge and, when that didn't work, erected high fences of barbed wire to stop people from jumping which remain to this day.

In its early days, L.A. attracted lower middle-class and middle middle-class retirees from the American Midwest, people drawn to the life of relaxed ease promoted in the booster ads of L.A.'s Chamber of Commerce. A further growth spurt came with the development of an industrial base in the 1920s. At the same time the recently arrived movie business began to attract a different sort of young person—attractive, ambitious, driven. One could argue that L.A. needed and invented Hollywood in order to provide itself with a different demographic and to achieve maturity. Then yet another element was thrown into the mix. After 1929 the character of immigration changed again as the roads into California filled with the armies of the indigent and the unemployed, riding in battered jalopies or hitchhiking. At the height of the Depression 1,500 arrived daily, many of them boys, said *The Nation*, "who beat their way out on freight trains and are in danger of becoming hopeless tramps or criminals."

In this defeated atmosphere, the expressionless blue of the sky and the unchanging rhythm of perfect days that followed each other one after the other added to the melancholy. "Outside the bright gardens had a haunted look, as though wild eyes were watching me from behind the bushes, as though the sunshine itself had a mysterious something in the light," wrote Raymond Chandler.

Cities have characters, pathologies that can make or destroy or infect you, states of mind that run through daily life as surely as a fault line. Chandler's "mysterious something" was a mood of disenchantment, an intense spiritual malaise that identified itself with Los Angeles at a particular time, what we call noir. On the one hand noir is a narrow film genre, born in Hollywood in the late 1930s when a European visual style, the twisted perspectives and stark chiaroscuros of German Expressionism, met an American literary idiom. This fruitful comingling gave birth to movies like *Double Indemnity*, directed by Vienna-born Billy Wilder and scripted by Raymond Chandler from a James M. Cain novella. The themes—murderous sex and the cool, intricate amorality of money—rose directly from the psychic mulch of Southern California.

But L.A. is a city of big dreams and cruelly inevitable disappointments where noir is more than just a slice of cinema history; it's a counter-tradition, the dark lens through which the booster myths came to be viewed, a disillusion that shadows even the best of times, an alienation that assails the senses like the harsh glitter of mica in the sidewalk on a pitiless Santa Ana day. Noir—in this sense a perspective on history and often a substitute for it—was born when the Roaring Twenties blew themselves out and hard times rushed in; it crystallized real-life events and the writhing collapse of the national economy before finding its interpreters in writers like Raymond Chandler.

In this book I evoke the time when Los Angeles came of age and found a defining tone. Many people—some famous, others not—will feature in an urban mosaic in which everything and everybody seems to be connected, and, in one way or another, is corrupt, is seeking corruption, or is trying to escape it. But, for me, the story belongs most prominently to two very different young men, both long dead and largely forgotten: Leslie T. White and David H. Clark. White, as we've seen, was for a while a D.A.'s investigator. In time he, like Raymond Chandler, would transform himself into a writer. For Clark, the veteran from WWI and high-flying attorney, the future would be very different. White, who was small and slight and peered at the world through horn-rimmed spectacles, proved himself undauntable. The tall and suave Clark, with his movie star looks and his huge promise, went wrong in a most spectacular way. These contrasting trajectories have much to say about Los Angeles, and maybe about America. The two men are symbols of light and dark, linked emblems in a city's scandalous process of becoming.

2

Dam Disaster

In 1928 the boom ran full tilt and the leaks in L.A.'s destiny had yet to appear. Nobody guessed yet that depression and a haunted future were around the corner, waiting to wash bright hope away. Leslie White was living in Ventura, about fifty miles north of the city. He was in his mid-twenties, recently married, and had his own photography business. Murder, and indeed Los Angeles itself, were far from his mind.

Ventura had a population of fewer than 15,000. It had a Main Street, a courthouse, one of the original Spanish missions, and two small newspapers. On an average after-noon, its air was thick with the smell of citrus. But this country town was being transformed by oil fields that had been discovered nearby. Several of these gushers had been brought in by Ralph Lloyd in partnership with Joseph Dabney, the former a friend of Raymond Chandler's and the latter who happened to be his boss in 1928. The existence of these Ventura fields, and a dispute concerning revenues from them, would be of great and surprising significance for Chandler's career as a writer. But that was in the future.

Leslie White came to Ventura in 1922. Born on May 12, 1903, he'd been raised in Canada—in Ottawa, Ontario. His father died when he was seven years old; his mother and aunts, strict Methodists, took the young boy to church three times a week, doing their best to point him in the ways of the Lord. He left school at fifteen, prone to ill health, and with an earnest and highly moral worldview. In Northern Canada he worked in a lumber mill and as a railroad fireman. He claimed, too, that he'd tried his hand as a prizefighter and traveled with a carnival. Certainly he loved adventure, and all his life he would be restless, searching for the next interest. On arrival in Ventura he secured a job as a park ranger, saying he knew how to ride though he'd never been on a horse. Mounting for the first time, he slipped and fell, breaking a collar bone. After he recovered, he went back to work, protecting land that had been bought for rich hunters. He became a deputy sheriff, despite admitting that what he knew of the law was "gleaned from Conan Doyle and motion pictures." His superiors called him "The Kid." He was touchy about his physique and youth, and he had a firecracker temper. Once he arrested a man for having carnal relations with a cow. On the lonely fog-swept promontory of Point Magu, he watched rumrunners armed with machine-guns bringing their crates of bootleg booze ashore. Gung ho, he was about to steam in to make some arrests when his superior warned him off, pointing out that the trucks into which the rumrunners were loading their stuff were driven and guarded by cops from the LAPD. This early brush acquainted White with how things worked in the big bad city where, as he would later write, "brains and money, or, better still, a combination of both, could sabotage the machinery of justice at will."

White shifted jobs frequently. The 1926 Ventura County directory lists him as a driver for Shell Oil and has him living on Poli Street, close to the courthouse. By 1928, however, he was married to Thelma, his first wife, and had opened the Leslie White Studio on Main Street. He loved gadgets and machines and had transformed himself into a photographer. He made portraits, or pictures of weddings and christenings, and did fingerprint and identification work for Ventura's newly inaugurated police force. His business did well. A wall-sized blowup of one of his street scenes is still featured in the main Ventura library. He was also learning to fly and was a fan of Clara Bow, whose film *Red Hair* finally reached Ventura in March 1928. White was a member of the Chamber of Commerce, the Rotary Club, and the Breakfast Club (at one meeting of which he caused a rumpus by releasing, as a prank, a tame circus lion!).

Leslie White was a success, and if truth be told, more than a little bored; but that was about to change.

At three minutes before midnight on March 12, 1928, in Los Angeles County, near the Ventura County line, an abutment to the St. Francis Dam gave way. Twelve billion gallons of retained water stirred into life. At that moment a motor-cyclist happened to be riding along the road at the reservoir's edge; he said the area of water, covering 38,000 acres and more than three and a half miles, appeared to grow still and shiver.

The water began to move, ripping through first one side of the dam and then the other, leaving only the dam's central section, a 200-foot-high hunk of concrete that lurched forward but nonetheless was left standing like an ugly tooth. On either side, a liquid avalanche was released, shaking the walls of the San Francisquito Canyon with a noise that was "a monster in the night, roaring like a tornado." Seventy families, mostly Mexican fruit pickers, lived immediately below the dam. They stood no chance.

Fifty miles to the south, the lights of Los Angeles flickered. For a few seconds, the entire city fell into darkness.

A power station lay a mile and a half from the foot of the dam. The wall of water took about five minutes to get there. "This was not the express train portrayed by pulp writers, but the generated destructive horsepower was impossible to visualize," wrote historian Charles Outland. "With a depth varying from 100–140 feet for the first few miles, nothing could withstand the violence of the flood wave. Huge pieces of the dam, some weighing 10,000 tons, were washed down the canyon." The massive power station was crushed as easily as an eggshell.

Drawn by gravity, thundering forward at an initial speed of twenty miles per hour, the flood reached the end of the canyon, slammed against the walls of the Santa Clara Valley, and kicked sharply to the right, creating a swirling funnel of water that completely erased the village of Castaic Junction, wiping it clean as a slate. "At Castaic there was nothing left to indicate that any habitation ever existed there," reported the *Santa Paula Chronicle* in an "extra" edition later that day. "Where the McIntyre service station, restaurant, garage, and camp buildings stood there is nothing but acres of mud and debris, in places 15 feet deep."

A tent city of construction workers, next in the way, was nearly obliterated. A few lucky men found themselves in tents snapped tightly shut that acted like balloons, floating on the flood. The water was now seventy feet high and bearing mangled bodies, trees, homes, and debris as it crossed into Ventura County, plowing toward the sea. Hundred-ton blocks of concrete rode the water like corks.

Ahead lay the towns and villages of Piru, Fillmore, Bardsdale, and Santa Paula, where people were just becoming aware of the disaster about to engulf them. Police sirens sounded and residents were told to flee to the hills. Telephone operators—"'Hello' Girls," the *Santa Paula Chronicle* dubbed them—stuck to their posts in Santa Paula and Fillmore, making call after call while the flood came closer.

Other tales of heroism, tragedy, and random luck took shape. George Bassolo of Fillmore drowned when the wave hit his car as he attempted to cross a bridge. "A passenger, whose name was unknown, escaped when he was thrown free of the car and washed up in an orange tree," reported the *Santa Paula Chronicle*. The Coffers, from Piru, were caught unawares as they slept. Mrs. Coffer drowned when her ship bed tipped over after banging into a tree stump, while her husband and son were saved. The four members of the Gordon Cummings family of Bardsdale got onto the roof of their house. The roof was torn away, but they floated on it like a raft—thinking for a few giddy, terrified minutes that they would survive—until the roof hit debris and broke

13

up, drowning them all. Another rancher blew a hole in the roof of his home with a shotgun, and while he was pushing his children out onto the roof, the entire house swirled away, bearing them all to unlikely safety.

Some who spoke only Spanish didn't understand the warnings they'd been given. Instead of fleeing they gathered on the long steel bridge spanning the Santa Clara River between Bardsdale and Fillmore. Perhaps they thought they'd be safe, or maybe they wanted to see what was happening. The bridge was torn from its foundations and hurled hundreds of feet when the water hit. One woman surfed the flood with her three children, floating on a mattress until it snagged on a tree and they were saved. A Mexican farmer raced in his truck ahead of the onrushing waters, taking many to safety—until he made one trip too many and his truck washed away and he drowned. One survivor lost his mind and was found wandering in the hills, naked, two days later. Highway patrolman Thornton Edwards was the night's Paul Revere, speeding up and down the valley in the dark to warn people.

The flood passed Santa Paula at 3:30 A.M. and surged toward the Pacific beyond Mantalvo. Back upstream, the St. Francis Reservoir had almost completely emptied itself, leaving a wet carpet of oozy mud, shimmering beneath the light of an aging moon.

Nobody knows how many people died as a result of the failure of the St. Francis. The *Santa Paula Chronicle* reported at first that more than a thousand people lost their lives, along with tens of thousands of animals. These days historians reckon the human loss anywhere between 400 and 700. Many bodies were never found.

"Never in the history of America has there been a disaster more tragic, nor one which came so quickly or brutally," was the conclusion of a later Joint Citizens Report. "The invincible wall of water, possessed it seemed of some malicious devil, struck without warning, in the dark of night, trapping scores of families asleep without means or hope of escape."

Behind the tragedy lay politics, human error, and, accused the *Santa Paula Chronicle*, "the actions of a foreign and selfish water board"—the Los Angeles Department of Water and Power (DWP). The dam should never have been built. Cracks had appeared along its surface months before, prompting locals, anxious about the muddy brown water seeping through the abutment, to resort to gallows humor. "I'll see you soon," they'd say, "unless she gives."

On the afternoon of March 12 the dam's architect, William Mulholland, the DWP's famed chief engineer, came out from the city to inspect the leaks. Mulholland had built the dam to provide Los Angeles with a year's worth of backup water supply, because people were dynamiting the titanic aqueduct system he'd built to bring water to the city from the Owens River Valley, some 300 miles away on the eastern side of the Sierra Nevada. Los Angeles had grown—and was continuing to grow, at ever greater speed—out of desert land, and its existence depended on any desert's most precious resource: water. Mulholland had completed his aqueduct in 1913. He turned on a gushing spigot, pointed to the water, and in a laconic and legendary pronouncement, said: "There it is. Take it." Farmers in the Owens River Valley, cheated of their water and livelihoods, had been angry ever since. Some sabotaged the aqueduct: there was, in effect, a war over water. To make matters worse, Los Angeles was enduring a cycle of drought—hence the need for additional supply, a reservoir or dam. Mulholland spurned other, perhaps more favorable, sites and opted instead for the San Francisquito Canyon. He was an arrogant and brilliant man; his drive and vision helped invent L.A. Perhaps he believed himself infallible. He began building the St. Francis Dam in 1924, finished it three years later, and at the end of his inspection on March 12, 1928, pronounced it safe and sound.

Only a few hours later, catastrophe struck. At first Mulholland blamed saboteurs, then shouldered the blame himself. People who knew him said his face aged twenty years. "Apparently we overlooked something," Mulholland would tell a coroner. "It's very hard for me to say it. And the only ones I envy are the dead."

The bursting of the dam put out electricity all over Ventura County, but the telephones were still working. Leslie White's phone rang at about 2 A.M. on the morning of March 13. On the line was his friend Roy Pinkerton, editor of the *Ventura County Star*, a new paper with a circulation of less than 5,000. "The St. Francis has just gone," Pinkerton said.

White grabbed his camera and headed to a local airfield where Pinkerton had arranged for a small plane to rush him to the scene. The plane flew south and beat its way through thick, low-hanging sea fog toward Santa Paula. As dawn crept into the sky, White saw "bridges swept away, homes floating in a muddy torrent where only the day before cattle had grazed. We could distinguish vague dots struggling in the turbulent surface. We could not understand, at the time, that we were watching people die below us." The swift high waters had whipped away almost every bit of vegetation from the valley slopes. Orange groves and apricot orchards and fields of beans and alfalfa were leveled. A few houses stood strangely intact, the flood having missed them by inches. Uprooted railroad tracks stuck out of the torrent like twisted spaghetti, sleepers hanging from them at crazy angles. Vultures already circled, swooping down to peck at animal and human debris. White took photographs that Roy Pinkerton sold to the *Los Angeles Examiner*. For White, though, this was only the beginning of his involvement.

In the flood's immediate aftermath, tempers ran explosively high. The subject is hot in the Santa Clara Valley even today. The nub was this: Los Angeles County water had killed Ventura County people. "This is no time to sit idly by in the midst of hysteria," said the *Santa Paula Chronicle*. "Los Angeles Should Pay." The big white chiefs of Ventura County—the politicians, the ranchers whose properties had been damaged or destroyed—called for restitution and prepared for a claim by commissioning a detailed record of the tragedy. Leslie White was recruited to number and photograph each body as it was found.

Mud-caked cadavers were stacked high in hastily improvised morgues, one of which was established in the Masonic Hall at New-hall, aka the Hap-A-Lan dance hall. An old sign above the door said

"Welcome"; inside were bodies with sheets thrown over them. "The force of the water was so great that none of the victims recovered on the first day had on so much as a stitch

17

of clothing," wrote White. He moved up and down the valley, driving from Newhall to a mortuary in Santa Paula, to a pharmacy in Piru where corpses were also piled. Many were twisted and battered, mauled by water and debris. They lay on long pine planks, where they'd been washed off with garden hoses so White could photograph them.

As the days went by, the work became more and more grisly. White photographed, for instance, the Cowdens, an entire family that had been wiped out. The bodies of father, son, and daughter washed up quickly but the mother, Corinna Cowden, was found days later, already in such an advanced state of decomposition that her eyes and nose were gone. Some corpses, buried in silt and protected from the air, were well preserved even when found more than a week later. Others were rotten with maggots and vegetation, nothing appearing human except the rows of grinning teeth. So little remained of some bodies that the pieces were stored in small baskets.

On March 20 White set out on a different kind of expedition. Together with Bernie Isensee, another Ventura photographer, and an armed deputy sheriff, Carl Wallace (a future intimate of J. Edgar Hoover), White crossed the county line back into L.A. County to photograph what was left of the dam. Isensee, soon to quit photography and become a highway patrolman (a later picture shows a handsome man in jodhpurs and aviator shades), owned a stereoscopic camera that produced negatives fifty inches wide. The men set up their equipment above the dam, with White shooting from the exact spot that Isensee covered in his wider version. Then they worked their way back toward the sea, along the path the flood had taken, selecting different vantage points from which to take more and more pictures. The eighteen huge images made by Isensee remain the most striking visual record of the scale of the flood, showing a skyscraper-high dam destroyed, an enormous reservoir emptied, an entire landscape and hundreds of buildings leveled.

At one point during the day, the men paused at the end of a washed-out road for a group photo. White set up his camera on a tripod, set a timer, and walked back into the shot so he could be a part of it. Indeed, he stands smack at the photo's center, a cocky little rooster of a guy, looking all business with his hat pulled down a little over one eye and his hands on his hips.

Los Angeles quickly agreed to make restitution. Money came from the DWP, from the Harbor Board, from L.A. County, and from individuals. Claims were adjudicated without going to court. Precise dollar and cent values were given for property loss and loss through death. A racial element came into play here: Nora McDougal, for instance, received a $15,000 settlement for the death of one adult, while Emilio Quezada received $500 for a similar loss. But Spanish-speaking victims signed off on the papers, receiving much less than their English-speaking counterparts, and L.A. got what it wanted—the chance to move on and start forgetting that the St. Francis Dam ever existed. Nobody knows exactly how much was paid—estimates vary from $5.5 million to $25 million in 1928 dollars. Roy Pinkerton wrote that $7 million had been paid by the mid-1930's. Meanwhile the water levels in the Hollywood Reservoir— held in place by the Mulholland Dam, a sister to the St. Francis and built along the same lines—were immediately lowered, and the dam itself was scaled back. Nobody wanted another disaster, least of all the DWP.

The first checks were handed to Ventura County victims and their families within months, while Leslie White went about the mournful task of helping to identify the corpses that were still showing up. "For weeks the authorities continued to bring in putrid corpses which had to be carefully examined and photographed, and for months skeletons were found on the great scar left by the flood," he said. What he saw would haunt him for the rest of his life.

White's young wife urged him to quit, but he stuck to the job. One morning, while he was preparing to photograph yet another fetid cadaver, he felt a sudden pain in his chest and a balloon of blood spurted from his mouth. His left lung had hemorrhaged and collapsed. Exhausted, he lay in a hospital bed. Doctors warned that he was developing tuberculosis and advised rest at a clinic in the desert near Palm Springs. White couldn't afford it. Instead he gave up his Ventura darkroom and moved with his wife down the coast to Los Angeles, for the dryness of the air. Odd as it may seem now, like many in the city's early days, he went to L.A. for his health.

3

A Hero
Named Clark

Illness and one of California's worst disasters combined to bring Leslie White to Los Angeles in the summer of 1928. On the other hand, David Harris Clark was a native son, born in Highland Park (near where Dodger Stadium is now) on April 4, 1898, thirty years before White moved to L.A.

Clark's father was named William Alton Clark, the "Alton" having been taken from the town in Illinois near where explorers Meriwether Lewis and William Clark (from whom this line of Clarks claimed distant descent) started their great westward journey of discovery in 1804. William Alton Clark was himself born in Maine in "about 1860." The 1930 U.S. census records note that he was unsure of the date. He married his childhood sweetheart, Anna Laina, and they traveled through the West before settling in Los Angeles in about 1890. They were probably intrepid, and experienced both adventures and hardships; but nothing suggests either was ever wild. Anna

Laina was stoic, not a talker (her mother was a Finn), and generally kept her smoldering temper in check. By all accounts she was, when young, a beautiful woman.

The 1898 City Directory for L.A. lists William Alton Clark as a clerk for the Southern Pacific Railroad, then the most important and reviled corporation in the state. The 1910 census lists his occupation as "railroad secretary." By the 1920 census, however, he was happy to describe himself more fully: "chief accountant for the Southern Pacific's freight division," an important job. He had bought a large home in Highland Park, on the fringes of downtown, and was supporting a large extended family: his wife's mother and father, his wife, and their five children—three boys and two girls.

He was a tall, lean, bespectacled man, proud of the steady rise he had achieved in a city that even then tended to promote spectacular and instant success. He'd survived and prospered amidst the various strategy shifts and upheavals and changes of ownership that the vastly powerful Southern Pacific had gone through in the early part of the previous century. He was diligent, hardworking, a churchgoer, and well positioned in L.A.'s business community. As a railroad man, Clark was also a representative of the past in a place that didn't like to look back, a city to whose bursting growth he had contributed but which already saw its future with the automobile. Still, the shrewd William Alton Clark had every reason to suppose that his children would prosper from the secure base he had provided.

Dave Clark, the second of his five kids, was educated at nearby Monte Vista Grammar School and Los Angeles High—the oldest high school in Southern California, then a big Gothic pile situated downtown on North Hill Street at

Sunset Boulevard. Among the school's future alumni would be Fletcher Bowron (a four-term mayor of L.A., from 1938–1953), Ray Bradbury, Charles Bukowski, Dustin Hoffman, and Johnnie Cochran (the attorney who defended O. J. Simpson)—as well as some who achieved darker fame.

Dave Clark excelled both academically and as an athlete. In 1917, on America's entry into WWI, Clark joined the United States Naval Academy at Annapolis. "Clark is able and disciplined and good material. He performs well, but must watch his temper," wrote one officer who taught him. Clark and a group of friends, fearful the war would end before they saw action, headed north to Canada and enlisted in the Royal Flying Corps. Clark became a fighter pilot. His service records show that he was based with the RFC's 5th Squadron on the Western front. Dispute would later arise about how much action Clark saw, but certainly he flew sorties, was shot at and shot back. The life expectancy of pilots on the Western front was brutally short—often only a matter of weeks. Harold Beaumont, one of Clark's American friends, was killed on July 17, 1918. "You have to carry on," Clark wrote to his brother, but noted too that in a rage during the mess that night he had smashed a bottle and cut his hand. "Damp hangars, muddy roads, crystal blue skies. I'll miss Harold. He was a crack pilot. I suppose now I'll have to kill a German for him." A photograph of the time shows Clark, dressed in uniform with a scarf trailing around his neck, leaning against the fuselage of a single-engined SE5 fighter. He's tall, broad-shouldered, dark-haired. His eyes look tired, but his expression is calm. He liked and needed action and didn't forget the spirit of the war. Always, after he'd returned from France to find an America that increasingly shrugged off wartime idealism in favor of realism and then hedonism, he wore an RFC badge on his lapel, a pin with a pair of wings.

Clark had a cool bravado that could amount to cruelty, but he was close to his family and never doubted he would return to Los Angeles. He was determined to succeed in the city where he had grown up, but questioned what career he should pursue. In 1920 he took a screen test with First National Pictures. "My head's not empty enough to be an actor," he told his brother. Or maybe Clark decided to pursue what looked like a steadier career. He spent the next two years studying law at USC and left, without graduating, as soon as he was admitted to the California Bar on March 3, 1922. Again, we might detect impatience here, the action of a man determined to get ahead fast—although forgoing law school graduation was frequent practice for law students in those days, when the route to a professional career was more flexible. It could be that he was strapped for cash—a common occurrence throughout his life. The handsome and socially connected war hero joined Wellborn, Wellborn & Wellborn, a small but established and powerful downtown law firm.

The Wellborns had for decades been players in the growth of Los Angeles. Olin Wellborn, Sr., a Confederate veteran of the Civil War, had been a three-time congressman in Texas who secured the federal judgeship for Southern California in 1895. For a while he partnered with oil magnate E. L. Doheny in a number of ventures. Though Olin Wellborn, Sr., died in 1921, his sons and grandsons continued the firm and still represented E. L. Doheny and had office space in Doheny's magnificent art-deco Petroleum Securities Building at Olympic and Figueroa.

It was here that Dave Clark went to work, seeing the

downtown building boom firsthand and learning his trade as the fast and brittle mood of the 1920s took hold. Women's skirts soared above the knee, the stock market scaled new peaks, a lot of people expected to get rich in a hurry, and Clark moved with ease among other lawyers, reporters, and cops. He was happy to throw off his coat and get down on the floor and play cards or shoot craps with the guys. Dick Steckel, a police captain who worked way down in Venice, was a particular friend. They golfed together. Clark was a championship level golfer, for years featured on the USC alumni team. He rode well and played polo too. He was charming, forceful, and perhaps vain—confident in his charisma and looks.

In 1926 he married Nancy Regina Malone, the petite and beautiful daughter of a New York judge. Nancy brought with her a little girl, Mary Lenore, her daughter from a previous relationship. During that same year Clark made another big decision, leaving Wellborn, Wellborn & Wellborn to join the fast-growing District Attorney's office. He wanted to make a name for himself as a litigator. For a starting salary of $375 a month, he became one of twenty deputies in the D.A.'s trial department, which was responsible for prosecuting more than 300 cases a month—burglary, robbery, grand theft auto, drunk driving, narcotics, assault, possession of a still, and murder cases, an increasing number every year. Crime in the 1920s, like pretty much everything else in L.A., was out of control. The LAPD simply couldn't cope, leaving many crimes undetected or unpunished. The murder rate more than tripled in the decade, rising to more than sixty a year. The upright and debonair Dave Clark knew that he'd be busy each morning when he strode into the lobby of the new Hall of Justice, the heels of his shining oxfords ringing on the marbled floors.

A courtroom is a theater, and L.A. had already known some star performers, notably Earl Rogers, who defended Clarence Darrow against jury-tampering in 1911, and was described by Darrow himself as "the greatest trial lawyer of his day." Rogers was a showman, a flamboyant and mesmerizing orator who, in his entire career, lost only three cases. He was also a reckless drinker and a womanizer, and died at age fifty-one in 1922, the year Dave Clark entered the law. Rogers was a legend, and perhaps for a young lawyer like Dave Clark, something of a role model. But Rogers's courtly, theatrical style already belonged to the past. Clark was something else again—leaner, harder, with a persona that seemed designed for the camera, not the stage. A 1926 photograph of the D.A.'s staff, taken just after the move into the new Hall of Justice, features Clark prominently; he's taller than everybody else, more tanned, and much better dressed—in a slick tailored suit with a silk tie tight at his neck, an immaculate white handkerchief folded in the outside breast pocket, that flyer's pin on his lapel. He has a pencil moustache and a gorgeous quality about him. Reporters likened him to John Barrymore, to John Gilbert, and later to Clark Gable.

On the morning of July 6, 1928, Dave Clark rose early, kissed his wife Nancy on the cheek, left their home in West Hollywood, got into his Model T Ford, and turned onto Wilshire Boulevard, heading downtown. He had a big day ahead. District Attorney Asa Keyes (pronounced to rhyme with "eyes") had given Clark important jobs before, but none as big as the one that faced him today, when he would begin prosecution of racketeer and bootlegger Albert Marco, called "L.A.'s Capone" by the *Daily News*.

"Marco's just a goon to me," Clark told the *News*, ridiculing the idea that the gangster might be given special consideration. "No stone will be left unturned and he will be sent to San Quentin."

"Tough words characterize this ice-cool prosecutor," wrote Gene Coughlin, a top writer on the *News*. Like many L.A. reporters of the day, Coughlin had served his apprenticeship in Chicago. He was friendly with Lionel Moise who, it's been said, taught Ernest Hemingway his trade on the *Kansas City Star*. Certainly Moise provided Hemingway, and Coughlin too, with a hard-drinking, hard-fighting journalistic persona that they adopted as their model. Coughlin was working the Marco story under instruction from *News* owner Manchester Boddy who had assumed control of the fledgling tabloid (L.A.'s first) in 1926, and immediately decided that the paper needed a circulation-boosting crusade. Vice, and Albert Marco in particular, became a target. "Albert Marco is loud, brash, and plumply complacent," wrote Coughlin in his gleeful and lurid way. "The whole of Los Angeles trusts that 'Debonair Dave' will rid our city of this menace."

It was a scorching summer day; by noon the temperature would reach 90 degrees. Crowds packed the Superior Court and jammed the corridors outside, barring what little breeze there was from the Hall of Justice. Charlie Chaplin, who loved a good trial, was given a numbered ticket so he could claim a seat. Albert Marco sauntered in and posed for photographers. "Seated beside his counsel Marco paid scant attention to the proceedings, glancing about the courtroom and smiling for friends," wrote Coughlin. "He was dressed in a gray suit, a skyblue silk bowtie with handkerchief to match, and wore a huge diamond in his lapel."

The D.A.'s office had tried to prosecute Marco several times before, but he'd always beaten the rap. Marco had friends in top places and was in no doubt that he'd secure an acquittal this time too. His courtroom demeanor mixed preening arrogance and feigned boredom. Albert Marco had once lost $250,000 in a single hand of poker to Nicky Arnstein, the famed gambler "Nick the Greek." Marco wanted the world, and Dave Clark, to know that a mere murder charge didn't faze him.

Marco had been born in 1887 in an Alpine village in northern Italy, where he'd been apprenticed to a hatmaker before deciding to try his luck in America. He, along with thousands of others primarily from Italy and Central Europe, passed through Ellis Island in 1908. He drifted west, roaming Nevada and Washington State as a pimp and confidence man. In Seattle he ran the prostitution business at a large and briefly successful gambling hotel. In 1919 he was arrested for burglary in Sacramento and served a brief sentence. The early 1920s found him in Los Angeles, already driving a Cadillac, wearing slick suits with a Panama hat pushed back on his head, and shipping bootleg booze into a Long Beach warehouse. In 1925 he drew a gun on an LAPD officer and brutally pistol-whipped him. For this, Marco got a $50 fine and was given his gun back. He had good reason to believe himself above the law. He was an important cog in The System, the cabal that ran the Los Angeles underworld.

"'Marco's been indicted,' was the whisper flashed from joint to joint," wrote Gene Coughlin in the *News* when Marco was arrested for attempted murder on June 28, 1928. "Many of the Marco hirelings, all of them strong believers in the racketeer's boast that he was ungettable, were hard to convince that the baron faced a potential penitentiary term." Marco, his clothes dried crimson with blood, had been caught on the roof of the Ship Café in Venice, trying to escape. He told the cop who arrested him. "I'm Albert Marco. I'm a big shot with the police downtown and if you pinch me you'll be sent to the sticks for life." A *Los Angeles Times* photograph shows him sitting on a police bench, staring at the camera with an expression of insolence and contempt. His dark hair stands almost straight up, a shock of vigorous, untidy curls rising above a long, meaty face. The double-breasted jacket of his smart suit is worn over a bloody undershirt; his dress shirt, presumably even more stained, had been left in the restroom where he'd been trying to wash it clean.

This, then, was Albert Marco: a thug, thickset and not pretty, but with blunt charisma. His trial—trials, rather, for there would be two—brought Dave Clark glory, but also would plant the seeds of his future doom.

Judge William Doran got proceedings under way amid rumors of jury tampering and stories that Marco had already reached a civil settlement with Dominick Conterno, the man he was accused of trying to kill. The first two days were consumed by the all-important ritual of jury selection before Conterno at last took the stand, with Dave Clark unsure whether this first, and most important, witness had already been squared away by the defense. That turned out not to be the case. Led by Clark, Conterno gave a telling and vivid version of what had happened.

The trouble began when a drunk Marco approached

Conterno's wife and was rebuffed, whereupon he called her a "lousy whore." Conterno, unsurprisingly, took exception and the argument swiftly escalated into a brawl, first in the restroom of the Ship Café, then outside, where Marco yanked out a pistol and fired two shots. The first slammed Conterno in the back, the second missed its target but winged Harry Judson (the singer with the jazz band that played at the Ship) who had stepped outside to observe the fun.

"I saw the flash of a gun and felt the bullet go through my body," Conterno said.

"How would you describe Albert Marco at that moment?" Clark asked.

"He was snarling like a dog," Conterno said.

Sitting beside his lawyer, an unperturbed Marco wrote something on a pad of paper on the table in front of him; he wasn't making notes, merely doodling.

Under cross-examination, Dominick Conterno admitted that he'd been so drunk on bootleg grape brandy that he could no longer remember exactly what had happened—a big point for the defense. Dave Clark countered with two witnesses who testified that they'd seen Marco fire the shots and a third who declared he'd heard Marco say, just before the shooting, "I'll kill you!" But then Evelyn Brogan, an attractive brunette who gave her profession as "legal secretary" (well, maybe she was Marco's secretary, and what she was doing now had something to do with the law), testified on Marco's behalf, swearing that she'd been Marco's companion that night and he'd had nothing to do with the shooting.

Judge Doran had placed the twelve jurors in sheriff's custody; they stayed in a downtown hotel at night. One morning the jurors piled into a bus and left downtown, heading west on Pico Boulevard, across empty countryside, and down to Venice Boulevard where Clark led them through the Ship Café, showing them the dance floor, the orchestra stand, the restroom where the fight had started, and the roof to which Marco had fled.

The weapon from which Marco was alleged to have fired the shots had disappeared, however; likewise had several witnesses who were, according to Coughlin in the *News*, "vacationing down Mexico way, courtesy of Albert Marco." Still, after the trial had been in progress for twelve days, Dave Clark reckoned he'd laid out a strong case. "Albert Marco fired those shots. He shot Dominick Conterno in the back, not caring whether he killed Conterno or not. It's true and it isn't pretty and I call upon the jury to find Marco guilty," Clark said in his closing remarks.

The jury went out, and stayed out, for more than two days; when they trooped back in, the foreman told Judge Doran they'd been unable to reach a verdict. Nine had been in favor of acquittal, while three believed Marco guilty.

Clark was shocked: *nine* had favored acquittal?

Marco smiled while his attorneys argued strenuously that the case should be dismissed, but the judge surprised Marco and his team of legal mouthpieces by announcing that there would be a retrial. Judge Doran was a lean, balding, bespectacled USC graduate who knew his own mind, a former member of the District Attorney's office who had argued cases against Earl Rogers and regarded himself as a mentor to Dave Clark.

Dave Clark's handsome face lit up with surprise and a smile; he'd been given another chance.

4

Angel City

Leslie White had been warned that another hemorrhage in his lung would most likely kill him. Doctors in Ventura County recommended confinement to bed and complete rest for at least a few months. White arrived with his wife at his aunt's house in Hollywood and tried to oblige. He lay on his back, reading books and the papers. He listened to the radio, sipped orange juice, and tried to sleep. Images from the St. Francis disaster—mangled corpses with twisted limbs and faces eaten away—kept flashing through his mind. He couldn't rid himself of the stench of decay that seemed to linger in his nostrils. He feared that he'd lost his mind as well as his health. He needed to be active, so when a different doctor told him he couldn't fight consumption lying on his back, White was only too glad to hear the news. He got to his feet and set about exploring "the great complex metropolitan machine" in which he found himself.

As White was walking down Hollywood Boulevard, where flashing neon signs proclaimed the Music Box, the Vine Street Theater, the Egyptian, the Chinese, the Plaza, the Roosevelt, and other big theaters and hotels, an old man stopped him, asking, "Are you saved, brother?" Outside a church an advertisement proclaimed an upcoming appearance by Rin-Tin-Tin, "the canine motion picture actor." Red streetcars rattled by and traffic lights gonged. Men in straw boaters and women in cloche hats bustled along the sidewalk. Everybody seemed breathless, White observed. Boxy Model T Fords were jammed into slant-wise parking slots. A jazz orchestra moaned ragtime in a dance hall.

Downtown, on Broadway, White paid thirty-five cents to watch Charlie Chaplin in *The Circus* in the United Artists Theater, which boasted a $200,000 refrigeration system and "Certified Cool Comfort." In the afternoon cool of another movie palace, he saw *Ladies of the Mob*, the very latest picture starring the "It" girl, Clara Bow, whom he liked. He was scarcely alone as a fan: Bow was then the world's most famous movie star, the first mass-market sex symbol, the object of obsessive curiosity and the recipient of 8,000 fan letters a week. In one of the small black notebooks he used as a diary, White wrote: "Saw new Clara Bow. She meets a bunch of crooks and gets sent to Folsom! Still feeling a little weak, but good to be on my feet."

The fever of the Jazz Age had spread from New York across America and was reflected back, magnified and amplified, by Hollywood. It was the era of daring short-skirted flappers, of wild parties and bathtub gin, of everybody needing at least one automobile. The country was in the midst of "the greatest, gaudiest spree in history," wrote

F. Scott Fitzgerald. Young women, for whom a star like Clara Bow was both symbol and role model, smoked and wore lipstick and freely had sex outside marriage. Radio and the tabloid newspaper, entirely new phenomena, chronicled the national obsessions—crime, sex, sports, and God. This revolution in manners, morals, and fashion played out against the extraordinary experiment of Prohibition—the attempt to turn America into a dry Utopia, which came into effect nationwide on January 16, 1920. Nobody drank less. Outlaw liquor—smuggled or illegally brewed—flooded the country by hundreds of millions of gallons each year, filling the land with crime and its adjunct, graft, creating a spirit of rebellion and a subculture of speakeasies and bootleggers like Albert Marco. Prohibition, though, failed to prohibit in ways that differed from place to place, from city to city. What happened in Los Angeles in the 1920s couldn't be more typically American, yet this history is also unique and particular.

Leslie White arrived in the city toward the end of July 1928, when the boom was soaring to giddy heights and Los Angeles was not merely expanding but exploding beyond recognition. "In L.A. tomorrow isn't another day," said *Los Angeles Times* columnist Lee Shippey. "It's another town." Modernity had arrived, in an awful hurry. At night the downtown neon billboards were so plentiful and incandescent that visiting *Harper's* correspondent Sarah Comstock said she longed "to hush them, to be rid of their blinding clamor, their deafening glare." This, from a woman who lived in Manhattan.

White saw scores of health cults and religious cults, churches of "Divine Power, of Divine Fire, of the Open Door, of the Blue Flames, of the Higher Things of Life." There were Temples of Light, Chapels of Numerology, Truth Centers,

Truth Studios. The frustrated Midwesterners who'd come to L.A. in droves, thinking that the city really was (as advertised by the Chamber of Commerce) "the white-spot on America's industrial map," sought almost any form of spiritual anchorage. Religion was what they knew, what they wanted; and religion in L.A. was like show business. Evangelist Aimee Semple McPherson had a radio station and was a star in her own right. With a husky voice hinting of sex, she entertained the "folks" with slide shows and healing sessions. She promised not fire and brimstone, but the overwhelming bliss of God's love as she presided over an enormous congregation that was a stew of life, a fantastic human muddle, a "heart-hungry" multitude. In pageants at her Angelus Temple she wore filmy, flimsy dresses and chased the Devil with his own pitchfork.

L.A. was a beacon to many, a nightmare for others, but already a phenomenon, not so much evoked as endlessly commented upon, by both locals and Easterners who arrived to work or indulge in a couple of weeks of intellectual tourism in this bewildering American city.

"It is a young city, crude, wildly ambitious, growing; it has halitosis and osmidrosis; and to kill the stench it gargles religious soul-wash and rubs holy toilet-water and scented talc between its toes," wrote Louis Adamic, a Slovenian immigrant who worked in the harbor pilot's office at Long Beach. Great ocean liners glided behind him while he composed magazine sketches that established him as the city's underground prophet and its first Boswell. "Los Angeles is America. A jungle. Los Angeles grew up suddenly, *planlessly.*"

The city that now drew the eyes of the world seemed to

have emerged out of nowhere, without much of a past. "The first 100 years were a kind of prehistory in which it moved from pueblo to cow town to hick town at a leisurely pace," said Carey McWilliams, who came to L.A. from Colorado as a young man in the early 1920s and in time became the most influential historian of the city in this period. "Then suddenly, in the 1920s, it achieved great-city status through a process of forced growth based on booster tactics and self-promotion."

It's true that L.A. evolved without an ordered architectural scheme such as Baron Haussmann brought to Paris or Christopher Wren to certain parts of central London, but in another way the growth of the city had been planned only too well—*plotted* rather, by a small group of men determined to create a metropolis and make money. Harry Chandler, generalissimo of the boom and publisher of the *Los Angeles Times*, and General Moses Sherman, the owner of the streetcar system, were among those who formed America's first Chamber of Commerce and established land syndicates so they could sell real estate, drawing people to the city by constantly promoting merits of climate and crimelessness. Chandler and Sherman, for instance, acquired 108,000 acres of land in the San Fernando Valley before sponsoring the building of Mulholland's aqueduct from the Owens River Valley. The aqueduct took the water from the Owens River Valley farmers and terminated, not in Los Angeles itself, but in the San Fernando Valley, thus irrigating the syndicate's lands and earning its members in excess of $100 million. This iniquitous plot was kept secret for years but would in time form the basis of Robert Towne's screenplay for the 1974 movie *Chinatown*. Towne set his story in 1937 so he could utilize the shapes of the private-eye story, a genre that didn't exist in 1905–1913, when these events took place. *Chinatown* has taken on a totemic power; it's a great movie, but misleading as history, a metaphor on many levels for the ways in which L.A.'s past tends to be hidden, erased, forgotten, rewritten, or present in our minds only through the filter of fiction. *Chinatown* does more than switch the dates; its replacement of social context by fictional construct creates a shimmer, a stylish and seductive surface beneath which run depths never spoken of. Thus the film's true subject is not the mystery that hero Jake Gittes tries to unravel, but the way Los Angeles thinks about itself.

"Los Angeles is a nut town run by rich bastards who hate the Wobblies like poison," somebody said to Louis Adamic, drawing attention to the oddity that, since the dynamiting of the *Times* building in 1910, this place of monotonous sunshine had become the focal point of America's anti-labor movement. By the 1920s L.A. was perceived in terms of its extraordinariness. Many tried to get a handle on the bursting city by looking toward its more outlandish manifestations. Edmund Wilson wrote of "the grooves of gorgeous business cathedrals," "the blue Avocado Building, bawdy as a peacock's tail, with its frieze of cute little cupids," "the regal and greenish Citrus Building, made throughout of the purest lime candy, which has gone a little sugary from the heat," "Aimee McPherson's wonderful temple, where good-natured but thrilling native angels guard the big red radio-tower love-wand and see to it that not a tittle or vibration of their mistress's kind warm voice goes astray as it speeds to you in your sitting-room and tells you how sweet Jesus has been to her and all the marvelous things she has found in Him."

Wilson, like Adamic, leaned toward socialism, but he was a cynic too, and L.A. got his glands going. "Nuestro Pueblo de Nuestra Senora la Reina de Los Angeles has more lovely girls serving peach freezes and appetizing sandwich specials with little pieces of sweet pickle on the side than any other city in the world," he wrote, and we wonder whether the girls or the sandwiches excited him more. The girls were there for early Hollywood, dreams of fame and stardom having added a whole new register to the city's palette of transformative possibility.

F. Scott Fitzgerald made his first visit to L.A. at about this time, and wrote a treatment for a movie that was never made. In 1928, though, he published "Magnetism," a *Saturday Evening Post* story using material he'd gathered from the trip. "This was perhaps the most bizarre community in the rich, wild, bored empire," Fitzgerald wrote. "Everything in the vicinity—even the March sunlight—was new, fresh, hopeful, and thin, as you would expect in a city that had tripled its population in fifteen years." Fitzgerald was no socialist but a sensitive and instinctively romantic observer. He fastened onto the oddness of the city's topography. Los Angeles was growing fast but the wide mountain-bordered basin in which it had been plunked was still largely undeveloped. Freeways were decades in the future. The boulevards that ran from downtown to the beach communities were wide and empty. L.A. wasn't yet the amorphous metropolitan area that it was to become, though already new neighborhoods mushroomed, geographically distant from what was then the undisputed center, the automobile making it easy for these suburbs to spin away from the pull of downtown. Movie studios were tactically positioned in the middle of nowhere, and Fitzgerald caught the sense of burgeoning sprawl: "George left and drove out by an interminable boulevard which narrowed into a long, winding concrete road and rose into the hilly country behind. Somewhere in the vast emptiness a group of buildings appeared," he wrote.

The movie business was a big part of the boom but not yet the dominant force in the city's life. Hollywood was coming of age and coming into its own but existed, geographically and psychologically, a little to the side—already aspired to and envied, a magnet. The crowds that flocked to searchlight premieres in the theaters built by Sid Grauman or Alexander Pantages on Hollywood Boulevard longed to see the destruction of movie stars almost as much as their elevation. Or perhaps even more. Celebrity culture was being invented. It began, in 1921, with Roscoe "Fatty" Arbuckle. Arbuckle was a comedian, the "fat owl" of the silent screen. Hugely successful and famous, he threw parties abundantly fueled by bootleg booze and drugs. Nobody ever claimed that these parties were good clean fun. After one party that lasted for several days at the St. Francis Hotel in San Francisco, a young model and actress, Virginia Rappe, was found dead. The L.A. press took several days to get hold of the story, but then William Randolph Hearst's *Examiner* started to dig, accusing Arbuckle of rape and murder. He was a "beast," "a moral leper" who drove "freak cars" and once held a "wedding for his dogs."

At the time of the Arbuckle scandal four other daily papers, in addition to the *Examiner*, served the L.A. market: the *Evening Express*, the *Evening Herald*, the *Evening Record*, and the *Times*. A frenzy of gloves-off coverage quickly ensued, each paper vying to top the other. There was no television, of course, and radio news coverage was barely beginning. Movie newsreels appeared days or weeks after big events, whereas newspapers ran brash stories and lurid images only hours after the events they depicted. It was a golden age for the press, which ran the spectrum from great writing to gutter journalism, often in the same story and under the same byline. In its coverage of the Arbuckle scandal, the *Examiner* featured photographs of Rappe's innocent face and her torn clothing. The *Express* noted that for Arbuckle "death would be too swift a penalty" and movie houses around the country dropped his films. Although a jury finally acquitted Arbuckle, noting that he was "entirely innocent and free from blame," the damage and the injustice had been done. Arbuckle's career was in ruins and would never bounce back. It was perhaps the first perfect mass-culture news story—involving sex, death, and the misdemeanors of a movie star.

L.A. newspapers sold by the million, and a pattern emerged. Sensational crimes—some involving Hollywood, others not—would result in circus trials and days of gleeful headlines. Competing papers sold the news in a series of editions that were published throughout the course of the day: the morning and afternoon papers ("AMs" and "PMs," Leslie White soon learned to call them) added "sunset" editions, "bulldog" editions, and "extra" editions if needed. When a big story hit, editors demanded fresh angles hourly and writers couldn't afford to be scrupulous about how they provided them. One top reporter recalled hiring a messenger to deliver an anonymous murder threat in the course of a trial so he could write about the recipient's reaction. Such shenanigans were the norm, and to study an entire day's outpourings from the L.A. press during this period is to see an ongoing and ever-changing crime epic in progress. The detail is more than novelistic; it's microscopic.

"L.A. was the hottest news city in America, probably the world," said Matt Weinstock of the *Daily News*, the tabloid that featured Gene Coughlin and had been launched in 1923 by twenty-year-old Cornelius Vanderbilt, Jr. The *News*—located in a building at the corner of Pico Boulevard and Los Angeles Street, downtown but farther south than the other papers—was new and fresh and different. Vanderbilt, the rich son of a famously rich family, loved the swift, jazzy tabloid style; but he tried to break away from the sensationalism that usually went with that style. He envisioned a penny paper that "may safely enter any home" and ordered his editors to look for international stories and human interest stuff that the great New York tabloids would ignore ("FOUR HUNDRED CHICKENS DISAPPEAR," ran one *News* headline). Circulation rose to 200,000 within a year but then slumped. The *News* foundered in 1926, and was plucked from the bankruptcy court by Manchester Boddy, a former book publisher and sales manager for Encyclopaedia Britannica. Boddy had $750 in his pocket, but proved to be the perfect man to put the young tabloid back on the map. He immediately removed Vanderbilt's quixotic ban on sex, scandal, and violent death, and circulation began to rise again.

"Los Angeles had the finest murders *ever*," wrote Carey McWilliams with a hint of pride. There was Walpurga Oesterreich, who kept her lover imprisoned in the attic for over fifteen years and then one day goaded him into killing her husband. There was college student Edward Hickman who kidnapped twelve-year-old Marion Parker and, having failed to extract a ransom, presented the corpse, with eyes and legs severed and eyelids sewn open, to the girl's father, asking: "Do you think I'll be as famous as Leopold and Loeb?" There was the murder of movie director William Desmond Taylor, shot through the heart with a single well-aimed bullet, perhaps having gotten on the wrong side of a dope dealer, or maybe one of the two gorgeous actresses he was bedding, or the mother of one of those actresses with whom he'd also been having an affair, or his ex-wife, or a gay lover. The bisexual Taylor, it transpired, had more people with reason to wish him dead than the victim in an Agatha Christie novel.

"Ideas grow as rank, coarse, and odorless as geraniums in the freakish atmosphere," wrote McWilliams. "When so many people have nothing meaningful to do with their time, nothing real with which to occupy their minds, they indulge in fantasy, in silly daydreams, in perversions, and, occasionally, in monstrous crimes." Incessant migration, rapid growth, and the swiftly repeated cycle of boom and bust and boom again had created a pathology of cults, cranks, and thousands of hastily improvised businesses and buildings—snakes for sale, frogs for sale, diners and stores that shot up in the shapes of owls, derby hats, shoes, airships, teakettles, windmills, and mosques.

"Los Angeles is the kind of place where perversion is perverted and prostitution prostituted," McWilliams observed. The city could seem like a vast melodrama of maladjustment. Climactic episodes took on an addictive character, and civic rituals turned inevitably into gaudy spectacle. Much of this now centered at the new Hall of

Justice, the thirteen-story Beaux-Arts building in spotless light-gray California granite that occupied an entire block at the corner of Temple and Spring.

The Hall of Justice was, and is, an impressive structure—solid, dignified, and elegant. When it opened for business in 1926, it was placed atop a hill with a handsome park in front of it, and with the enormous letters HALL OF JUSTICE chiseled in stone above the lofty entranceways. It was designed and erected at a time when the fathers of this most recklessly modern and American of cities felt they needed a Parthenon, a statement of civic intent and seriousness.

The Hall of Justice cost $6.5 million in 1920s dollars. A barrel-vaulted entrance foyer swept through the entire length of the building, and visitors, like the folks who worked there daily, couldn't fail to be impressed by the gold marble walls, enormous marble columns, marble floors, and gold-coffered ceiling. Elevators rose to the offices of the District Attorney on the sixth and seventh floors, the courts on the eighth, and the jury and press rooms on the ninth. Above that was the County Jail, a full three floors of cells. Most days the place was a bustling hive. The people of L.A. demanded not only fictional but real-life entertainment. The Hall of Justice, envisioned for a cast of thousands, soon became not something Greek, but the city's equivalent of the Roman Coliseum, a grand arena of life and death.

This building would soon become the center of Leslie White's professional life, as it was of Dave Clark's. Both would be players in the great crime circus of L.A. in the late 1920s and early 1930s; both would be touched by murder and scandal, although only one would survive intact. White had come to Los Angeles during the first Marco trial, and he'd read about a number of racket-related murders that had occurred since then. Jack Palmer, a Washington State rumrunner, another newcomer to town, had been killed in a downtown rooming house. Palmer's flapper girlfriend said nonchalantly that he'd been shot by gangsters. Another man, Augie Palambo, was killed in the back of a San Pedro taxi cab. The *Evening Express* showed a picture of Palambo's straw hat with a bloodstained bullet hole in it. These underworld rumblings were connected with the opening of a gambling ship, the *Johanna Smith*, off Long Beach. Marco was a part owner of the ship, along with his associates "Farmer" Page and former LAPD vice cop Guy McAfee. Were these men fighting among themselves, or were outsiders trying to muscle in? Reporters didn't know, or if they did, they weren't writing about it. The *Express* did note that the number of unsolved murders in the city was soaring. There had been fourteen since the beginning of the year.

White, intrigued, took a streetcar downtown and entered the Hall of Justice for the first time, riding the elevator to the eighth floor where, outside the doors of Judge Doran's Superior Court, he joined the line of early spectators awaiting the start of Albert Marco's second trial on the morning of August 24, 1928.

5

The Gangster Goes Down

Dave Clark faced an uphill struggle. As proceedings got under way, a string of witnesses either didn't appear or dropped out. Walter Eaton, an LAPD cop who had evidence of how the enraged Albert Marco had smashed chairs in the grand jury room, and Louise Bardson, a member of Marco's party at the Ship Café, simply didn't show up. Dr. George T. Dazey, who had dug the bullet out of Dominick Conterno's back, had "gone to Europe." Marco grinned when Dazey's absence was announced in court, while Clark, furious, demanded a thorough investigation.

Marco had gotten himself a neat new haircut. He wore a dark blue suit with a muted chalk stripe, but his swagger was still unrestrained. He yawned and laughed. He slumped in his chair beside his attorneys, doodling and buffing his nails. He "smiled at secret thoughts," as Gene Coughlin wrote in the *Daily News*, and treated the trial like a joke. He probably had good reason. Two of the key prosecution witnesses seemed to have developed eyesight and memory problems when they took the stand. Dominick Conterno said he'd been fighting with Marco, pummeling the vice-king over the head when a blow rendered him almost unconscious. The blow broke his hold on Marco, and he staggered backward. It was at this moment, he said, that he saw a flash and felt the bullet punch into his back—but he didn't see who fired the shots. Harry Judson testified that he had no idea who fired the shot that wounded him in the foot.

Leslie White recorded some of his impressions. "Marco is an ugly brute. His neck is so thick it threatens to tear apart the collar of his shirt. The young prosecutor's name is Clark. He's got an impossible job, I think. Everybody thinks Marco is guilty and everybody thinks he'll win his acquittal in a trial that seems fixed."

White was still weak and walked with a stick. He sat at the back in the stuffy courtroom in case the heat made him faint and he needed to get out. Allied Architects, the designers of the Hall of Justice, had put big windows in the courtrooms, failing to consider the sheer amount of light that would strike them. On an average day Los Angeles received fourteen times more sunlight than New York. Fans had been installed in Judge Doran's court, and venetian blinds that threw slanted patterns on the floors; but on summer days, the room still cooked.

Dave Clark, immaculate as always, looked cool in the heat, though he felt this shambles of a trial slipping out of his control. That weekend he and his wife Nancy accepted an invitation from Baron Long, the owner of the Ship Café. Long and a syndicate of other investors had recently opened a gambling resort across the Mexican border outside Tijuana, in the picturesque hills at Agua Caliente. The resort, set on 655 acres, had its own airport. Clark and Nancy flew down in Baron Long's plane, and Clark walked for the first time among the sumptuous and soaring spaces of Agua Caliente. He saw the huge ballroom, the immense mosaic-tiled spa, the vast floors of the Gold Bar and Casino, where he gambled with chips made from solid gold. There were no windows or clocks, and security men watched from tracks above the paneled and coffered ceiling.

"Paradise in the midst of hell," was how the writer Ovid Demaris described Agua Caliente. For years the resort—with its hotel, bungalows, swimming pools, golf course, spas, stables, and racetrack—would serve Hollywood and Southern California as an exclusive retreat. It was over the border where American laws didn't apply and L.A. reporters knew not to snoop. Charlie Chaplin, Mary Pickford, Douglas Fairbanks, and Clark Gable would be frequent visitors; likewise Harry Cohn, Jack Warner, and other studio bosses. Margarita Cansino, later known as Rita Hayworth, would be discovered there, dancing in the cabaret. Designed by the young architect Wayne McAllister, Agua Caliente was a prototype for Las Vegas, where McAllister would later create The Sands casino and hotel.

Dave Clark's diaries were strictly appointment books, lists of names and times and places. He wrote few letters and left no commentary on his life. He wasn't self-conscious in that way and remains impenetrable and hard to read. But we know that he fell in love with Agua Caliente because he would return there again and again, rubbing shoulders with the high rollers and the Hollywood aristocracy. The resort was like a gorgeous movie set that suited, perhaps, Clark's inner sense of his own drama and glamor. He had a high opinion of himself—with some reason, for he was a man whose gifts and guts had already taken him far.

Clark came back refreshed from Agua Caliente, and the second trial of Albert Marco entered its second week. Meanwhile, a wild buying orgy sent stocks soaring on Wall Street; at San Quentin hundreds sought tickets to see the Los Angeles murderer Edward Hickman hang; and on a busy street in Chicago, Tony Lombardo, Al Capone's aide and consigliore, was killed, struck by two dum-dum bullets that ripped away half his head. In L.A. the spate of unsolved underworld murders went on: Bobby Lee, "Chinese flapper bride," was gunned down in Chinatown; the bullet-ridden body of Bozo Lancer was found on the floor of his North Broadway restaurant; Philip Rubino, the "proprietor of a grapejuice and bottle supply company," was killed by a shotgun blast outside his Compton home. In connection with Rubino's killing, the *L.A. Examiner* used the word "mafia," perhaps for the first time in the paper's history. "The Mafia supposedly never forget," LAPD Captain William Bright told reporters. There's rich irony here, for later it would be revealed that two LAPD cops had in fact killed Rubino, acting under orders from somebody in the Los Angeles "System"—maybe Marco himself.

Clark rested a prosecution case that he knew to be weak. His best efforts had been undermined at every juncture, and the defense began to call its witnesses. Among the first was Earl Kynette, an LAPD lieutenant who testified that he knew Albert Marco well. "The defendant is a peaceful man," Earl Kynette said. Ten years hence, in 1938, Kynette—by then a captain and the head of LAPD's notorious Red Squad, a unit that was set up to monitor and arrest Communists but became a tool of the underworld—would himself be prosecuted for attempted murder, having placed a bomb in the car of a private investigator hired by civic reformers. But in 1928, the LAPD's connection with the rackets was not the open secret it would become, nor were the Marco trials seen as they would later be perceived—as an early chapter in the long, turbulent story of citizens trying to regain control of city politics.

Next witness for the defense was Evelyn Brogan, the "legal secretary," who testified that when the shooting broke out at the Ship Café, Marco had been so scared she'd had to hold his hand. Sitting in his chair, looking plump and complacent, Marco smirked.

"Who did fire the shots, if the defendant didn't?" Clark asked.

"I didn't see," Evelyn Brogan replied, and Marco smiled again.

It was at this moment that Marco's attorneys, perhaps overconfident, made their big mistake. Joseph Moore, the hulking chauffeur of Marco's Packard, shambled onto the stand. Far from smart, he nonetheless gave his evidence with unblushing effrontery. "It was I who shot Dominick Conterno," he said.

Sitting in his usual spot at the back of the courtroom, Leslie White said he was unsure whether to laugh or gasp as Moore told how he'd just finished parking the car when he heard a commotion in the Ship Café.

"I ran to the swinging doors and looked in. I saw four or five men beating Marco up," Moore went on. He said he ran

49

back to the car to get a jack or something, a weapon. "The first thing I saw in the car was the gun, a .32 caliber pistol, and I grabbed it and ran back up into the café."

Moore described how he stood beside Marco, with the gun placed beside Marco's hip, and opened fire when the assailants tried to attack his boss again. "I was trying to scare them. I didn't mean to injure anybody," he said. "Afterwards I ran onto the beach and buried the gun in the sand."

Dave Clark, in his cross-examination, asked Moore whether he could remember exactly where he'd hidden the gun. Moore said yes—it was close by the Ocean Park lifeguard station. Clark then called for an adjournment, so that he, Moore, and officers of the court could search for the weapon. A trip westward duly ensued, and the automatic was retrieved. An expert's examination established that the gun had been in the sand only a matter of days, not for the two months that had passed since the shooting.

"This story is an utter and ridiculous fabrication, a device that the defense seems to have cooked up with the help of Broadway," Dave Clark said when proceedings resumed. He was referring to a recent play, *The Racket* by Bartlett Cormack, in which a stooge takes the blame for his underworld boss. "I'll prove that Joe Moore wasn't within fifteen miles of the Ship Café when the shootings took place."

Moore, called back to the stand, now kept his mouth shut, refusing to answer any more of Clark's probings about his phony confession, and was promptly arrested for perjury.

"Moore was a 'goat' who'd been paid $10,000 to take the rap, plus an additional $10,000 for each year he spent in the pen at San Quentin," wrote Gene Coughlin in the *Daily News*.

Albert Marco appeared unconcerned; he went on doodling and chatting with his friends, unaware that the trial was about to take one more sensational twist.

Judge Doran, convinced that certain jury members had been bribed, threatened, or otherwise tampered with, called counsel for both sides into his chambers and told them he was planning to dismiss all twelve of the present panel.

Dave Clark jumped on this. "If you take my advice, Judge, you'll get rid of them and never let them come back."

Howls of protest came from the Marco side—to no avail. In a scene reminiscent of Brian DePalma's Prohibition gangster movie *The Untouchables*, Doran marched out one jury and swore in another before rushing the trial to its conclusion.

This gave Clark the opportunity to draw on a skill learned from Earl Rogers, who is credited with inventing the art of cross-examination in its modern form. In the famous 1902 Catalina Island Murder Case he cajoled, badgered, and lulled a witness into admitting his guilt concerning the killing for which another man was on trial. When Albert Marco took the stand in his own defense, Clark had no need for melodrama. Standing in front of him was an ideal candidate for cross-examination, a defendant who was surly and ill-prepared yet believed himself invulnerable. The trial transcript reads wonderfully:

Clark: "Did you fire the shots?"
Marco: "No."
Clark: "But you were at the Ship Café that night."
Marco: "Yes."
Clark: "You heard the shots?"

Marco: "Yes."

Clark: "Where were you at the time?"

Marco: "I can't remember."

Clark: "Many witnesses have testified that you did indeed fire the shots. You took aim and shot Dominick Conterno in the back."

Marco: "I didn't fire those shots. But if the jury believes I did I want them to know I was acting in self-defense."

Evidence was reprised, closing statements made. The new jury went out, and though expected to remain out for at least a day, returned within hours, finding Albert Marco guilty on all counts, whereupon, Gene Coughlin reported in the *News*, Marco's "wry smile turned to a sneer."

Marco's attorneys sought a new trial, but Judge Doran refused it and found himself facing death threats. So did Dave Clark. Undeterred, Clark pressed for the maximum sentence and a week later Doran handed Marco fourteen to twenty years in San Quentin.

"BIG PAPA SENT TO PEN!" said the headline in the *News*.

It all ended in such a hurry that Leslie White missed the moment when the jury delivered its verdict. He'd been struck most of all by the sheer theatricality of the trial, and how different it had been from those he'd seen in Ventura County. "Here in Los Angeles nobody spoke of the truth—they spoke of testimony and evidence. If a witness tried to tell a straightforward story, he was heckled by both the defense and the prosecution until he was too bewildered and confused to remember anything," he wrote. He recorded, too, further impressions of Dave Clark. "A big city attorney. Young, standing upright. Brave, with a real military bearing."

Dave Clark felt the heat of fame. His picture appeared in the papers and he showed that he knew how to milk the moment. "Marco went to extreme measures to try to ensure his freedom," he said. "But the jury came back with the only verdict twelve intelligent people could return. This serves notice on gangland—Los Angeles won't tolerate racketeers big or little."

"The blue-eyed prosecutor did his job courageously and honestly," reported Gene Coughlin, whose path would one day cross Clark's again in very different circumstances. "The people of this city should congratulate the gangbusting lawyer and handsome poloist."

Dave Clark wasn't Earl Rogers yet, but this was more than a beginning. He was the lawyer with guts enough to take on the underworld and brains enough to win.

6

Oil, Law, and Scandal

Albert Marco had worked with, and for, Charlie Crawford, the "kingpin politician" of whose murder Dave Clark would be accused in 1931. Yet, throughout the entire course of the Marco trials, and in all the reporting of those trials, Crawford's name was never mentioned. He occupied a higher rung than Marco on the ladder of the L.A. System, but for the moment remained where he wanted to be—in the background, in the shadows, known only to those by whom he wished to be known, or those who wouldn't or didn't dare to mention his name. Crawford's power lay behind the scenes, and relied on secrecy. This would change, much to Crawford's dismay. The brazen corruption of which he was a part would soon be flushed out into the open. Leslie White had arrived in L.A. at the time when crime and the integrity of those who should have been enforcing the law had become a major issue. Forces of reform were fighting back.

"Albert Marco has finally discovered that his money, his power, his more or less respectable political contacts, his threats, his promises and his pleas are unavailing in the face of simple honesty and unassuming integrity and courage. The lesson he has learned will not be confined to himself; it will permeate the entire realm of criminal thought and activity here," claimed the *L.A. Times*, sounding a hopeful if pompous note. "Had he been able through the unlimited fund at his command to set aside the just disposition of his case he would have afforded to those of his kind a shining example of what can be achieved by the unscrupulous use of wealth and influence."

The Women's Republican League of Van Nuys, in supporting Judge William Doran for reelection, spoke more forcefully of "a terrific struggle by all the influences of evil, subtle and bold, from the lowest depths of society to the high circles, to flaunt the law. Los Angeles is facing a crisis in the battle between civic righteousness and the underworld."

In November 1928 the city elected a new District Attorney, Buron Fitts, who would keep the job until 1940. Controversial and tenacious, Fitts would see out the death throes of L.A.'s adolescence and survive the depressed years of the city's early maturity. He would be a key and ultimately compromised figure both in that transition and in the struggle for reform. He was big-nosed, big-talking, anti-labor, anti-radical, anti-liquor, still—at age thirty-three—young, and a favorite of Harry Chandler, publisher of the *Times*. Photographs show a shaven-headed, bright-eyed, mean-faced man gazing at the camera, unsure whether to snarl or smile. Soon after his election, he struck out a city ordinance that had legalized slot machines and staged raids on downtown nightclubs and gambling ships off Long Beach, making sure that the press tagged along. Throughout his career, Fitts knew the value of a photo op. He was more a politician than a lawyer.

Fitts reshaped the D.A.'s office, getting rid of the previous regime's deadwood and retaining a staff nucleus of only thirteen assistant D.A.s, a number to which he would quickly add new recruits. Dave Clark—fresh from the Marco triumph—was among those kept on, and Fitts handed Clark both a salary increase and greater responsibilities within the trials department. Clark celebrated by buying a couple of new suits, and driving with Nancy to Agua Caliente for dinner; they danced in the ballroom and toasted with champagne.

Fitts also restructured the D.A.'s investigative unit. He brought in a friend, Lucien Wheeler, a one-time presidential bodyguard and former Los Angeles bureau chief of the Federal Bureau of Investigation (BOI, the predecessor of the FBI), to head up the show. Wheeler let go many of the incumbent staff and started to recruit a new team. Within weeks he had more than 3,100 applications on file for some thirty jobs.

Meanwhile, Leslie White had been wondering what to do with his life. One day at his aunt's house in Hollywood, he was delighted to be visited by friends from Ventura County. They came in with long faces because the word back in Ventura had been that Leslie White was at death's door. They were amazed to find him on his feet and hear him say he was itching to get back to work. One had heard about Buron Fitts's new investigative unit and suggested, "Why not apply?"

Armed with letters of recommendation, White went again

to the Hall of Justice, this time riding the elevator to the seventh floor and the D.A.'s office. He was young and green, but his experiences as a deputy in Ventura and during the St. Francis Dam disaster worked in his favor. He'd photographed and identified hundreds of corpses so was at least unfazed by the sight of death. He landed a job specializing in the gathering of material evidence. Police forensics was then in its infancy. Fingerprint classification, corpse temperature graphs to determine the time of death, and the comparison microscope for bullets were still relatively new techniques. In 1923 the forward-looking August Vollmer, then briefly head of the LAPD, had created America's first crime lab. Now Fitts's office would have one too. Leslie White would become, in his way, a pioneer and a crusader. "Politically Los Angeles was in a panic. The reformers were sweeping into every office, looting and pillaging the old system. Having reached the saturation point of corruption, the old regime had been driven from power and the 'revolution' was on," as he later wrote. "I was for the 'cause' and loved a fight."

Buron Fitts's first big objective was the prosecution, not of some racketeer or notorious murderer, but the previous District Attorney, Asa "Ace" Keyes, the man who until recently had been Fitts's boss. Behind this unlikely turn of events lay the most spectacular fraud in L.A.'s history. "The Julian Petroleum debacle, in which thirty thousand investors were milked out of untold millions of dollars, touched off the fuse which blew the politicians out of the limelight," wrote Leslie White. "The grafters had been in power a long time and Los Angeles was in a bad state of affairs. The Julian Pete symbolized it all."

The story began years earlier, in 1885, when Chauncey C. Julian, later to be known as "C.C.," was born in Manitoba, Canada, the son of an impoverished farmer. As a boy he sold newspapers. As a young man he drove a milk wagon, clerked in a clothing store, sold jewelry and building supplies, worked in real estate, and in the oil fields of Texas worked as a rigger. In 1921 he arrived, penniless, in L.A. and started peddling stock in oil leases. His first promotion fizzled. Then he had a massive stroke of luck: on a four-acre lease he drilled five wells and all five came in, producing gushers. His first investors earned money, and he gained a following. Soon he was acquiring more leases, opening gas stations, and selling millions of dollars in stock. He had his own radio station and pilloried the big oil companies. He called his own gas "Defiance"—a nice touch.

Breezy as a door-to-door salesman, brandishing his fist or pointing his thumb and forefinger in the shape of a pistol, Julian had shrewd insight into the mind-set of the small American investor, confronting head-on the accusation that he was a con man. His daily press advertisements became a feature of city life. He told those who couldn't afford to take a chance not to bother while urging the adventurous of spirit to plunge. "Come on, folks, you'll never make a thin dime just lookin' on. I've got a surefire winner this time, a thousand to one shot. We just can't lose. We're all out here in California where the gushers are and we just ought to clean up. Come on, folks, get aboard for the big ride," he said. Or: "I've got a wonder coming up, folks. She's not only warm, she's 'red hot'—right off the coals. How big? Oh, I don't know—she looks like a hundred million dollars."

Julian became for a couple of years as grand a celebrity as any in L.A. Reporters tracked his every step, gleeful when Chaplin decked him after a spat in the nightclub Café Petroushka or when he gave a Cadillac to a hatcheck girl. To continue doling out dividends, and to pay for his four homes and the gold-lined bathtub into which he plunged each morning, he kept issuing more and more stock, turning his original operation into a scheme of the sort recently made famous by Charles Ponzi. Ponzi, a smiling, skimmer-wearing, cane-wielding con man who ran a get-rich-quick scheme in Boston, had promised that investors would double their money within three months. To fulfill this pledge, he only needed ever larger numbers of investors, and for a while they flocked forward. It was a classic pyramid scheme, earning Ponzi $2 million a week at one point, typical of the money-mania that swept America in the 1920s and seen more recently in the Bernard Madoff affair. But taking from Peter to pay Paul can't last forever: Ponzi's scheme collapsed and he was sent to jail.

Likewise, by 1925 C. C. Julian was in trouble. He bowed out, or was pushed out, handing over control of his companies to a group of businessmen, "nimble-witted magicians" according to the *Times*. They were led by S. C. Lewis, a lawyer from Texas, and his sidekick Jake Berman, alias Jack Bennett, "the boy Ponzi of the Pacific Coast," "a two-name man as dangerous to a community's state of mind as a two-gun man."

Lewis and Berman kicked the Julian Pete into another gear, intent on fraud from the start. The swindlers stepped in, bought brokerage houses, and invited celebrities and rich investors (shakers and movers like Charlie Crawford) to form privileged "rings," boosting the stock they then watered. Over four million shares were sold at a par value of $200 million. Punters were gullible, and besides, this was one of those times in American economic life when it was possible to buy into a scam and still make money—so long as you got out in time, or were on the inside.

Some 40,000 Angelenos—high and low, and almost everybody in between—invested in the Julian Pete. Local reporter Guy Finney wrote: "They knew their city was galloping along at dizzying speed. The easy money carnival spirit gripped them. They sang it from every real estate and stock peddling platform, in every glittering club and café, in banks and at newsstands . . . The dollar sign was on parade. Why marvel then that like epidemic measles among the young it spread from banker to broker to merchant to clerk to stenographer to scrubwoman to office boy, to the man who carried his dinner pail . . . The mass craving wanted its honey on the table while the banquet was on. It simply couldn't await a soberer day."

A single word explains this story of a city gone nuts: oil. In the 1920s L.A. was primarily an oil town. Oil derricks rose high in the middle of major boulevards while nodding donkeys dotted the hillsides. Thirteen hundred or so oil wells operated throughout the Los Angeles Basin, in places "as thick as holes in a pepper box," producing scores of thousands of barrels a day, one-fifth of the world's oil output at that time. Amazing.

A 1923 photo of Signal Hill in Long Beach shows hundreds of oil derricks bristling above a few blocks of California bungalows. Water, and the theft of water, allowed L.A. to grow, but oil was the bonanza. Oil promised swift and transforming wealth. Oil created Los Angeles as a plausible business hub and prompted the development of an industrial base that would later manufacture much of the world's aircraft and automobile tires. Promoters ran bus trips to the oil fields where salesmen bore down bearing "sandwiches, cookies, and huge cups of coffee," according to the *Saturday Evening Post* (in the central part of a 1923 series about the L.A. boom titled "Mad from Oil!"). It was the free chicken dinner school of finance. People bought oil stock because they saw derricks and wells and blowouts right there in their backyards. "It was like drilling for oil at Fifth Avenue and Forty-second Street in Manhattan," said one Texas oil man. Lawns and parks and houses were constantly plowed up so new wells could go down. Homeowners banded together to sell their properties to big developers. When Upton Sinclair wrote his 1927 muckraking novel set in the city, he didn't call it *Movies!;* he called it *Oil!* Nobody wanted to be bothered with memories of struggling, frugal days. "Little people were suddenly seized with the vision of becoming big people and were driven half-crazy with a mixture of greed and fear," said Sinclair's wife, May Craig, observing the madness. "We were right in the center of an oil cyclone."

The Julian Pete grew and grew until on Friday, May 6, 1927, the inevitable happened. "This hapless May day . . . expressed by the nature of things in Los Angeles in the serenity of sunlit skies and outward peace . . . saw the Julian Petroleum stock mirage crumble to earth . . . saw one of the most spectacular and unreal promotional dreams ever fostered in the great, upclimbing Pacific Coast go into swift eclipse . . . saw frenzied stock gamblers, conscience-heavy bankers, wide-eyed, anxiety-driven business and professional men running around in fear . . . saw an explosion blast more than 40,000 stockholders who unwittingly had dumped their savings on the swindling bonfire," wrote Guy Finney.

The great Los Angeles bubble had burst and trade in Julian Pete stock was suspended. Those 40,000 investors awoke to the realization that they'd been fleeced of $150 million; many of them had been ruined, and almost at once they raised angry cries for justice and revenge. What had happened? Who had done this? To District Attorney Asa Keyes fell the task of rounding up the fraudulent malefactors. Indictments against Lewis, Berman, and a host of others were issued by a grand jury in the summer of 1927. But when, after a succession of delays, judicial proceedings finally began in January 1928, Asa Keyes—shuffling, uncertain, apparently indifferent—recommended to the jury sitting in a courtroom in L.A.'s fancy new marbled Hall of Justice that charges against the accused be dropped. And so, amid chaotic scenes, the case of the *People of California v. Lewis, Bennett, et al.* collapsed.

Judge Doran (he also presided over the Marco trials) knew the result should have been different and expressed his surprise in scathing terms: "I feel that diligence on the part of District Attorney Keyes would have brought a different verdict," he said. All hope of retribution against those who'd plundered the Julian Pete seemed to have been lost.

The verdict divided the city's press. The *Examiner* seemed unconcerned, arguing that this was how the nitty-gritty of business sometimes worked and business, after all, was America's lifeblood. The *Times*, on the other hand, had an axe to grind against Asa Keyes. Rumors had long persisted that, back in 1926, Keyes took a $30,000 payoff following the sensational disappearance of the evangelist Aimee McPherson. A pile of clothes was found on Ocean Park Beach in Santa Monica and for thirty-two sensation-packed days, the world wondered where she was. Several of her distraught followers killed themselves, and the city spent vast sums organizing a search. Then McPherson reappeared with a tale of having been kidnapped, although it soon came out that she'd been shacked up in a hotel with the man who was her radio operator and lover. "Her followers were kneeling in the sand, praying for her to come back walking on the water," wrote reporter Adela Rogers St. Johns, the daughter of Earl Rogers. "Instead she came up in the desert in Arizona with a young man named Ormiston." Asa Keyes brought McPherson to court and charged her with obstruction of justice then did an about-face and dropped proceedings. Now, for the *Times*, it seemed the same had happened again, this time within a situation that reached deeper; the Julian Pete swindle had touched most of the city's population one way or another.

The *Times* got proof of Keyes's corruption in the shape of a diary, a little black book that had been kept by Milton Pike, an assistant to a prominent downtown tailor named Ben Getzoff, whose shop at 609 Spring Street was near the courts and the business district. In his diary Pike had recorded the various comings and goings, and the shady transactions, that took place in the back of Getzoff's shop, all of which he observed through an angled mirror. Prominent Julian Pete players had been frequent visitors, likewise Asa Keyes, "often half-lit" on the bootleg booze kept there. Pike alleged that he'd seen Keyes accept lavish gifts and bribes. At first Keyes denied the charges and refused to resign, but accumulating evidence forced his hand. Asa "Ace" Keyes, the Los Angeles

District Attorney, a public servant of twenty-four years, had taken money and thrown the most important trial on his watch. Some were shocked, but many perplexed and faith-shaken Angelenos thought this outcome logical. "So pock-marked was this slimy business with fraud and faith-lessness, so infiltrated with shuffling and trimming, with bad faith and treachery, money-juggling and moral back-sliding, that few citizens were greatly surprised at this dramatic turn," wrote Guy Finney.

Enter Buron Fitts, elected with a mandate to get Keyes and clean house. Making Julian Pete prosecutions would become the holy grail of Fitts's first term as D.A. In time he'd learn that the Julian Pete was an unending and unfathomable story. The scandal symbolized the crazy prosperity of the 1920s boom and presaged the despairing time that was to follow. Its consequences would ripple on and on, gaining force until they became bewildering for Fitts and, in the end, deadly for the likes of Charlie Crawford.

7

Our Detective
Learns the Ropes

The trial of Asa Keyes, former District Attorney for the County of Los Angeles, gave Leslie White his first important assignment in his new job with the D.A.'s office. Jake Berman (aka Jack Bennett, the "two-name man") and one of the leading Julian Pete conspirators, had turned state's evidence in exchange for the immunity Buron Fitts granted him. As a result, Berman found his life under threat and White was to be his bodyguard. Forensics was nowhere on White's agenda. As he later wrote, "When trapped by the reform administration, Berman sold his confederates down the river. In this wise, he gained his release and my particular task was to keep either his former friends or the thousands of victims from killing him."

Jake Berman was twenty-eight, only a few years older than White, but the two men could not have been more different. Berman grew up in the Brooklyn ghetto, worked as a runner on Wall Street, and served time for fraud in a New Jersey prison. He'd arrived in L.A. with nothing but a suitcase and the friendship of S. C. Lewis. He had a round face and thinning hair, but his soulful brown eyes made him handsome as a gigolo. He sported silk neckties with a stickpin bearing a diamond the size of a dime. He'd proven himself a master manipulator and salesman, capable of making ten suckers grow where previously there'd been only one. He'd thrown $20,000 parties with champagne and movie starlets on hand to gladden the hearts and soften the purse strings of big investors. In one sixteen-month period—January 1926 to April 1927—his bank transactions totaled $67 million. "Gossips say the boy wonder had $2 million in $10,000 bills in a body belt on his person," wrote Lorin Baker in 1931. When Julian Pete crashed, Berman had eluded capture, fleeing to Europe on the ocean liner *Berengeria*, carrying $625,000 in that same chamois leather belt. He landed in England and outfoxed the Scotland Yard men sent to catch him. In time he returned to America of his own free will, traveling first class on another liner, the *France*, and surrendered to Buron Fitts in L.A. His soft-leathered shoes were natty and expensive, his suits cut from the finest cloth. He was a classic conman: people came to him in droves, wanting something for nothing; he gave them nothing but took plenty.

White and his partner, the more experienced Blayney Matthews, kept Berman holed up in an apartment house at Hollywood and Vine. Next door a nightclub dancer played jazz on the phonograph all day long. Berman tapped on a table, beating the rhythm. He was restless, irritated by this confinement, and kept ordering White to fetch him coffee and sandwiches. No doubt this rankled, as did Berman's grinning certainty that he could manipulate the law with ease. He had bilked investors out of millions, yet he expected to walk away. "You'll help me do it," he told White.

"Berman was sleek and flashily groomed; he reminded me of a wharf rat that has just climbed out of the water. He had brazen bulging eyes," White wrote. "He was a bumptious Jew."

An FBI report notes Berman's "hebraic features," and White's remark to some extent reflects standard race prejudice for the era. It still sticks in the throat. Here was material for a comedy: the country boy, new to the city, boxed in a room guarding the life of a man he professes to despise but perhaps secretly envies—the smoothest of smooth urban operators. White earned $55 a week, not a bad wage at the time, but Berman had between two and three million dollars salted away in safe deposit boxes all over town. White hated Berman with a vengeance; Berman, when he noticed White at all, treated him with a mixture of arrogance and contempt, laughing in White's face when White said he believed what politicians told him. "It's all just a show. Wind to rope the suckers," Berman said.

Jake Berman's defection decided the fate of Asa Keyes. The trial's result was never really at issue. First, the prosecution put Milton Pike on the stand. Pike ran through the allegations that had already been published and closed his testimony by reading his diary entry for July 28, 1928, the last day he worked for Ben Getzoff, when he saw Asa Keyes drive up to the tailor's shop in a brand new Lincoln coupe. This prepared the way for star witness Jake Berman, "debonair and with a multitude of diamonds flashing on his fingers," said the *Examiner*, who told how Keyes came to get that new Lincoln, and much more.

Keyes, acting through Getzoff, had put on the squeeze, first demanding $10,000 from Berman to cover gambling debts. Then Keyes wanted a gift for his house, a chaise lounge with fabric chosen from Brooks Brothers. Then a new car, a Chevrolet, for his daughter, "as it will please me and help the situation along." Then the Lincoln, and an additional $10,000 so that Keyes could get the property he'd just bought in Beverly Hills out of escrow. One day Getzoff suggested that Berman might buy Keyes a set of golf clubs, and forced Berman to wait while he got Keyes on the phone—choosing makes, weights, and sizes. The clubs, inlaid with the initials "A.K.," were then delivered in a splendid leather golf bag to Keyes's home. All this suggests that the Roaring Twenties underworld as evoked by Damon Runyon corresponds more closely to the real thing than we might suppose. These "jungle-dwellers," as Louis Adamic called them, had a sense of mischief about their greed.

Berman bribed Asa Keyes to the extent of $40,000. On the witness stand, Keyes attacked the crooked character of his accuser but couldn't dent Berman's credibility. Judge Ben Butler, entirely sold, reckoned that Berman was as persuasive a witness as any he'd ever seen.

Dave Clark was part of the prosecution team. No doubt this was a way of proving his loyalty to his new boss Buron Fitts. And it was another high-profile trial, a way of continuing to build his career. Clark joined in the fun, describing Keyes "on his way to heaven, wearing a smoking jacket, listening to an $1150 radio with a set of golf clubs in one corner, a Lincoln roadster on behind as a trailer, and in his hands a sheaf of Ben Getzoff's liquor prescriptions."

Buron Fitts had none of Dave Clark's experience or flair

as a trial lawyer. Still, he knew how to play a courtroom hand as strong as this. He protested all along that he'd been hoping and waiting for his old boss Asa Keyes to prove his innocence. "He has utterly failed," Fitts said. "He has debased and rendered contemptible this county in the eyes of the world. He has made the Temple of Justice a den of thieves. By your verdict you will say whether this sordid, rotten, putrid scheme of things as carried on by Asa Keyes will continue in Los Angeles County."

In the evening of February 8, 1929, the jury deliberated only ninety minutes before finding Keyes, and co-conspirator Ben Getzoff, guilty on all counts. Keyes turned ashen, knowing that he would be sentenced to San Quentin, where many of the murderers and crooks he himself had prosecuted were still serving time. In San Quentin Keyes became prisoner number 48,218. His hair was shorn, like that of a common thief. He was photographed, fingerprinted, and put in a cell in the old men's ward. "What is life?" he said, passing through the prison gates. "We have an hour of consciousness and then we are gone."

Ben Getzoff, on hearing the verdict, was less philosophical. Crushed, he slumped in his seat, exclaiming: "That settles it!"

The verdicts rocked L.A., confirming what many had feared and suspected: the Julian Pete had been a huckster's paradise in which a chosen few had looted the pockets of the average Joe. Now the chosen few were fighting among themselves like dogs. Some joined with Fitts in his hope that the irreputable city was at last becoming reputable. Others agreed that this might be a new beginning, but saw the events as a foreboding—as if the next cycle would see not a coming together but a falling apart that would prove still more violent. L.A. was on the verge of something.

"The trial of Asa Keyes and his co-defendants was a spectacle I shall never forget. The courtroom was always jammed with celebrities, many from the film colony," White wrote, fascinated and horrified by how a smart courtroom attorney like Dave Clark could heckle, bewilder, and confuse a well-meaning witness. Clark would start a witness off slowly, letting him relax, and "then abruptly hurl question after question at him until the poor devil did not know what was happening." White resolved that when the time came to take the stand himself, he would adopt the trick of counting to three before answering even the simplest question, such as his name or address, so that when the tougher and more confusing questions came, his pauses wouldn't be conspicuous.

The tailor Ben Getzoff, meanwhile, sick with ulcers and groaning with pain, feared that he was about to die. Dramatically he called for Buron Fitts and named more names, men who'd been part of a fixing ring that centered around his shop. Getzoff's goal was to extricate himself from the slammer, and Fitts seized on the chance to gain more column inches. The story Getzoff told "will shake this county to its very foundations," Fitts said, making political hay. The names Getzoff coughed up included politicians, attorneys, and one "who held a higher position in the community than any of the others," Fitts said.

The saga of Julian Pete entered a new phase.

Jake Berman, meanwhile, wanted to start living again and was determined to go out to dinner. White and Blayney Matthews usually let Berman go out the door first. On the evening after the trial, however, Blayney Matthews himself led the way and saw a gunman open his coat and pull out an automatic pistol. Matthews slammed shut the door just as the gunman readied himself to shoot. Two bullets punched through the door and into a wall.

"To kill Berman would have been an act of justifiable homicide, but we defended him at risk to our own lives," wrote Leslie White. His innocence and principles were no pose; he sincerely believed that if enough individuals refused to be corrupted, the system could be changed. Berman was the first of his reality instructors, but White couldn't yet respond to Berman's blithe, opportunistic cynicism. Instead he saw problems that needed to be solved. White's idealism was like a thick rope, tough to cut.

8

Shots in the Night

Just a few days after the conclusion of the Asa Keyes trial, on February 17, 1929, Leslie White received another phone call in the middle of the night, around 2 A.M. Lucien Wheeler, head of the D.A.'s investigative unit, was on the line.

"Les, young Doheny has just been murdered. Get out to their Beverly Hills home as soon as possible," Wheeler said.

Half-asleep, White again struggled to understand the immensity of what he'd just heard. "You mean E. L. Doheny's son?"

"The same. I'll meet you there," said Wheeler, and hung up.

White scrambled into his clothes, gathered his cameras and fingerprint gear, loaded his car, and drove into the night. He didn't need to be told the address—his aunt had often pointed out the Doheny mansion, Greystone, looming high in the hills. Everybody knew where the Dohenys lived. They were, along with the Chandlers of the *Times*, among the most powerful families in L.A.—the elite, the ruling aristocracy. E. L. Doheny, the old man of the family, was one of the richest men in America; his life story recalled a Western dime novel, but his power reached throughout the realm, rivaling that of J. P. Morgan or John D. Rockefeller. He was a legend.

It had been Edward L. Doheny who, flat broke and still hopeful after almost twenty years of scrambling for gold and silver throughout the West, first struck oil in L.A. back in 1892. Within a year he had sixty-nine more wells pumping, most in residential districts, setting in motion the oil boom. "He had developed the Midas touch," the *New York Times* would observe. "Gold flowed out of the grounds at his command." With the California market in hand, Doheny ventured into Mexico, gained a lease on a million acres around the port of Tampico, on which he built roads, railways, shops, warehouses, and living quarters, creating a whole city around the oil he struck. What he'd found in California was nothing compared to his great Mexican wells—Cassiano 6 & 7, Cerro Azul 4. They were like oceans, producing hundreds of thousands of barrels a day, turning the vivid colors of the tropical jungle glistening black. Thus Doheny became the most successful prospector in history, much more successful than he or anybody else had become through gold, silver, or gems. When the Mexican Revolution began in 1910, Doheny bribed officials and financed a private army to protect the region he controlled, lobbying hard in Washington to bring the objectives of the U.S. government in line with his own. He was involved in plots, uprisings, and attempted coups d'etat. Some of his contemporaries believed him responsible for the assassination of Mexican President Venustiano Carranza in 1920.

By the early 1920s E. L. Doheny was worth more than $300 million. He was short and slight, with stooped shoulders. He had sharp blue-gray eyes and a thick, graying moustache. He spoke quickly and was impulsive and overbearing. Always willful and driven, he'd beaten down almost overwhelming obstacles. Success had made him both pigheaded and feared, like a Napoleon in Los Angeles.

At the turn of the century he'd bought a mansion in Chester Place, then the city's most exclusive district, where big homes were grouped around a park. When he moved in, he decided this should be his own kingdom, and bought all the other houses so he could rule as he pleased. Singlehandedly he funded the building of St. Vincent's, the magnificent Roman Catholic Church that still stands at Adams and Figueroa, near his Chester Place compound. Doheny hobnobbed with presidents and heads of state. His companies were major suppliers to the U.S. Navy and the Cunard Line. Gas stations—their signs bearing the Doheny symbol, a green shamrock—had sprung up all over Southern California. As president of the American Association for Recognition of the Irish Republic, he was the country's leading funder of Sinn Féin and the Irish Republican Army (IRA). Promoters, eager to thrill people with the idea of wealth and to hammer home the dream of money, took their prospects on bus tours of L.A., pointing out both the old wells Doheny had brought in and the palatial Chester Place residence, "home of the *multi*-millionaire." William Randolph Hearst, the newspaper magnate, complained that it was tough to hire journalists because Doheny had put so many of the best ones on his own payroll—protecting Doheny interests, supporting Doheny positions.

Doheny had a sense of humor and was used to bending entire nations to his purpose. He so hated to lose that he routinely appeared in court to fight speeding tickets, having fun torturing the judge a little before handing over the fine, a detail that Upton Sinclair seized upon and gave to his fictional oil magnate J. Arnold Ross in *Oil!* B. Traven, the socialist author of *The Treasure of the Sierra Madre*, had featured Doheny's Mexican plots and counterplots in another of his novels, *The White Rose*. Doheny, then, was admired, reviled, a figure of awesome accomplishment and domineering arrogance—an emblem of American success in all its profligate and controlling glory.

In the early hours of the morning of February 17, 1929, speeding in his Model T Ford through the dark streets, Leslie White sat with his back straight, peering shortsightedly through his horn-rims, gripping the steering wheel tight, and smelling the cool fragrance of the Los Angeles night through the open window. He was nervous and excited, knowing that he was calling on power. This, for White, was something entirely strange and new—a real taste of the big time. He was aware, too, that the situation would touch upon not only the supposed murder but an already existing scandal that had rocked the country and wrecked a presidency.

The First World War confirmed that oil—possession of oil, control of oil—was central to military power. Washington politicians increasingly sought E. L. Doheny's opinion and support through the decade 1910–1920, when his influence and the twenty million barrels of oil he provided yearly for ships, airplanes, cars, trucks, and tanks became crucial. As early as 1917, Doheny appeared before a Senate Committee, arguing that oil-rich American lands laid aside for the U.S.

Navy should be commercially exploited. Josephus Daniels, then Secretary of the Navy, opposed the idea. He quizzed Doheny about Mexican oil he was providing for American ships. This oil had a high sulfur content that, when burned, made much more smoke than Doheny had promised it would. Doheny replied with a twinkle: "I lied about it."

Warren Harding, on his election as president in 1920, appointed a new Navy Secretary, Edwin Denby, who, unlike his predecessor, was pro-oil and anti-conservationist. Doheny stepped up efforts to get hold of federal lands located in Elk Hills, California, and Teapot Dome, Wyoming; and Denby soon handed over control of the matter to another Harding appointee—the new Secretary of the Interior, Albert Fall.

Now the story became pleasingly plot-heavy and intimately corrupt because Albert Fall was Edward L. Doheny's oldest friend in the world. They'd played poker together and been partners back in the early 1880s in the wild mining town of Kingston, Arizona. There Fall, a big fellow with piercing black eyes, had never been without a gun and liked to boast that he'd killed men. Since then Fall had done well as a lawyer, and prospered as part of the Santa Fe property ring that ordered the assassination of legendary lawman Pat Garrett, himself the killer of Billy the Kid. Later Fall became senator for the fledgling state of New Mexico—another story, apparently, of the frontier spirit surviving to triumph in the twentieth century. Fall, like Doheny, gained power; but unlike his friend, he didn't know how to hold on to his money. He lived high and was always short of cash. In 1921, when he took office as Secretary of the Interior, he owed taxes and was heavily in debt—inconveniences he was just managing to keep secret.

Fall arranged for Doheny to meet President Harding, and soon handed his old friend the Elk Hills lease, which Doheny reckoned would be worth more than $100 million. In exchange Doheny agreed to build the vast oil storage facilities that would allow the creation of a deep water port for the U.S. Navy in Hawaii—Pearl Harbor.

All this was incestuous, corrupt in the predictable way of the world, but would have been "perfectly legal," as Doheny later said, were it not for one detail: on November 30, 1921, Doheny's son, twenty-eight-year-old Edward L. Doheny, Jr., acting on his father's instructions, withdrew $100,000 from a New York bank account, stuffed it in a black leather satchel, carried it by train to Washington and, in a room at the Waldman Park Hotel, presented the money—five $20,000 bundles bound with rubber bands—to Albert Fall.

Unknown to the Dohenys, Fall made a similar deal with oilman Harry Sinclair for the Teapot Dome lease, and suddenly awash with ready money, paid off his back taxes, put $40,000 into improvements to his New Mexico ranch, and even bought some adjoining property. Journalist Carl Magee, struck by the mystery of Albert Fall's sudden new wealth, did some digging and before long uncovered the messy story. Fall resigned and Warren Harding died in disgrace, but not before memorably remarking: "I can take care of my enemies; it's my friends who are causing me trouble."

By the beginning of 1929 the presidency of Calvin Coolidge was finished, and Herbert Hoover was about to take office. But "Teapot Dome," as the scandal was known, refused to go away; on the contrary, it became a national symbol of Jazz Age greed and graft, an even more far-reaching version of the Julian Pete. Albert Fall's ham-fisted attempts at a cover-up only made Doheny's situation worse. More than seven years after the $100,000 had been handed over—after an endless series of congressional investigations, civil suits, contempt cases, and acquittals that led only to further criminal prosecutions—Doheny faced yet one more trial, with the certainty of further public controversy and disgrace coupled with a real possibility of jail time.

And now Doheny's son, the deliverer of the black leather satchel, had been killed. On the one hand Leslie White knew all this as he whizzed toward a moment of destiny; on the other hand, he had no idea what he was getting into. He was about to face whole worlds of money and machination that were beyond him. Jake Berman had been a beginning; soon White's education and disillusionment would really speed up.

9

Beverly Hills C.S.I.

In the early 1900s—when President William McKinley was gunned down in Buffalo by the anarchist Leon Czolgosz, when America danced to the syncopated beat of ragtime and women's dresses still brushed the ground, when the automobile was already transforming the life of the century and E. L. Doheny was at last achieving the sort of wealth of which he'd always dreamed—Doheny had decided he needed a nearby getaway place, a haven where his family could ride horses or enjoy a picnic. He bought 400 acres of land south of the San Gabriel Mountains, several miles from downtown, in an area that was then just countryside: Beverly Hills. As the years went by, and Beverly Hills became populated and a desirable location for residences, Doheny built houses for various family members on his 400 acres. In 1926, after one of his Teapot Dome acquittals, he planned a house for his son Ned, daughter-in-law Lucy, and their five children. Not just any house: this would be the grandest in L.A., rivaling any personal residence in the United States. Doheny gave fifty or so of his Beverly Hills acres for a site and held a competition before settling on society architect Gordon B. Kaufmann to do the design, which turned out to be mock-Tudor, but on a military scale.

"The huge (over 46,000 square feet), magnificent structure rose high over Sunset Boulevard, sited on a promontory," writes Margaret Leslie Davis, Doheny's most recent biographer. "Its grounds would include an enormous stable (close to 16,000 square feet), dozens of riding trails, a two-bedroom gatehouse, formal gardens, terraces, a sixty-foot swimming pool, several greenhouses, badminton and tennis courts, and a waterfall that cascaded down an eighty-foot-high hillside before filling an artificial lake gloriously landscaped with white water-lilies. The estate's interior was equally awe-inspiring: it contained several Georgian fireplaces, a thirty-seat motion picture theater, a two-lane bowling alley, a recreation room and a gymnasium, a walk-in fur and jewelry vault, a temperature-controlled wine cellar, and a billiard room with a hidden bar that, in this Prohibition era, retracted into the wall at the push of a button . . . Greystone's three-foot-thick gray Indiana limestone walls gave the mansion its name. Its steeply pitched roof, framed with steel-reinforced concrete, was covered with solid Welsh slate. Many of the windows of the home featured an inspiring view from downtown Los Angeles to Santa Monica Bay."

The mansion was completed in late 1928, at a cost between three and five million dollars (worth perhaps fifty times as much today). Greystone cost plenty, but then Doheny *had* plenty, and the building and stuffing and staffing of the mansion no doubt provided a welcome distraction from the imbroglio of Teapot Dome. The writer Raymond Chandler would in time get lots of mileage out of the Dohenys; their story fascinated him—haunted him, it's fair to say—and Greystone appears as the home of General Sternwood in *The Big Sleep* and the Grayle residence in *Farewell, My Lovely*, in which he writes: "The house itself was not so much. It was smaller than Buckingham Palace, rather grey for California, and had fewer windows than the Chrysler Building . . . and inside, if you could get inside, a special brand of sunshine, very quiet, put up in noise-proof containers just for the upper classes."

If you could get inside . . . In Mexico, Doheny had hired an army to protect an entire region against insurgents and unpredictable revolution. In Los Angeles, he turned the family homes into fortresses. "Beverly Hills residents came to regard Greystone as a self-contained principality," writes Margaret Leslie Davis. "The estate had its own gatekeepers, watchmen, mechanics, house staff, field crews, and even its own fire station. A neo-Gothic garage, which housed ten of Ned and Lucy's cars, featured its own gas pumps, lifts, and machine shops. Among the staff were cooks, housemaids, a kitchen maid, laundresses, a maintenance worker, a painter, ten gardeners, four chauffeurs, and two operators who ran Ned's two telephone switchboards."

Among the staff . . . Even the wealthiest can't work or live alone—not if they wish (like the Dohenys did) to live with style and show. Cocoons are really only effective for the recluse. For a while Doheny Sr. employed as one of his private secretaries a smart, educated young woman named Miriam Lerner, the daughter of a department-store owner, a girl from a good family. No doubt the fact that she was gorgeous helped too. Lerner was a mistress of the photographer Edward Weston, and became the subject for some of his most famous nude studies. Among Lerner's other lovers was a young artist and beginning screenwriter, John Huston. In the early 1930s, while living in the South of France, she helped Emma Goldman write her autobiography. At this time, in the late 1920s, she turned her Los Feliz house into a salon for writers, artists, bohemians, whose money problems she soothed by fixing cushy jobs with the Dohenys. Thus, the future bookdealer Jake Zeitlin trimmed the Greystone lawns, and for a while Louis Adamic had jockeyed gas from a Greystone pump.

All this was innocent; and perhaps Doheny knew of, and smiled at, the game beautiful Miriam Lerner was playing. But the urge for self-containment and self-protection sometimes has ironic, unforeseeable consequences. Even if you build a fairy-tale palace with, as Margaret Davis notes, "a gift room where Lucy Doheny could wrap fabulous presents for her family, friends, and staff at Christmas time," you still live with whatever perhaps not-so-fabulous gifts that are unknowingly seeded within. Much can be controlled by money, but not everything—not even by $300 million. E. L. Doheny discovered this on that fateful night in February 1929—for his son was killed by a member of his staff, a trusted and put-upon servant.

"With the accelerator squeezed against the floor boards, I raced my car through the semi-deserted streets of Hollywood and Beverly Hills to the palatial Doheny mansion on Doheny Drive," wrote Leslie White. To his amazement he found the estate surrounded—not by the police but by private detectives, another of Doheny's armies. A *Times* photo taken later that morning shows the men still in place around Greystone, toting pistols and shotguns.

"It would be simpler to crash Buckingham Palace," wrote White, making the joke that Chandler would later tweak and polish. Three of the guards stopped White at the gatehouse, barring his entry until word came down and they waved him on. "I drove up to the house and was admitted by one of those frozen-faced butlers, properly and immaculately garbed despite the hour and the tragedy."

Once inside White set down his camera and equipment for a moment, took off his spectacles and polished them. He was struck by the silence as Greystone's hushed solid-stone splendor heightened the weird reality, almost surreality, that attends murder's official aftermath. Whole teams of law enforcement spoke to each other in whispers. This, as it happened, was the first murder the newly formed Beverly Hills Police Department had faced, though neither the Beverly Hills cops nor the L.A. County Sheriffs' Department deputies, who were also there, showed any desire to claim jurisdiction over a case that was clearly explosive and filled with career-ending potential. So the D.A.'s office had taken over, in the commanding shape of Lucien Wheeler.

While at Notre Dame, Lucien Wheeler had been on the rowing crew and had played in the brass band. He was a handsome, powerful man of medium height. He had large, shrewd eyes, a small mouth, and huge skills. As head of the U.S. Secret Service's presidential guard, he'd ridden on the running boards of automobiles, keeping a watchful eye for anybody who might step out of a crowd and try to assassinate Theodore Roosevelt and Woodrow Wilson. He'd visited Los Angeles as early as 1911, as the advance man for President Taft, meeting the railroad people, the police, the organizers of the parades, and the managers and bellboys of the hotels where the president would stay. He arranged the guards and plotted the routes and the guest lists. In 1929, at age fifty-three, this subtle and unflappable man was the most experienced and accomplished law enforcement guy in L.A. The brash young Leslie White was a little in awe of Lucien Wheeler.

"He met me in Greystone's huge hallway and calmly briefed me," White wrote. "He told me to do my work and report back only to him."

White, small and intrepid, lugged his gear down a long, dim corridor, and went through a door into a guest suite. On the floor he saw not one corpse, but two. "They were just as dead as any of the score or more 'bindle-stiffs' I had found in the jungles," White wrote. He used the term "bindle-stiff," slang for the victim of a drug overdose, to give the impression that he'd seen scores of corpses, and he had; nonetheless, beneath the tough-guy pose, he was shaken. Here was violent death, frightening and intimate. "In a luxurious bedroom lay the corpse of Doheny, clad only in his underwear and a silk bathrobe. There was a hole through his skull from ear to ear and he lay on his back. Blood was crisscrossed in a crazy pattern over his finely chiseled face."

White set about his work.

The second corpse was that of Hugh Plunkett, Ned Doheny's secretary. Spread-eagled on his stomach, Plunkett lay face down in a pool of blood that welled from a hole in his head. His brains had spattered the wall, and the rug at his feet had been shoved sideways as he fell. His right arm was stretched out, empty; the fingers of the left hand, lying at his side, had been burned by the half-smoked cigarette they still held.

White wondered about the cigarette, the first of a number of details he would find strange. He located the bullet that had passed through Ned Doheny's brain. It was buried in an exterior wall at a height of six feet. Carefully, with tweezers and the blade of a penknife, he eased the bullet out of the flaking plaster and dropped it in an envelope. He finger-printed both men, taking their lifeless hands in his own, rolling the finger and thumb ends on an ink pad, and pressing them against paper. He lifted Plunkett's body and found a still-warm gun, a Bisley .45 Colt revolver. He wrapped it in a cloth, planning to take prints from it later.

With his camera and flashgun, White took crime scene photographs that have lost none of their power. They show an expensively furnished room with Ned Doheny lying in a pool of his own blood next to an overturned chair. Drying blood covers his face like a mask and his bare feet are tucked into shiny leather slippers. An unlit cigarette lies at his fingertips. A glass tumbler, unbroken, has fallen to the floor. An opened bottle of Johnnie Walker is on a table. Plunkett, dressed in a pinstripe suit, is in the background, prone in a doorway. He, too, lies in blood. The two men are close, as they had been for years, yet separated by a crucial distance.

Ned Doheny had a life of privilege from the start, very different from Plunkett's. From the storybook frontier uncertainty of his own father's, Ned grew up rich in Los Angeles, attending a private Catholic school, then Stanford University and USC law school. On graduation from USC in 1916 he joined Doheny Sr.'s oil business as a partner and became a multimillionaire instantly. Probate would value his personal estate at $12.5 million. In WWI he served as a lieutenant on a Navy cruiser and later behind a desk in Washington. In Los Angeles he was a member of the University Club, the Los Angeles Athletic Club, the Los Angeles Country Club. He had given handsome endowments to USC and sat as a university trustee; he was a part of the city's aristocratic furniture—friendly, though spoiled and with flashes of his father's temper.

Theodore Hugh Plunkett, on the other hand, was born poor on March 28, 1895, in Illinois, and came to Los Angeles in 1912. His parents, like many Midwesterners, had been seduced by the boosters' promise of sunshine, health, and wealth. He got a job at a downtown service station owned by the family of Lucy Smith, soon to marry Ned Doheny. It was here that Plunkett and Ned Doheny first met. Plunkett changed the tires on one of Ned's cars (Ned already had many) and the two struck up a friendship. Plunkett became a chauffeur for the Doheny family, and his WWI draft card shows that he enlisted in L.A. on the same day Ned did: June 16, 1917. Plunkett's signature is clumsy, and the draft card states that he had blue eyes, light brown hair, and was of medium height and slender build. He served as a machinist's mate on a submarine chaser, and, when the war was done, went back to work for his friend and boss. He was completely loyal to the Dohenys and they trusted him and treated him almost as a member of the family. He helped supervise the building of Greystone and wrote hundreds of thousands of dollars' worth of checks in Ned's name to pay the contractors. Plunkett was married, but he and Harriet, his wife of ten years, were estranged and without children. At the time of his death she was living in a retreat high in the Verdugo Hills, a neophyte dressed in Indian robes in one of Southern California's many religious cults.

"Ned and Plunkett went everywhere together," E. L. Doheny had said in one of the earlier trials.

"He acted as secretary to Ned, but their relationship was more than that of friends," Frederic Kellogg, one of Ned's attorneys, told the *Times*, a strangely formulated statement that hints at more than Kellogg probably intended. Leslie White would hear many rumors. One of them was that Plunkett and Ned Doheny had been lovers, killed by Ned's wife, Lucy, out of jealousy.

Plunkett's story belongs to another of those genres typical of L.A., which remains utterly class-ridden despite seeming so up for grabs. He was the employee who became an intimate, privileged yet doomed, part of the entourage. He'd been with Ned Doheny in the New York bank in November 1921, when the teller rubber-banded the notes into five $20,000 bundles; he'd traveled with Ned Doheny with the black leather satchel on the train to Washington; he'd fixed drinks for Ned Doheny and Albert Fall while the cash was handed over and the men laughed and talked at the Wardman Park Hotel. He'd played an important walk-on in Teapot Dome; and his role had been about to return to haunt the Dohenys.

Teapot Dome litigations had been dragging on for more than five years at this point. Doheny had lost the Elk Hills lease, and had been forced to make substantial reparation. Both he and Fall were acquitted of conspiring to defraud the government, but they were soon to be tried for bribery. The two cases would be heard separately—first Fall's, then

Doheny's. Were Fall to be found innocent of taking a bribe, then *ipso facto* Doheny couldn't have given one, and he'd be completely off the hook; but if Fall were found guilty, then Doheny would himself stand trial one more time. In Fall's trial, much would hinge on Hugh Plunkett. For the first time Plunkett was being called upon to testify. The Dohenys had been trying to persuade him to check himself into Camarillo State Mental Hospital and dodge the subpoena.

In the days prior to the killings Plunkett had been, according to differing accounts, only "slightly nervous" or "almost completely unhinged." His state of mind, anyway, was subject for concern. He'd been taking Veronal and Dial, addictive barbiturates, to help him sleep. He'd bought clothes and serviced his car, perhaps in readiness for the trip to Camarillo. "The one thing that appeared to be constantly on his mind was the upcoming criminal trial," said Mrs. George Johnson, Lucy Doheny's personal secretary. For the exhausted Plunkett, the options looked grim: give false testimony at Fall's trial, perjuring himself; tell the truth, betraying his friends and risking jail; or head off to the insane asylum. He had Doheny interests so much at heart he would lie awake thinking of them.

Such was the background.

10

Cover-Up

Leslie White's job, as forensics investigator, was to put together a picture of the crime strictly from the physical evidence. For more than two hours he took photos and fingerprints and combed the room, making a minute study of every article of furniture and every inch of wall and floor space. When done, he gathered his gear and walked back down the long corridor. In Greystone's lofty hallway he reported to Lucien Wheeler.

Plunkett, it seemed, had come to Greystone at about 9:30 P.M. the previous night, letting himself in with his own key. By then Ned and Lucy were already in their own bedroom, getting ready to sleep, so Ned put on a dressing gown and told Plunkett they'd talk in the guest apartment. The conversation lasted more than an hour and grew heated. Plunkett—emotional, unwell, apparently almost hysterical—was digging in his heels and refusing to check himself into the sanatorium at Camarillo. Ned Doheny tried to change his mind. Plunkett grew enraged, produced a revolver, and shot his friend. Others heard the noise; they said it was like "furniture banging." They came to investigate, whereupon Plunkett shot himself. This happened at about 10:55 P.M. It was a case of murder and suicide: Plunkett killed Doheny and then took his own life.

"It was a crazed man instead of the trusted secretary who sent the death-dealing bullet into the young Doheny's brain as the oil king's son pleaded with him," the *Times* would report.

This version depended almost entirely on the statements of Ernest Clyde Fishbaugh, a doctor who'd been treating the Doheny family for seven or eight years by then. Fishbaugh told how he'd been summoned from his seat at a Hollywood theater with the news that Plunkett was at Greystone and acting crazy. The call had come from Ned Doheny, via Fishbaugh's message service. Fishbaugh hurried from the theater and had his chauffeur drop him off at Greystone, where Lucy Doheny met him at the door and led him toward the room where Ned Doheny and Plunkett were arguing.

"Plunkett stepped to the door and surprised us by saying, quite gruffly, 'Don't come in here!' or words to that effect," Fishbaugh told the *Times*, varying and cleaning up a little what he'd told the *Examiner* a few minutes before—when he'd described the door shutting softly, as if blown by a ghostly wind.

"As I recall it, he shut the door hard," Fishbaugh went on in his *Times* interview. "And it seemed that he had no more done that than there was a shot fired. I told Mrs. Doheny not to come in, but went in myself. I found Plunkett lying on the floor a few feet inside the door, his feet toward the door. He was shot through the head. He was not breathing. I quickly stepped into the guest room and saw Mr. Doheny stretched out on the floor near the foot of one of the twin beds. An overturned chair was near him. A pool of blood was near his head. He had been shot through the head."

Fishbaugh said that Plunkett must have shot Doheny as Fishbaugh was coming up the driveway. Earlier that Saturday afternoon, Fishbaugh said, he'd been with Ned and Lucy Doheny while they all tried to persuade Plunkett to check himself into Camarillo.

Fishbaugh told how, in recent months, he'd treated Plunkett for abscessed teeth, sleeplessness, and chronic nervous disorders. The swiftly adopted idea that Plunkett had been on the verge of breakdown, or already insane, stems almost entirely from Fishbaugh's statements. Others, even at the time, flatly contradicted the insanity notion, saying that Plunkett, while under strain, was well enough. But Fishbaugh hammered his line: "We all urged Plunkett to take a rest. He simply sat there. Hands clenched. Jaws set at times. He said he would come out of it all right. I could see it was no use to push him further."

This was how the story was shaping up, and Lucien Wheeler was too cool and experienced to venture an opinion at this point about whether he believed it or not. He did suggest, though, that something was odd in the testimony he'd heard from the maid, the nanny, the guards, the night watchman, and the liveried butler (whose splendid name was Albert Doar). Their tellings had grooved too neatly, as though all the staff had been schooled in a story and ordered to stick to it. He told White to go with the meat wagon and learn as much as he could from a detailed examination of the corpses.

Shortly before dawn White arrived at the Beverly Hills mortuary to which the bodies of both men were first taken. Already the corpses had been stripped and laid out on adjoining drainage tables in a room of sparkling tile. White took more pictures, flashbulbs fizzing in the silence. He put his face close to the flesh of the dead men. "I found powder burns around the bullet-hole in Doheny's head, proving that the gun was less than three inches away at the moment it fired. I found no such markings on Plunkett's head," he wrote. However, according to Fishbaugh, whose evidence the *Times* relied upon to make an elaborate, cartoon-like reconstruction of the crime scene, Plunkett had shot Doheny from a distance of several feet, while both men sat on chairs. This theory, always a little bizarre, was thus disproved by White even as the *Times* went to press with it.

Other details nagged. Both victims had clearly been drinking, though Fishbaugh, Lucy Doheny, and the Greystone household staff had denied it. This was minor, though; the cigarette that had been between Plunkett's fingers worried White more. He didn't quite see that even an insane man would shoot his best friend, open a door, retreat from the people he saw approaching, and shoot himself in the head, all the while holding a cigarette as though he were a character in a drawing room comedy.

White was inspecting the corpses when a uniformed L.A. County sheriff sauntered in and perched on one of the drainage tables. This amiable dude with a moustache had been sent to check up on him, White realized. He thought of the discrepancy, the little crack that Lucien Wheeler said he'd noticed in the schooled Greystone tellings. According to Fishbaugh, the shots that Plunkett fired were spaced apart by several minutes; but one of the maids said she'd heard the shots fired all together, "One-two-three." Now these various details bundled themselves together and White's growing unease found a focus.

"Something's warped about this case," he said. "I don't think Plunkett killed Ned Doheny."

Silence fell. The deputy gave White a wry little so-what smile.

"We've got to get to the bottom of this," White said.

Now the sheriff's man shook his head. "There's no 'we' about it, kid," he said. "Old man Doheny's too big to monkey with."

White left the morgue and drove away. He spent the rest of the night and the early part of the morning at the lab in the Hall of Justice, inspecting and firing the murder weapon. He found no fingerprints on the Bisley, not even partials or smudges. This was odd. Nor could White explain to himself why the gun had been hot when he removed it from beneath Plunkett; the leaking body warmth of the corpse didn't account for it. White had no choice but to conclude that somebody had wiped clean the gun and otherwise tampered with it.

At 10 A.M., when White phoned Lucien Wheeler with his findings, Wheeler listened without comment and told him to report in person to Buron Fitts. So for White it was yet another ride in the Model T, back across the city, to Hollywood and leafy Marmont Lane, high above Sunset Boulevard where Fitts then kept his home.

"He was a young man, forceful and filled with a mixture of

idealism and practicality. Few people really knew Buron Fitts, for his personality changed in direct ratio to the number of people in his presence. I liked him best when I met him alone," White wrote.

On this Sunday morning White found Fitts with a Bible in his hand; he'd just come back from church. In WWI Fitts had been a marine officer. Shrapnel blew off part of his right knee at the Battle of the Argonne and he'd also suffered mustard gas burns, episodes he didn't hesitate to rehash for the benefit of the press and additional column inches. Fitts had ridden to power on the back of his status as veteran and hero, supported by the American Legion and Harry Chandler. While running for D.A., Fitts had undergone surgeries resulting in the loss of his wounded leg and its replacement by an artificial one, a series of procedures reported daily in the *Times* as the campaign rolled on. Buron Fitts "limped noisily into office," as one cynic put it.

"He was a fighter," White wrote.

For White himself this had been the most extraordinary night in a youthful life that was already rich with incident. Though exhausted, he buzzed with adrenaline, certain he was on to something big. He took out the crime scene photographs that he'd developed and laid them out, telling Fitts he just didn't believe that Plunkett had killed Doheny and then himself. At the very least, he said, the shootings couldn't possibly have happened in the way claimed by Dr. E. C. Fishbaugh.

"The physical facts and the testimony of witnesses don't jibe," White said. He was tired and irritable and, as often, a little too eager. "I understand, too, that some people believe the Doheny family are too influential to tamper with."

Now Fitts, in turn, grew testy. His sharp eyes glittered. "There isn't a man in the United States big enough to stop me conducting a criminal investigation," he said. "But if Plunkett didn't kill Doheny, who did?"

That was the question. White said he didn't know, but he did know that they hadn't discovered the truth—yet.

"We'll damn soon find out," said Fitts, the fighter, the "soldier prosecutor." He got Lucien Wheeler on the phone, ordering him to get all the Doheny witnesses down to the Hall of Justice for further questioning. Leslie White sat in, and when E. C. Fishbaugh came into the interview room, he seized his chance.

"Doctor, you were approaching the house at the time the shooting took place and you rushed into the bedroom within a matter of seconds," he said. "Is that correct?"

Fishbaugh nodded.

"Doheny was dead when you arrived?"

Again, a nod.

"And the body was not disturbed in any way?"

Fishbaugh was defensive. "It was not disturbed in any way."

"Then, Doctor, as an experienced physician, will you kindly explain how blood could run *up* from the ears and cross back and forth over the face of a man who never moved off his back?"

This was White's coup, his big moment in the Doheny investigation. Blood had streaked in a crisscross pattern on Ned Doheny's face. White's crime scene photographs show the covering, dried, and in places thick. This wasn't conjecture, but hard evidence. The patterns made by Ned Doheny's blood flatly contradicted Fishbaugh's story.

Fishbaugh was trapped and he knew it. In a low voice he admitted that young Doheny had lived for approximately twenty minutes after the shooting. His pulse had been faint and he was bleeding from both sides of the head with blood trickling from his mouth. Fishbaugh tried to save him by moving him on his side and clearing his breathing passages—to no avail.

Buron Fitts slammed his fist on a table. If Fishbaugh had lied about this, and he had, he might have lied about other things too. Yet his story had already been peddled to the scrum of newsmen at Greystone and accepted wholesale. Fitts didn't like the smell of it. Still angry, he told Fishbaugh to get out of his sight, promising there would be "a sweeping investigation."

White saw reason to be satisfied. An inexperienced forensics man, he'd nonetheless done a thorough and competent job. Now he was happy to turn the whole thing over to the older and wiser brains of Lucien Wheeler and Buron Fitts. But within hours a different Buron Fitts—Fitts the survivor, Fitts the politician who knew where his bread was buttered, Fitts the man who was already plotting a run at the governorship of California—called a press conference, declaring that county authorities had already signed death certificates for both men, labeling the tragedy as a murder and a suicide. "My office has concluded beyond all doubt that Hugh Plunkett, while insane, shot Ned Doheny and then turned the gun on himself," Fitts announced.

No inquest would be held, and Ned Doheny's body would undergo no autopsy.

The case was closed.

It was a staggering turnaround.

E. C. Fishbaugh modified his story about how he found Ned Doheny, telling the *Times*: "He was breathing but unconscious. A telephone directory was lying on the bed opened to the page where my name is listed." A Doheny attorney added further spin, suggesting that Plunkett had arrived at Greystone intent on suicide and Ned Doheny had nobly tried to talk him out of it.

One moment the "sweeping investigation" had been about to step up several gears; the next, it was over. "The newspapers dropped the Doheny story as if it burned their fingers," White wrote. This was the most sensational of the many murders in L.A.'s history up to that time, and for twenty-four hours the press handled it as such: screaming headlines, pages of photographs and crime scene constructions and character artwork—thousands of column inches. Then silence. Coverage stopped dead.

White would believe until the end of his life that Doheny's power killed the story. Certainly Doheny knew how to use the media. He'd spent time and money in the assemblage of his own myth, that of the free-spirited, free-roaming frontiersman who made good through adventure and luck and ceaseless striving. More recently he'd been chasing Cecil B. DeMille to turn selected episodes of his life into a movie and offset the damaging publicity generated by Teapot Dome. He was a calculating and autocratic man. Harry Chandler and William Randolph Hearst, owners of the city's most influential papers, were close friends and had been, at various times and in different ventures, business partners. To study the press treatment of the Greystone tragedy is to be stunned by the speed with which a massive story went away.

Only the publishers of underground rags (there were scores of them in L.A. at the time, short-lived and energetic, often scandalous) questioned the official version. "DEATH TRAGEDY CONNECTS TO TEAPOT DOME," reported the editors of *The Truth*, a fortnightly whose ill-printed and disintegrating pages are categorized as "California Ephemera" in the Special Collections department at UCLA. "District Attorney Buron Fitts would have us think that a chauffeur went mad and killed a rich man and then himself at the Doheny's palatial home last Saturday night," *The Truth* noted in its issue for March 2, 1929. "We are not satisfied that this is the whole, or accurate story—and we call upon Mr. Fitts to tell us THE TRUTH about Hugh Plunkett and his role as a $100,000 bagman in the famed Teapot Dome affair. Did Hugh Plunkett's mind really 'go suddenly mad.' Or was he himself murdered by a ruthlessly applied death-dealing bullet?"

Doheny biographer Dan La Botz, writes: "Today, years later, it seems clear that Ned Doheny and Hugh Plunkett were the victims of old man Doheny's ambition . . . He had used his son and his son's friend to carry out the dirty business of bribery and deceit . . . No matter whose hand did the deed, it was Doheny's character that killed them, his egotism, his hubris."

Doheny's malfeasance returned to punish him in a way that does indeed seem plotted to achieve the maximum effects of tragedy and irony, snatching from him that which he wished to preserve above all else: the integrity and future of his family. Ned's death shattered Doheny. He'd been at Chester Place when the call came through from Greystone. He'd hurried over, driving through the silent streets of Beverly Hills, insisting against advice on seeing the bodies, hoping there'd been a mistake. Then the reality had sunk in. "Yes, it is Ned after all," he said.

A *Times* reporter captured the sad scene: "He gazed at his son's body for a moment, and then knelt beside it. He shook with emotion as he reached down and took young Doheny's right hand. 'Ned, my Ned,' he sobbed as he was half carried from the room."

"He came staggering into his son's house like a ghost, hardly able to walk. He crept up the stairway. There he collapsed," wrote the *Examiner*. "The favorite of madcap fate, in the evening of his life, found himself the plaything of destiny."

11

Good Time Charlie

Ned Doheny's funeral was held on Tuesday, February 19, less than sixty hours after the shootings at Greystone. E. L. Doheny wanted this done in a hurry, but with the style and pomp that he felt was his son's due. The funeral, coming so quickly after the tragedy, and at a time when press coverage was peaking, seized the imagination of the whole city. The outside of St. Vincent's, the massive church at the corner of Adams and Figueroa that Doheny had paid for, was draped in black. Squads of LAPD men struggled to restrain the thousands of people who crammed and thronged the streets, hoping to get inside, where the congregation filled every seat and overflowed into the aisles, standing rank on rank.

Dave and Nancy Clark arrived early, and Clark found his wife a seat on the right side of the church, close to the pews that were roped off for family members. He himself joined those who stood, looking back over a sea of hatless heads toward the great oaken doors of the church. Clark knew the Dohenys. While at Wellborn, Wellborn & Wellborn, he'd helped prepare for one of E. L. Doheny's earlier trials, in which Doheny had been accused of conspiracy to defraud the U.S. government. Clark was part of a large and expensive legal team that eased Doheny off that particular hook. He'd met the old man on several occasions in the corridors of the Petroleum Securities building. He'd known Ned Doheny, having helped draw up the contract with Greystone architect Gordon B. Kaufmann. Clark had attended USC alumni events with Ned, and they'd golfed together at the Los Angeles Country Club. Clark was proud of his connection with the city's most powerful family; it fitted his vision of himself as an Angeleno who was going places and destined for big things.

At ten o'clock Clark heard the organ of St. Vincent's rise and swell, and the service began. Some of E. L. Doheny's closest business and political associates walked in front of the casket, honorary pallbearers: Ezequiel Ordonez, the Mexican geologist; Frank J. Hogan, Doheny's Washington attorney in the Teapot Dome trials; Albert Bacon Fall; and Rufus B. von KleinSmid, the head of USC. The presence of these men reflected, perhaps, a son whose life had belonged too much to his father. Clark also noted that Olin Wellborn III, his friend and former boss, was one of the six men actually shouldering Ned's coffin. Behind the casket walked Lucy Doheny, the widow, her face hidden by a veil that reached almost to the ground. E. L. Doheny himself, shaking and walking on unsteady feet, held his daughter-in-law's arm—for support, it seemed, rather than comfort. Doheny was white and haggard, and his vacant eyes kept slowly closing and opening, as if his mind was broken.

The service, hushed and respectful, proceeded nonetheless with all the splendor that E. L. Doheny had wished. John J. Cantwell, a close friend of the Dohenys and the bishop of the diocese of Los Angeles and San Diego, was presiding, clad in purple and seated on a massive throne covered with a canopy of red and gold. Father Martin O'Malley, the pastor of St. Vincent's, delivered the main address, offering words of gloomy consolation. "Death, bitter death," he said, the words falling slowly and inexorably through the vaulted reaches of St. Vincent's and into Dave Clark's ears. "This is sober truth, this is bitter death. But to you whom Ned Doheny loved, to you who are crushed by the burden of the cross that the loved ones must bear"—and here O'Malley turned toward the weeping widow and the crumpled old man at her side— "to you there is but a few words that might make less and soothe the burden. These are the words that Ned learned at the altar as a child when he was confirmed. Jesus said, 'I am the resurrection and the life. He who believes in me, although he is dead, shall live, and he who liveth and believeth in me shall not die for ever.'"

Dave Clark glanced toward his wife, but Nancy had her head bowed in prayer. Nancy had grown up in a Catholic household and still had her faith, attending mass twice a week. Dave Clark's parents were still active in their local Highland Park church but he'd ceased to care about religion. Nancy believed in permanent and passionate commitments. Dave was more footloose.

"God grant Ned Doheny eternal rest and let the eternal light shine upon him," said O'Malley.

E. L. Doheny seemed to stare unseeingly before him. Lucy Doheny was slumped in her pew, a handkerchief to her eyes, sobbing. The two were helped from their seats for a last glance into the casket. Then Doheny once again held tight to his daughter-in-law's arm as they walked out of the church.

Ned's body was taken by hearse to Forest Lawn and interred in the Doheny family mausoleum, a vast marble temple brought by Doheny from a church in Rome where it had once held the remains of a second-century Christian martyr. Predictably, less ceremony would attend Hugh Plunkett's funeral, which took place the next day, though he too was laid to rest at Forest Lawn, barely thirty feet from the Doheny mausoleum where Ned lay entombed. The two men were as close in death as they'd been in life, and as far apart.

After the grandeur of St. Vincent's, Ned Doheny's burial was private, a strictly family affair, and Dave Clark wasn't among those who witnessed it. Besides, on that Tuesday morning, once the requiem mass was concluded and the congregation filed out of church and into the streets, he had business to attend to. He kissed Nancy on the cheek and hurried downtown to attend a hearing in the grand jury room on the seventh floor of the Hall of Justice. Clark was as yet unaware that these proceedings would have grave implications for his own future, though he did know that the hearing concerned another older man who was at the center of power in Los Angeles: Charlie Crawford.

Charles Crawford—"Good Time Charlie," the *Examiner* called him—was in his early fifties by 1929. Like E. L. Doheny, Crawford came from Irish stock. Like Doheny, he was born of pioneer parents. His basic education in a one-room schoolhouse was followed by a drift westward. Crawford fetched up in Seattle in the late 1890s, soon after prospectors found gold "like piles of yellow shelled corn" up in Alaska's Yukon Valley, on the banks of the Klondike. "GOLD! GOLD! GOLD! GOLD!," screamed the *Seattle Post-Intelligencer.* "STACKS OF YELLOW METAL!" Within days, the last great gold rush was born; the whole continent went Klondike crazy, and Seattle became the port of entry for those heading to the mining camps. The American economy had been hit hard by financial panic in 1893. Unemployment was widespread and there was growing strife between industrial employers and emerging unions. The prospect of sudden, easy wealth was even more seductive than usual. Within a year of the discovery of gold in Alaska, more than 100,000 people came to Seattle, fanning north into the Yukon territory toward Dawson City. In time 12.5 million ounces of gold were taken from the ground. The writer Jack London recorded the hardships endured, the adventures enjoyed; and Charlie Chaplin's 1925 silent film *The Gold Rush* would be set on the Klondike. Another uncharted region of the West was put on the map.

"Prosperity is here," said the *Seattle Post-Intelligencer* at the time, and a hastily formed Seattle Chamber of Commerce, led by the ingenious Erastus Brainerd, plotted a successful campaign to seize the bulk of the gold rush trade.

Seattle roared, and Charlie Crawford was there, having realized that Klondike entertainment and crime would be even more profitable than Klondike prospecting. Hard-working miners rarely held on to their stake. Gambling parlors and brothels sprang up all over town, and Crawford made his first small fortune, booking dance-hall and vaudeville entertainers into local theaters, dance halls, and saloons. He became a vice-lord in Seattle's Tenderloin, "a bottomless cauldron of sin," according to *McClure's* magazine in 1911. Lawyer and city councilman Hiram Gill handled the interests of Crawford and other underworld captains. In 1910 Gill ran for mayor on a "wide-open town" ticket, arguing that vice was both natural and lucrative but should be regulated and confined to one section of the city. "Hell, this is a sea port, ain't it?" Gill said. His campaign was successful, at which point, said *McClure's*, "The city transformed itself almost magically into one great gambling hell." It was Charlie Crawford's kind of town. On Beacon Hill he built the Northern Club, with 500 rooms the biggest and most elaborate gaming hotel in the country, prefiguring Las Vegas in its grandeur. Roulette, blackjack, craps, faro, poker, and slot machines featured at ground level, while prostitution roosted above.

"Everywhere the wheels were clicking and the bones were rolling, and a particularly impressive sight was a heavily gold-braided police captain who benignantly elbowed his way in and out of the throng," said *McClure's*. The Northern ran for fifty-four days, with three shifts of dealers and barmen and girls working around the clock seven days a week, netting Crawford $200,000 before reformers discovered that the club was built on land actually leased from the city itself. This was too much, even for Seattle. Hundreds of respectable citizens roused themselves, marching past the Northern Club with banners raised, to the accompaniment of a Salvation Army Band. It was another classic Western scene. Hiram Gill's mayorship was recalled, largely through the vote of newly enfranchised women. Police chief Charles "Wappy" Wappenstein, another

Crawford supporter, earned himself three to ten years in the state pen at Walla Walla, and a new police unit known as "The Purity Squad" patrolled the streets, rousting single women from hotel rooms and arresting even married couples who strolled the streets after dark.

For Charlie Crawford, Seattle was over. In 1911 he headed south, to a town that still seemed wide open: Los Angeles. Downtown, át 230 East Fifth Street, he opened the Maple Bar, another handsome Barbary Coast affair with a casino downstairs and a whorehouse above. "In those days he was a picturesque, hard-fisted, garish figure, shrewd, generous, and following his own course," wrote the *Examiner*. "His saloon was the meeting place of a strange assortment. There were ward heelers, police officers, men of shady and questionable reputation."

L.A., though, wasn't Seattle; the atmosphere was different. "Toil broken and bleached out, they flock to Los Angeles, fugitives from the simple inexorable of life, from labor and drudgery," wrote Louis Adamic of the Midwestern surge into the city. These immigrants—"half-educated, materially prosperous, but spiritually and mentally starving"—had left behind the freezing winters but brought with them habits of religion and temperance. L.A.'s Anti-Saloon League was well organized, and the city voted itself dry in 1917, more than two years before the federal Prohibition amendment took effect.

The "great experiment" of Prohibition changed everything, forcing Crawford in theory to shut the Maple Bar. But by now he was an adept operator in the shadows where the city's politics and police department mixed seamlessly with crime through the simple expedient of money. Civic historians are uncertain when "The System" actually came to L.A. It's not the kind of historical event that gets marked with a plaque. Many American cities of that era had their own style of graft—Minneapolis was an example of complete police corruption, while in St. Louis "boodlers" (businessmen who paid off officials for public works contracts) ran the show. In Pittsburgh, known as "Hell with the lid off," industrialists were in control. The way in which business became politics and politics was turned inside-out by money differed subtly from place to place, and it's likely that Charlie Crawford brought The System with him from Seattle, where he'd operated in a boom town by causing his man, Hiram Gill, to be elected mayor.

In L.A. Crawford found his enabler in Kent Kane Parrot, a former USC football star and graduate of USC law school. Parrot was a tall, handsome man, a suave dandy who liked urban politics, "because it's lots of fun." His first wife had been the screenwriter Mary O'Hara, the future author of *My Friend Flicka*. Parrot had friends everywhere. He "mastered the art of the unorthodox floating coalition, merging liberals with conservatives, church leaders with underworld figures, union officials with open-shop zealots, and prohibitionists with liquor interests," writes historian Jules Tygiel. Parrot's alliance included important preachers, members of the Better America Foundation, a couple of important judges, a local figure who could deliver the black vote on Central Avenue, political fixer "Queen" Helen Werner, and Charlie Crawford.

The key moment came in 1921 when, defying predictions and the opposition of the *Times*, the Parrot alliance put in their own man, George Cryer, as mayor. In 1925 Parrot and his crew once again routed the entrepreneurial elite and kept Cryer in power. Parrot embraced municipal ownership of water and other utilities. He promoted a growing city that was businesslike and conflict-free. He believed that people would drink, gamble, and frequent whorehouses whether national and local governments permitted them or not. Tourists were an important part of L.A.'s economy and some tourists expected to enjoy tourism's more dangerous pleasures. Therefore vice went on, sanctioned and protected, low-key and lucrative, controlled and almost monopolized. A corrupt corps of men in the LAPD didn't fight crime; they protected it because those who ran the rackets had city government on their side. Practical politics meant not rocking the boat, greasing the palm, and keeping the machine grinding. Parrot let Charlie Crawford work the way he knew. Kickbacks and bribes got things done. Money had to be made and the boys had to be looked after. Vice wasn't a racket, it was a business; and corruption was merely a part of the grown-up fallen world.

"The huge diamonds that covered his fingers and gleamed from his tie vanished," wrote the *Examiner*, describing how Crawford grew into his role of power. "His clothes became subdued and his conduct underwent the same change. In his own way, Crawford had graduated."

Another contemporary observer noted: "He dressed differently, moved with a different stride, walked with a different companionship. He was no longer a ward heeler and a tenderloin boss. He was the man next to the throne and he had the native ability to assume the part."

Crawford brought down Albert Marco from Seattle to help him run things. Crawford met regularly with Kent Parrot in

Parrot's apartment at the Biltmore Hotel. Parrot stood closest to the figureheads, the elected officials. Crawford kept tabs on the police and the underworld captains, orchestrating the business between them. "Crawford was the general behind the collections, and the stream of gold that flowed from commercialized vice and the protection thereof flowed through the hands of Crawford," wrote a contemporary. "Commercialized vice was yielding more profits to those protecting it than the combined salaries of all police officials on the beats."

This was the L.A. System, the entrenched graft that the *Daily News* and reformers sporadically sought to attack. Crawford further burnished his image by opening a real estate and insurance office, though the red ledger on his desk, often showing a daily income of $15,000, told of "Mrs. Flora Carroll, $2,500" and "Mrs. Belle Stocking, $2,500"— these were rents from or protection for brothels. Crawford had a wife, Ella, who was a good deal younger than he, and two small children, both girls. The family lived in an elegant two-story villa with a high, arched portico on North Rexford Drive in Beverly Hills, then (as now) a ritzy neighborhood of grand properties and wide green lawns.

Crawford met a beautiful and capable young prostitute, Beverly Davis, and established her as the madam of an opulent brothel in Hancock Park. The brothel was designed for the "rich, sporting element, the studio crowd," and Davis became Crawford's mistress and spy. "He was a big, bluff, handsome man," she said. Crawford was a survivor, a fixer who preferred to outsmart his opponents. "He was never a gunner," said his friend, the ex-Seattle police chief "Wappy" Wappenstein. "He knew everybody," the *Evening Herald* wrote. "Judges, lawyers, bankers, beautiful women, theatrical magnates, chauffeurs, politicians and bootblacks were familiar acquaintances and friends. He was genial, happy, and at home wherever he found himself." A "politician" then, in the 1920s sense. Even so, Crawford tried to dodge publicity, saying that his mother was "92 years old and wouldn't stand it."

Crawford's muscle, his chief enforcer through most of the 1920s, was Dick Lucas, an LAPD lieutenant later described as "a racketeer with a gun buttressed by the authority of a police badge." At the time no journalist would dare print such a statement. Lucas was a big man, over six feet tall and weighing 250 pounds, and was often seen casually toting a Thompson sub-machine gun. He made great copy, personally driving Eastern gangsters out of the city by threatening them with the Thompson and suggesting they had until the next evening to get back to New York or Chicago, or else find themselves on a slab in the morgue.

"One day in 1927, Al Capone and his entourage came to town, allegedly to sniff out prospects. The gendarmerie buzzed," wrote Matt Weinstock of the *Daily News*. Capone was already a prime symbol of what Prohibition had come to mean, a swaggering multimillionaire bootlegger and gang-lord who had gained control of a Chicago suburb, Cicero, while his henchmen afflicted the entire city with a new style of wholesale murder, rubbing out rivals with bombs and machine-guns. Capone lived like a king, occupying several floors of a plush hotel, and driving through the Chicago streets in an armor-plated car with bullet-proof windows. He was the kind of flamboyant gangster that Los Angeles didn't have, the kind of ruthless, all-powerful gangster and rival that the more discreet Charlie Crawford, especially, didn't want. So Crawford sent Dick Lucas to call on Capone and ask him what his intentions were. Next day Capone took the train to Chicago and the *News* headlined its story: "CAPONE TOLD TO BLOW. GANG CHIEF ROUSTED."

Another time Lucas and his partner Harry Raymond waited with machine-guns in the garage of a bootlegger who had made the mistake of hijacking some of Albert Marco's supply. When the bootlegger came home and opened the garage door, they killed him. Applause greeted the effort, though the public didn't know the cops were on the payroll of politician-racketeer Charlie Crawford. Lucas and his men committed other murders that were then blamed on Italian gangsters who were at that time marginalized in L.A. and kept out of the richest pickings of The System.

In 1923 reformers managed to put in place August Vollmer, the nation's foremost police intellectual, a major influence behind the introduction of crime labs, fingerprinting, lie detectors, and method-of-operation files. Vollmer, invited down from San Francisco to reorganize the corrupt and demoralized two thousand-strong LAPD, set up a series of lectures and symposia at USC and UCLA. During one of these think-tank meetings, LAPD Captain Clyde Plummer said: "The Chinese have no excuse for existence. They are gamblers and dope fiends. They are a menace to our community." Another ranking officer, Lieutenant James Lyons, noted: "The organization I represent is known as 'The Crime Crushers.' We are the fellows that go out and knock their ears down. We chastise them." Los Angeles needed August Vollmer badly. He analyzed what was wrong and issued a progressive manifesto in a big and handsomely bound volume that was promptly discarded. Vollmer was sent on his way, ousted in less than a year by Kent Parrot's faction.

Attempts at police reform stopped when Vollmer left, and a quarter-century of neglect ensued. Through the rest of the 1920s corruption was tolerated so long as L.A. didn't appear to be out of hand in the way of, say, Chicago, where Capone's friends and enemies blasted each other in the streets and blew each other apart with bombs that killed innocent bystanders too. The LAPD had a number of other chiefs during this period, one of whom, Louis Oaks, was fired when found drunk with a naked woman in the backseat of his car. The most important was James Edgar Davis, another big man, a crack shot who posed for publicity shots surrounded by beauties in swimsuits. Davis, described by one newsman as "a burly, dictatorial, somewhat sadistic, bitterly anti-labor man who saw Communist influence behind every telephone poll," had the support of Harry Chandler at the *Times* (Chandler feared organized labor and Reds, not racketeers of The System, who were at least capitalists) and of Mayor Cryer, whose aide was Kent Parrot, close friend of Charlie Crawford. Wheels-within-wheels: "See Charlie—that was the answer to a request for a political favor," wrote the *Evening Herald*, and at the height of his power and influence, in the mid-1920s when most people in L.A. had never even heard of Charlie Crawford, he had much of the city's political structure in his pocket—city hall, cops, reporters, too, dipped their beaks.

In the grand jury room of the Hall of Justice, on that morning after Ned Doheny's funeral, Dave Clark saw that Charlie

Crawford was with Jerry Giesler, another young attorney making a name for himself. Giesler had come to California in 1907 where he'd studied law at USC, and had apprenticed himself to Earl Rogers. Some of Giesler's future cases— involving the defense of Errol Flynn, Charlie Chaplin, Bugsy Siegel, and the stripper Lili St. Cyr—would provide headline copy for nearly half a century. But at this time, it's fair to say, Dave Clark was the more famous and better regarded lawyer. The Marco case had given Clark a glow, and here was a chance to add to it.

Back in 1927 a reform-minded city councilman, Carl Jacobson, had approached the *Daily News* and handed over the addresses of various brothels on Sunset Boulevard. The *News* then published these addresses as part of its anti-vice campaign that was being spearheaded by reporter Gene Coughlin and chiefly directed against Albert Marco. The brothels, though, were a part of Charlie Crawford's empire. Crawford assumed that Jacobson was corruptible, like almost everybody else, and sent over Albert Marco to offer him $25,000 if he'd stop being a pest. Jacobson refused. Soon thereafter he found himself befriended by Mrs. Callie Grimes, a blonde widow with obvious charms. Grimes invited Jacobson to her home on Beagle Street, to a "vine-covered bungalow" that was soon to be famous. Jacobson was there with Callie Grimes one afternoon when the door flew open and cops burst in, together with reporters and photographers with flashguns. Among the cops were Dick Lucas, Harry Raymond, and others who were on Charlie Crawford's payroll. It was later disputed whether Jacobson was dressed only in "red flannel underwear" or whether, as he himself claimed, Lucas and Raymond upended him and stripped off

113

his pants while the lovely Callie disrobed to pose for pictures.

This little farce, which came to be known as "The Red Flannel Raid," happened on August 5, 1927. Jacobson was charged with a morals misdemeanor and found not guilty. He claimed he'd been framed, and went on causing trouble. Some fifteen months later Callie Grimes herself was persuaded to support him. She sold her story to the *News* for $2,500 then proceeded to the D.A.'s office and swore out a sensational affidavit, listing the men who, she alleged, had conspired with her to stage the raid and bring down Jacobson.

Albert Marco was among those Callie Grimes named, as was Charlie Crawford; it was a big moment in the reformers' struggle with the serpentine power of the L.A. System. The grand jury followed through: conspiracy indictments were returned and arrest warrants issued. Marco was by now already in county jail, awaiting transfer to San Quentin, having been prosecuted by Dave Clark. But Crawford reported to the grand jury room with Jerry Giesler to answer his warrant and hear the date when he would be required to enter his plea and then face trial. Dave Clark arrived a little late, having hurried from St. Vincent's, but in time to play his part in the formalities.

Charlie Crawford was a big man, still handsome, long-faced, soft-voiced, with eyes of startling blue and silvery hair. He had ruddy cheeks and big ears with long fleshy lobes. It's been suggested that golf, the great connector in Dave Clark's social and professional life, had brought the two men together before this, and it's indeed likely that their paths had crossed. Certainly Clark, like everybody in the D.A.'s office, already knew a great deal about Charlie Crawford.

This day's proceedings were routine. Dave Clark filed for a trial date. Crawford posted $2,000 bail and was granted his freedom. For Crawford, the worst part of all this was the exposure. On the afternoon of February 19, the *Evening Express* felt free to name him "the city's outstanding underworld boss." The Gray Wolf was no longer in the shadows. Soon Clark would be facing Crawford in court, foreshadowing their later confrontation over a gun barrel.

12

Systems Under Siege

Within days of the shootings at Greystone, Lucien Wheeler, the head of the D.A.'s investigative unit, ordered young Leslie White to investigate the death of a prostitute. She'd been found in a gutter in Chinatown, killed by a bullet from a gun that lay nearby. The LAPD reported a suicide. Wheeler wondered whether White, having been "so successful" with the Doheny case, might prove her death happened otherwise. At the morgue White found the woman's corpse covered with bruises, apparently made by the toe of a shoe. She'd been kicked almost to death before being shot from an angle and distance that precluded any theory of suicide. It was murder, but White soon discovered that nobody gave a damn. "Her case was dropped not because she had too much money to tamper with, but simply because she did not have money enough," he wrote.

White felt like, one way or another, he too had "taken an

awful beating." His anger bubbled over and he confronted Lucien Wheeler.

In the early 1920s, while bureau chief for the Federal Bureau of Investigation in Los Angeles, Wheeler had orchestrated the capture of former Mexican general Enrique Estrada, who was amassing machine-guns, armored cars, and various other weaponry in Southern California, planning to march back down into Mexico and start a counter-revolution. Along with Estrada, 104 other insurrectionists were arrested, and the Mexican government sent engraved watches to each of Wheeler's men who'd helped thwart the half-baked though dangerous scheme. BOI agents (like FBI men subsequently) were forbidden from accepting such gifts so Wheeler gathered together all the watches and returned them. This was all very well and proper. On the other hand, Wheeler had been a beneficiary in one of the Julian Pete rings, happy to line his pockets.

In 1927, J. Edgar Hoover, the new head of the BOI, threatened Lucien Wheeler with a transfer. Hoover liked his agents young and eager and kept them on their toes by shifting them or firing them at will. Wheeler was too experienced to submit to Hoover's tyranny. Besides, he had other irons in the fire. He resigned, and was replaced in L.A. by Frank Blake, who would in time orchestrate the trapping and slaughter of the bank robbers Bonnie and Clyde and become one of Hoover's top men. Meanwhile Wheeler set himself up as a private investigator. One of his first clients was Jake Berman, aka Jack Bennett, the two-name "Boy Ponzi" whose antics and demeanor so annoyed Leslie White. Wheeler, on becoming head of Buron Fitts's investigative unit, brokered the deal whereby

Berman received immunity in exchange for turning state's evidence.

Lucien Wheeler was more than savvy; he was a part of the power structure that he knew how to juice, and when White summoned up courage and confronted him, asking "Who do *you* think killed Ned Doheny?," he refused to answer. He was giving White a lesson in realpolitik or, more likely, just protecting his own position. In L.A. the accomplished Lucien Wheeler swam in the same mixed-up waters as everybody else.

"What was I supposed to do?" White asked.

"You were wrong, Les," Wheeler said. "You should have let sleeping dogs lie until you could prove definitely what *did* happen."

"How can I prove a thing like that unless I'm allowed to investigate it?" White asked.

Lucien Wheeler shrugged.

White was walking out of the Hall of Justice, going down the steps when he met Dave Clark coming in. It was a cool and cloudy afternoon. White had seen the handsome Clark often enough by now and the two men usually exchanged nods and greetings. This time, though, Clark stopped. He'd heard that White's wife was expecting a baby. "Congratulations," he said, and he touched White on the shoulder in a friendly way. The two men—the one tall and dressed with his usual elegance, the other short with his hat pushed back on his head—stood there chatting. It was a scene White would remember and record in his diary.

Just about a week before, at around the time of the Greystone killings, Alfred A. Knopf had published *Red Harvest*, Dashiell Hammett's first novel, in which an unnamed narrator, a private investigator called the Op (short for "operative") is summoned to a mining town where, to solve his case, he plays off all sides against each other, cops against gangsters, gangsters against gangsters, cops against cops. "I've got a hard skin over what's left of my soul, and after twenty years of messing around with crime I can look at any sort of murder without seeing anything in it but my bread and butter, the day's work," says the Op, launching a sour yet hugely seductive and influential world view, a quintessential American style: the hardboiled. Hammett, the former Pinkerton man, had once been offered $5,000 by the Anaconda Copper Mining Company to kill labor leader Frank Little. Hammett viewed himself as a formerly dangerous man living in a perpetually corrupt society; his starting point was worldly disillusion, and his Op is "a fat, middle-aged, hard-boiled, pig-headed guy."

Leslie White, on the steps in front of the Hall of Justice in February 1929, was a very different sort of detective. Sickly, smart, dedicated, and eager to do good, he recalled an earlier character type, such as those created by Balzac or Charles Dickens. Both authors wrote novels about naïve young men recently arrived in the big city, about to undergo adventures they only think they want, but might not survive. White was the subject of a real-life *bildungsroman*, and Dave Clark—what Dave Clark said and what happened to him—would be a part of his education. Dave Clark was, in ways both urbane and ultimately tragic, a reality instructor.

The two men talked about the Doheny case and Lucien Wheeler. "You stood out for what you believed," Clark told White. "That's unusual. It frightens people."

Clark warned White that he could expect some ridicule

from the older detectives, the broken arches. "Not because you were wrong, but because you were naïve," he said.

Clark also told White a story. One time he'd been inside the Doheny Mansion at Chester Place with his then boss Olin Wellborn III. He'd seen Doheny open a desk drawer filled with neat stacks of $100 bills and hand Wellborn $50,000 as casually as though it had been a nickel.

"You might not like that kind of power but you have to know that it's there," Clark told White. "It makes things happen."

Clark liked E. L. Doheny. He admired not so much the empire the old man had built or the way he pushed people around but his indomitable spirit. He sympathized, too, with Leslie White's predicament, knowing that crusades were hard work. People tended not to thank you for embarking on them.

"Have you heard of Charlie Crawford?" Clark asked.

Indeed White had. "Even before I learned that a city, any city, is invariably under the dominance of a 'boss,' I knew of the existence of Charles Crawford, sometimes known as the 'Gray Wolf' because of a whitish-gray thatch of hair," he wrote. "He was almost a legendary figure about whom all sorts of rumors and mysterious stories were told. Boss of Los Angeles County, when he wiggled his fingers the puppets we knew as politicians danced to his lyrics."

Clark brought up the subject of the so-called "Red Flannel Raid" and the upcoming conspiracy trial in which Crawford would be among the defendants. Buron Fitts wanted to target The System and was making a big deal of the case. Clark said some preparatory investigative work needed to be done.

"Would you be interested in tackling the job?" Clark asked.

White said yes, and Clark spoke to Lucien Wheeler about it. Two days later Wheeler approached White, who collected his gear and drove to 4372 Beagle Street where he climbed the creaking and uneven steps that led up to Callie Grimes's cottage. He took pictures of the room where Jacobson's pants were supposedly removed. He made a map of the neighborhood. A photograph from this time shows White himself, stern and owlish in his horn-rimmed spectacles, pinning material to a board in the Hall of Justice.

Callie Grimes failed to appear at various pre-trial hearings; she'd vanished, and rumor suggested that Crawford had given her a payoff and arranged for her to leave town. Lucien Wheeler put wiretaps on the phones of Grimes's friends and family. When Grimes contacted her mother, the call was traced to El Paso, Texas, where Grimes was then surprised in a room at the Sheldon Hotel, propped up among pillows and wearing little besides a string of pearls that she claimed Charlie Crawford had given her. Lucien Wheeler chartered a plane to bring her back to L.A. She arrived in time for the beginning of the trial, with silverware and towels she'd stolen from the Sheldon Hotel hidden in her suitcase. Callie Grimes was in no mood to testify. "Why should I be bothered?" she asked grandly. "My plans are my own."

Callie Grimes, clearly, would be less than reliable as a witness. The trial began in late March, with Dave Clark and the two other deputy D.A.s who were working the case bitterly denouncing the "subtle alliance" that existed between the police and the underworld. For one afternoon the court was removed to Beagle Street, where Leslie White gave a tour of the cottage, pointing out objects and locations that would feature in proceedings, and rubbing shoulders with Callie Grimes and with Albert Marco, who had been let out of jail for the day. Here White gained his first close-up look at Charlie Crawford. White had expected a villainous roué. Instead he found "a soft-voiced old gentleman, big of stature, with a bland expression and a lock of silvery hair that curled over his forehead and gave him, somehow, a priestly look."

Crowds grew daily as the trial went on. Dave Clark was quick to admire Jerry Giesler's cool and witty conduct of Crawford's defense. Giesler wasted no chance to exploit the humor of the case; remorseless, he piled indignities on Carl Jacobson, arguing that the councilman had been guilty of improper conduct. "Entrapment is no defense," Giesler argued. "Carl Jacobson made love and improper advances to Callie Grimes."

Jacobson wept on the stand. Recalling what had happened, he said he felt something, "a slap on the neck," and stumbled onto Callie Grimes's bed. "Next thing I remembered there were four flashlights in the room, like lights coming out of a dim fog. A policeman was standing in the room with my trousers over his arm. I had one shoe on and the other off. My glasses had been knocked to the floor," he said.

Giesler said that Jacobson had been like a mouse after cheese in a trap: he got his neck broke.

Jacobson told how Marco had offered him the $25,000 bribe in a room in the old City Hall. Jacobson was voluble, but not convincing; he hadn't reported the attempted bribe at the time the offer was made.

Callie Grimes refused to back up the accusations she'd made in her affidavit and Giesler argued that charges against Crawford and Marco should be dismissed because there was no legal evidence linking them to the conspiracy. The judge accepted this, and Crawford rose to go, sweeping out of court with a smile, while Marco was returned to his cell in the county jail. The trial of the LAPD men went on, however, and resulted in a hung jury and the ordering of a retrial.

"The case was laughed out of court," Leslie White wrote. "I was satisfied that Crawford was a vicious old scoundrel."

Afterward, in the Hall of Justice waiting for the elevator, White confronted Dave Clark. "That was a farce," White said. "You know that Crawford was guilty."

The suave Clark smiled. "He's fully capable of framing his own grandmother," he said.

"You don't seem bothered."

Clark shrugged: you win some, you lose some, he seemed to be implying. "It was the right time for our office to run with the informers. And Crawford might not have won after all," he said.

Clark had a point. The result looked like a triumph for Charlie Crawford but really wasn't. The timing of the trial was crucial. A mayoral election was in progress and public airing of the underworld's intimate connection with City Hall and the LAPD (the gap between these entities now having been shown to be less than the width of a councilman's undershorts) gave plentiful ammunition to Crawford's enemies, and to the enemies of Kent Parrot and George Cryer, who decided not to run again, on grounds of ill health, and was replaced as a candidate by another Parrot/Crawford stooge, William G. Bonelli. Eminent among Crawford's enemies was the Reverend Robert Pierce Shuler, known as "Fighting Bob," a charismatic figure in one of the city's increasingly powerful arenas: religion. Shuler was a brilliant and powerful evangelist who charmed his massive audience though a whiff of manure seemed to cling to his shoes. This one-man moral backlash fought a form of class warfare on behalf of his "folks" against the corrupt downtown grandees and the sybarites of Hollywood. He was not so much the conscience of L.A. as its puritan subconscious sprung to vivid and resentful life.

"The Rev. Bob Shuler was born in a log cabin in the Blue Ridge. His people were mountain whites, all poor and most of them illiterate. As a boy, he worked with oxen in the fields. His clothes were made by his mother on a spinning wheel out of flax grown behind the barn," wrote Edmund Wilson in the *New Republic* in 1931. Bob Shuler cut wood, hoed corn, tramped the railroad looking for jobs, became a Methodist preacher and, upon arrival in L.A. in the early 1920s, a celebrity. Like his rival Aimee McPherson, Shuler was a rousing preacher whose wealthy followers provided money for a radio station. Unlike her, he had a passion for politics, and used his huge radio audience accordingly, rallying them against evolution, graft, the Jews, Hollywood, and the perceived lawlessness of the rich and famous and powerful. "I've found very few millionaires who didn't get their money in a manner that I doubted if God would own or bless," he said. With his hillbilly vernacular, Shuler played to the conservative Midwesterners whose exodus had first peopled L.A.

"Bob Shuler's appeal was perfectly gauged for these retired farmers and their families, who, finding themselves, after the War, unexpectedly rich from their wheat and corn, had come out to live in California bungalows and to bask in the monotonous sun, but for whom listening to sermons was one of their principal pastimes," wrote Wilson. "Side by side with sporting oil-millionaires, an exotic California under-world and the celluloid romances of Hollywood, they were glad to get an intimate peek into the debauched goings-on of their neighbors, and at the same time to be made to feel their own superior righteousness, and even—what was probably most gratifying of all—to have a hand in bringing the wicked to judgement."

Fighting Bob became "Christ's ambassador in a wicked city." At his red brick Trinity Church he preached in front of banks of flowers and beneath an enormous American flag. Two nights a week he turned over the airwaves of his station, KGEF, to "civic betterment." Translated, this meant dishing the dirt. Shuler was the most powerful gossip in L.A. and the best informed. He was outspoken, magnetic, a charming fanatic, a zealot who wore loose brown suits and flapping ties and saw conspiracies everywhere. He'd seen one in the fall of Julian Pete, believing that hucksters disguised in the respectable robes of business had robbed blind tens of thousands of his radio congregation; he was right about that, and he rode this insight to greater power, attacking the "Julian thieves" endlessly, slamming Asa Keyes for booze parties and shady meetings with luscious secretaries, and mocking the successive LAPD chiefs who, he saw, were mere pawns of Kent Parrot and Charlie Crawford.

Through the months of April and May 1929, in the wake of the dismissal of the conspiracy charge against Crawford, Bob Shuler used his radio station and his magazine to lobby hard for John Porter, his own candidate for mayor. Shuler had plucked Porter, a junk dealer and one-time Ku Klux Klansman, out of nowhere—or rather, from the ranks of the grand jury that had indicted Asa Keyes. Porter, therefore, had some loose association with reform, and with Buron Fitts, whom Shuler idolized. A master of innuendo and the personal slur, Shuler liked to single out specific individuals— not just the vague targets of immorality. As the mayoral election reached its climax, he declared that he would "as soon baptize a skunk as Charlie Crawford." Crawford was "the greatest artist of the double-cross that California has ever seen, a snake," Shuler said, "no, lower than a snake, a slithering reptile force smearing his loathsome reptile scales on the cleanliness of our city."

The rhetoric, going out citywide, had a gathering effect, and in the elections on June 4 the Parrot/Crawford slate met with defeat. John Porter was elected mayor by a wide margin. Further, nine of the candidates nominated by Shuler as city councilmen were put in office. Overnight "Fighting Bob" Shuler became, in effect, the new political boss of L.A.

It looked like a shattering blow to The System. Mayor Porter quickly replaced LAPD chief Edgar Davis with Dick Steckel, Dave Clark's good friend. Steckel fired Dick Lucas and Harry Raymond, Crawford's strongarm men. In swift order Crawford had lost his City Hall clout and the backbone of his protection. Nor was that the end of his problems or threats to his power.

On February 14, 1929, sandwiched between the end of the Asa Keyes trial and the deaths of Ned Doheny, Jr., and Hugh Plunkett, seven men had been gunned down in a warehouse on Clark Street in Chicago, a now legendary moment in the history of crime: the St. Valentine's Day Massacre, when Al Capone struck at his rival Bugsy Moran.

At the time, though, what had happened was far from clear. "Chicago's Massacre Unsolved," declared the *Times*, in a story that ran alongside the breaking news of the Doheny killings on the morning of February 18. "Police Opine Canadians May Be Gang Killers." The massacre, coming as part of a liquor war, and hard on a wave of bombings and hijackings, made Capone's enemies think about getting out of Chicago; some of his allies, too, expecting a clampdown, wondered about swapping the windy city for balmier climes. Both groups eyed California, specifically Los Angeles—the new wild west. The Mafia now began to make a more concerted effort to move into L.A., using as allies those Italian racketeers—Jack Dragna, John Rosselli, and the rumrunner Tony Cornero—who were already active in the city, but had been cut out of Charlie Crawford's System.

Like E. L. Doheny, Charlie Crawford was a figure from the Old West who'd survived into another time and prospered. Like Doheny, he'd been instrumental in the development of the city he'd made his home, and his arena, in middle-age. Crawford's role was in the shadows, but he and Doheny had known each other in a casual way for a long time. They both juiced the city's hidden power lines. Now both of them saw enemies in every corner. Soon after his son's death, E. L. Doheny boarded a train that took him from L.A. to Washington, D.C., for the bribery trial of Albert Fall. "My friend will be on trial back there and I'm going to testify in the case—that's about all there is to it," he told the reporters who watched him depart.

Attorney Owen J. Roberts, acting for the prosecution in the case of *United States v. Albert B. Fall*, summed up the affair: "It is all simple," he said. "There are four things of a controlling nature for you to remember. One is that Doheny wanted the lease of the Elk Hills. The second is, Fall wanted money. The third is, Doheny got the lease, and the fourth is, Fall got the money."

The aging Fall collapsed and onlookers feared that he might be about to die when the jury delivered its guilty verdict. Fall didn't die; instead Judge William Hitz fined him $100,000 and sentenced him to a year in jail. Doheny, "stiff and ashen" as the *Times* reported, knew now that he would be tried for giving a bribe to a man who had already been found guilty of accepting it.

It wasn't in the nature of either E. L. Doheny or Charlie Crawford to throw in their hands and quit. They were accustomed to power and command, and their careers had been a process of successful adaptation. They would go on fighting, even as an era drew to its end and history got ready to sweep them away.

13

Reach for a Typewriter

In June 1929 Leslie White's wife gave birth to a son. Fatherhood added to White's feelings of uncertainty. Aspects of his work, and the closed-off avenues he was warned not to explore, worried him and nagged at his conscience. He'd put down a deposit and taken out a mortgage on a small house in the suburb of Glendale. He commuted into the city each morning, often sharing the ride with his friend, Casey Shawhan, a crime reporter on the *Examiner*. The two talked freely about law and graft in L.A., and White aired his insecurities. He had a baby and a bad lung he had to nurse along. For all he knew, he would be let go if another D.A. was elected. The current D.A., Buron Fitts, had set up the expanded investigative bureau as a brand new deal, and with Fitts the bureau might fall. "I had studied hard and was already a qualified court expert on finger-printing and photography, and something of an expert on the examination of questioned documents," White later wrote. "At best the job was an interlude."

For a while White considered joining the LAPD, a job that wouldn't go away and came with a pension; but, within weeks of his son's birth, he was called upon to investigate a murder. A Mexican teenager, Christobal Silvas Sierra, had been found dead in an empty lot with two bullets in his back. Apparently he'd been shot by a friend, Robert Ocana. But White and the D.A.'s office soon discovered that Sierra had in fact been killed by an LAPD officer, Bill Bost, a beat cop with a nasty drinking habit and a berserk temper. Bost's LAPD comrades at the Boyle Heights station had covered up for him, framing Ocana.

Bost was tried, but convicted only of manslaughter. White felt he should have hanged. Under the circumstances, though, the manslaughter verdict was a victory, and White received pats on the back and a letter of commendation from Fitts. He was struck by how *un*surprised everybody seemed. This very nasty case attracted little press, the LAPD's clannishness being regarded, perhaps, as a necessary evil, or a problem too engrained to tackle.

Joining the LAPD was thus removed as a possibility. White doubted his ability to stay in line or even alive within the organization. But he still faced the problem of how to plot his future. Needing advice, he called a friend in Ventura, and when the friend's business next brought him to L.A., the two men met in a cafeteria on Broadway, down the hill from the Hall of Justice.

Over coffee White found himself looking into a round, moon-like, almost bland face with unexpectedly sharp eyes that squinted and glittered at him from behind wire-frame glasses. His friend's name was Erle Stanley Gardner. In

Leslie White (centre), cocky and self-assured, poses with colleagues
days after the St. Francis dam disaster. *(Museum of Ventura County)*

A mass grave for St. Francis victims. *(UCLA Special Collections)*

Dave Clark (second from right) – tall, tan, white-hatted, and "frigid-eyed" – strides on a downtown sidewalk with other attorneys.
(UCLA Special Collections)

A major scene of the action—the Los Angeles Hall of Justice, which opened in 1925. *(UCLA Special Collections)*

Buron Fitts, district attorney for Los Angeles County and a formidable power player, enjoys a photo op. *(UCLA Special Collections)*

Oil promoter C. C. Julian – his dealings characterized the crazy 1920s boom. *(Los Angeles Public Library)*

A bloody Albert Marco, pictured after his arrest at the Ship Café. *(UCLA Special Collections)*

Oil magnate E. L. Doheny – political scandals in which he was enmeshed led to profound tragedy. *(UCLA Special Collections)*

A forest of Los Angeles oil derricks from 1926. *(UCLA Special Collections)*

Greystone Mansion in Beverly Hills, the morning after the shootings.
(UCLA Special Collections)

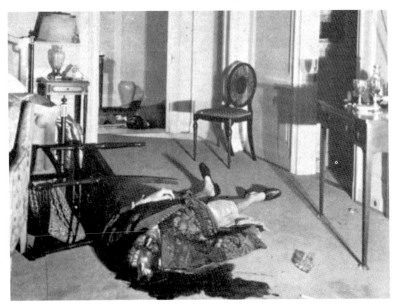
The corpses of Ned Doheny (foreground) and Hugh Plunkett.
(Boston University)

Journalist and murder victim
Herbert Spencer.
(Los Angeles Public Library)

The Rev. "Fighting Bob" Shuler –
in jail and milking the moment.
(Los Angeles Public Library)

Erle Stanley Gardner – when
he was still a Ventura County
attorney.
(Museum of Ventura County)

Raymond Chandler in the 1930s,
at the outset of his writing career.
(Los Angeles Public Library)

Charlie Crawford, smiling benignly at one of his trials and counting on his customary acquittal. *(UCLA Special Collections)*

Clara Bow – dressed as demurely as possible – at a court appearance.
(UCLA Special Collections)

Dave Clark with Daisy DeVoe during her arraignment.
(Los Angeles Public Library)

Charlie Crawford's bronze and silver burial casket was the costliest to be found in Los Angeles at the time. *(UCLA Special Collections)*

A poker game in the holding cell at the Hall of Justice – Dave Clark looks cool as usual. *(UCLA Special Collections)*

The brand-new Colt that killed Charlie Crawford and Herbert Spencer. *(UCLA Special Collections)*

Guy McAfee in Las Vegas, breaking ground for one of his clubs – he gave "The Strip" its name. *(UCLA Special Collections)*

The Octopus

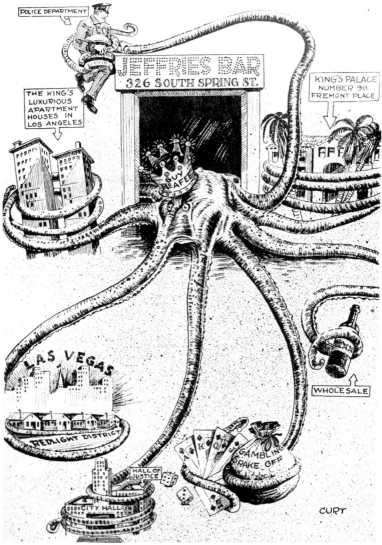

The cartoon that appeared in Herbert Spencer's magazine *The Critic of Critics* and caused a lot of trouble – the octopus Guy McAfee is pictured with his tentacles around all of Los Angeles.
(UCLA Special Collections)

Dave Clark, on the stand during his first trial. *(UCLA Special Collections)*

Leslie White, giving evidence. *(Los Angeles Public Library)*

Dave Clark and his wife, Nancy, outside his cell at the Hall of Justice.
(UCLA Special Collections)

appearance Gardner was nondescript, like somebody's uncle, but White knew the man had the energy of a bursting dam. For years—Gardner had just turned forty—he'd toiled in the courts and law libraries of Ventura and Oxnard. In L.A. he was known to be a clever and determined attorney, a country boy who came to town and occasionally bested the metropolitan legal stars. But White didn't want to talk to him about law; he wanted to talk about writing. He knew that Gardner supplemented his income to the extent of $15,000 a year by creating fiction. Gardner slept as little as three hours a night, instead staying at his typewriter until he had produced the 4,000-word daily target he set for himself. Gardner was a writing machine, a story industrialist. He had yet to create Perry Mason, the character that would make him famous—and for a long time, the world's bestselling author—but in recent years he'd hammered out millions of words and sold hundreds of stories: about Speed Dash, human fly; Sidney Zoom and his police dog; Ed Jenkins, the phantom crook; confidence men Lester Leith and Paul Pry; Key-Clew Clark, consulting criminologist, and Major Copely Blane, freelance diplomat; the Patent Leather Kid; Hard Rock Hogan; Señor Arnaz de Lobo; and a host of others.

White had always wanted to write. It seemed to him the ideal sort of existence: a chance to think as he liked, to travel, to escape the sordid side of life. But he'd been afraid to mention it to Gardner until now, and was still nervous about doing so. Instead he poured out his frustrations about the Doheny case, about the LAPD, about money. In Ventura, Gardner's office had been just down the street from White's photographic studio. The two had met while Gardner had been fighting, and winning, a pro bono case on behalf of a farm laborer sentenced to hang. White admired Gardner's energy and go-getting practical attitude.

"I'm thinking about trying fiction," White blurted out finally. "But I have no education. I don't know where to start."

Gardner regarded White with brusque impatience. "Forget about education. You've got a whole library of stories inside you," he said. His voice was calm but forceful. "That 'sordid filth' you say you want to get away from—it's material."

Erle Stanley Gardner would remain a friend, and this brief conversation would change Leslie White's life. White was by nature an enthusiast. In later years he turned himself into an expert on the breeding of beef cattle and the building of model railways, about which he wrote *Scale Model Railroading*, a standard text. He threw himself into things. Having received this encouragement from Gardner, he went home to Glendale that night and walked out to a newsstand to buy some of the publications Gardner was writing for and selling to: the pulps, so called because they were printed on rough, wood-pulp paper, not expected to last. White found them crowding the newsstand, hundreds of magazines, seven by ten inches with gaudy covers and trashy titles: *Thrilling Detective*, *Dime Detective*, *Crime Busters*, *The Shadow*, *The Underworld*, *The Whisperer*, *Weird Tales*, and so on. It was a different America: millions read these all-fiction magazines every week, and hundreds of writers made money selling stories to them, at one to three cents a word. The pulps had usurped the dime novel's place in the culture.

White began his studies with *Black Mask*, the best in the market, founded in 1920 by H. L. Mencken and George Nathan, but by then under the editorship of the legendary Captain Joseph T. Shaw. White saw that Gardner himself had a story, titled "Spawn of the Night," in the current issue, for August 1929. Also advertised was the upcoming serial of Dashiell Hammett's new novel, *The Maltese Falcon*. Gardner had told White that Hammett was *Black Mask*'s ace performer, a private eye who had learned about writing, not a writer who was faking it. Hammett wrote in a style that was lean and stripped down. His stories had plausible hooks and twists and convincing motivation. He showed the underbelly of American life without illusion. He was creating a whole new kind of crime fiction.

White set up his typewriter on the kitchen table, at the far end of the house from where the baby was sleeping. He rolled in a sheet of paper, paused for a moment, and began to tap away. He found, to his surprise, that the words came easily. He finished a story in a single burst, mailed it out the next day, and watched it come back over subsequent weeks with a series of rejection slips, from *Black Mask* and other pulps. It didn't really matter, because by then he'd already written several more stories and sent them out too. On November 3, 1929, he found a letter from New York in his mailbox. "Dear Mr. White," wrote editor Harry Goldsmith. "I enjoyed reading your story, 'Phoney Evidence,' and it is an accept for DRAGNET. In your letter you asked for suggestions, but the story was very good in every direction. Please keep working along the lines which you have started and I am confident you will sell to DRAGNET regularly." Enclosed was a check for $50.

White was on his way. From then on he made regular sales. He was no stylist like Hammett, but his stories moved quickly. In "Phoney Evidence," a doctor covers up a murder by daubing another man's blood on the face of his victim—shades of E. C. Fishbaugh. In "The City of Hell!," a story that White did sell to *Black Mask*, renegade cops take down a crime machine that has an unnamed city by the throat; the cops kidnap racketeers, lawyers, the chief of the grand jury, and a judge, and hold vigilante trials in the sewers. Then they save the state and taxpayers a lot of money, shortcutting the necessity of more formal legal proceedings with a staged nightclub shoot-out: "All hell broke loose! With the deafening chatter of the twin machine guns, came the screams of stricken men."

The speed at which White wrote these early stories revealed the nature and limitations of his talent. He had verve and a quick gift for story. He leaned in the direction of hokum and melodrama. Like any crime writer, he gave away parts of his inner fantasy. Dashiell Hammett's Sam Spade takes several steps further the cynical bastard Hammett hoped he was. Georges Simenon's Maigret provides the answer to a question Simenon posed himself: What if I were a decent man? White's detectives have none of the depth of these characters. He didn't write realistic versions of himself or Lucien Wheeler or Blayney Matthews. Instead he created comic book avengers, upright and merciless conquerors of wrong, as if on the page he wanted to fix and make right a world he was coming to regard as irreparable.

During the day, working for the D.A.'s office, White's attitude changed. He gave up worrying about making a mistake in forensics or in court. The trickier and more sensitive the case, the more he wanted to get involved. He was no longer merely an odd kind of cop; each morning, as he entered the Hall of Justice, striding through the barrel-vaulted entrance hall that ran the entire length of the building, he knew something else was going on beside the investigative challenges he faced with a new eagerness. He was research-ing, gathering material. He was writing pulp fiction.

14

Raymond Chandler— Oil Man!

In the summer and fall of 1929, Raymond Chandler, who would get to know Leslie White and within a few years easily surpass him as a writer, was further removed from a literary career than at any time in his life. He was forty-one years old and his marriage was on the rocks. He was drinking heavily, and one day checked into a downtown hotel room and called his wife to tell her that he was going to jump from the window. This suicide threat (and there were others) wasn't perhaps entirely serious but more a tortured cry for attention from an unhappy alcoholic subject to wild swings of mood. Yet Chandler was a professional success, earning in excess of $13,000 yearly at a time when rent for a decent apartment was $50. Chandler earned more than, say, Buron Fitts, and Chandler's prosperity had nothing to do with writing. A photograph of the time shows him dressed in a suit at the Bureau of Mines and Oils Annual Banquet at the

135

Biltmore Hotel. He was a high-placed executive in the oil business and about to involve himself in the seemingly never-ending saga of Julian Pete. He was helping bring a lawsuit.

Chandler, when he achieved fame, would say that he was conceived on the high plains of the West, in the frontier town of Laramie, Wyoming; but he was born on July 23, 1888, in Chicago, Illinois, and spent most of his childhood in England, where he was educated at Dulwich College, a fancy public (that's to say fee-paying) school. This background in part accounts for Chandler's lifelong restlessness and his divided personality. He was an American who loved England, a snob who understood low-life and base instincts, a man who could be both hardboiled and sentimental, a man attracted to women yet frightened of them.

Chandler first arrived in L.A. in 1912, when the population had just climbed over 300,000. Mulholland's aqueduct was unfinished and no water came as yet from the Owens River Valley. The streetcars with their hundreds of miles of track connected the downtown center to the newly incorporated city of Hollywood and distant Santa Monica and Venice Beach. Downtown street corners had hitching posts and watering troughs. Bel-Air, Brentwood, and Pacific Palisades were unheard of. Pico and Olympic Boulevards were barley fields. A few primitive automobiles smoked and roared through the streets, but was still mostly propelled by horse and buggy. This was a time so distant as to seem almost science-fictional. The city still reverberated from the dynamiting of the *Times* building by iron worker unionists on October 1, 1910, an explosion that killed twenty people and injured many more, the result of a desperate and increasingly violent struggle between capital and labor. At stake was the future of the city and, in a way, its very soul. Would L.A. become socialist or remain the businessman's creation? For a while the question was real, the result uncertain. Battle lines were drawn, and two men, John J. and James McNamara, came to trial for the act of terror. Across the country many believed the McNamaras had been framed. The legendary trial lawyer and labor attorney Clarence Darrow was persuaded, at great expense, to defend them. But during the course of the proceedings, Darrow was himself accused of bribing a juror and the McNamaras changed their plea to guilty, giving socialism in Southern California, and arguably in America as a whole, a blow from which it would never recover. Capital won the day, and a key chapter in Los Angeles history was written. Trials arising from the case dragged on well into the time when Raymond Chandler was already in L.A., showing him how power worked in the city and perhaps already starting to shape his vision of what only looked like paradise.

"I used to like this town. A long time ago. There were trees along Wilshire Boulevard. Beverly Hills was a country town. Westwood was bare hills and lots offered at eleven hundred dollars and no takers. Hollywood was a bunch of frame houses on the inter-urban line," Chandler's fictional hero, the detective Philip Marlowe, would remember much later, in 1949. "Los Angeles was just a big dry sunny place with ugly homes and no style, but goodhearted and peaceful. It had the climate they yap about now. People used to sleep out on porches. Little groups who thought they were intellectual used to call it the Athens of America."

Chandler himself belonged to one such group, The Optimists, formed by his friend Warren Lloyd, a lawyer with money from oil who had befriended Chandler on a boat coming over from Europe and had invited him to L.A. The Optimists met weekly at Lloyd's house on South Bonnie Brae Street. Music was played, poetry declaimed, literature and philosophy discussed, and at one of these soirees Chandler first met Julian Pascal, a concert pianist and music professor, and Pascal's wife Cissy.

"Cissy was a raging beauty, a strawberry blonde with skin I used to love to touch," Chandler would say later. "I don't know how I ever managed to get her." It took a while, because Cissy resisted Chandler for years.

Chandler fought in France in WWI and came back (or was drawn back) to L.A. in 1919. Julian Pascal agreed, after much argument and discussion, to bow out of the picture; but Cissy and Chandler didn't marry until 1924, when Chandler's mother, with whom he'd been living, died at last from an agonizing cancer. Only then, it seems, did Chandler learn that Cissy was not eight years older than he, as he'd thought, but *eighteen.* He was then thirty-five, and he'd married a woman of fifty-three.

"All this is the stuff of passion and novels," noted Patricia Highsmith in an essay. Highsmith's first book, *Strangers on a Train*, would be adapted by Chandler for a 1952 Alfred Hitchcock movie. "But little of the formidable emotional material that Chandler had at his disposal actually found its way into his writing." That's not quite true. Chandler was too troubled ever to be truly happy, and too inhibited and mannerly to be a freely autobiographical writer. This, for him, was good; his heightened sense of his own pleasures and dismays would translate into the way he captured L.A. in his writing, the changing city that wouldn't let him go. But that was in the future.

In the early 1920s Warren Lloyd helped Chandler secure a job with the Dabney Oil Syndicate, a group of companies that operated one hundred fields in the city that was then producing so much of the world's oil. Chandler's boss, Joseph Dabney, was a multimillionaire, a native Iowan who had roamed west and struck oil, developing big fields in Ventura County and at Signal Hill in Long Beach. Dabney, like many a rich man before and since, soothed his conscience and bought a reputation through charity, making big cash donations to the Salvation Army and the California Institute of Technology (Caltech), the future home of scientific geniuses such as Albert Einstein and Richard Feynman. Chandler would eventually characterize Dabney as a petty tyrant, though this was later, after their relationship went sour. For years Chandler was one of Dabney's most important employees. He'd been with Dabney only a short time when he realized that the company's auditor had stolen $30,000. "His method would only be possible in a badly organized office," Chandler wrote. "But I found him out and at his trial I had to sit beside the Assistant DA and tell him what questions to ask. The damn fool didn't know his own case."

Chandler rose quickly, was promoted out of accounting "to become a director of eight companies and a president of three . . . They were small companies but very rich." He had two cars—one a big eight-cylinder Hupmobile, a very upscale automobile—and his handsome salary. He wore slick, custom-made suits. He had a big office and a team of secretaries in the Bank of Italy building on South Olive Street. He hired and fired the staff and reckoned himself an excellent judge of character. As an executive, Chandler could err on the side of arrogance. He managed the services of six lawyers. "Some were good at one thing, some at another. Their bills always exasperated the chairman," he wrote.

Much later Chandler would remark that business was tough and he hated it, but business—what he saw business do, and what business did to him—was key to the writer he became. Business possessed L.A., and because he was a part of a business machine, he came to know the city so well that it started to belong to him too. Business taught Chandler cynicism, revealing to him the inner workings of power. A part of him grew up and became hardboiled. He later wrote about one experience in particular that contributed to his education:

I remember one time when we had a truck carrying pipe in Signal Hill (just north of Long Beach) and the pipe stuck out quite a long way, but there was a red lantern on it, according to law. A car with two drunken sailors and two girls crashed into it and filed actions for $1,000 apiece. They waited almost a year, which is the deadline for filing a personal injury action. The insurance company said, "Oh well, it costs a lot of money to defend these suits, and we'd rather settle." I said, "That's all very well. It doesn't cost you anything to settle. You simply put the rates up. If you don't want to fight this case, and fight it competently, my company will fight it." "At your own expense?" "Of course not. We'll sue you for what it costs us, unless you pay without that necessity." He walked out of the office. We defended the action, with the best lawyer we knew, and we proved that the pipe truck had been properly lighted and then we brought in various bar men from Long Beach (it took money to find them, but it was worth it) and showed that they had been thrown out of three bars. We won hands down, and the insurance company paid up immediately about a third of what they would have settled for, and as soon as they did this I cancelled the policy and had it rewritten with another company.

A nice drama, and a foreshadowing of *Double Indemnity*, the James M. Cain novella that Chandler would later help turn into a screenplay. In London, back at the turn of the century, Chandler had written poetry that was wistful and sadly noble. Now he lived and worked in a highly ignoble city where drunk people smashed into a car and, having taken out an opportunistic lawsuit, expected to cheat the insurance company and get away with it.

Chandler took pride in his clear-sighted victories. He enjoyed jousting with insurance men and attorneys, finding some refuge from his personal unhappiness at the office. He played tennis with work colleagues and journeyed with them up the coast to college football games. He chased show girls at gala dinners and his weekend-long benders became notorious. This desperate behavior suggests F. Scott Fitzgerald, with whom Chandler has more in common than might at first be supposed. He was a Jazz Age guy in crisis, though at this point he still held his high-level job.

Joseph Dabney had lost hundreds of thousands of dollars in the Julian Pete debacle. Unlike most who'd been bilked, he was an enormously rich man with power to seek redress. Opportunity came along in the shape of Arthur Loeb, a Julian Pete victim who nursed a special grievance, having lost an eye during a struggle at a stockholders' meeting. Loeb had been on an unsuccessful mission of vengeance ever since. Now he was looking for partners to contribute the $20,000 he needed to pay a lawyer and initiate a suit that would charge numerous brokerage houses, and the Los Angeles Stock Exchange itself, with continuing to sell Julian Pete shares long after they knew of the over-issues. Dabney told his right-hand man Raymond Chandler to look into the matter. Having met with Loeb and Loeb's attorney, a former Superior Court judge named Guy Crump, Chandler advised Dabney to go ahead, and Crump went to court on behalf of Dabney, Loeb, and various other Julian Pete stockholders.

This lawsuit, demanding $15 million, would end in blackmail, robbery, fraud, and several murders: Leslie White would be sucked into its aftermath, as would Charlie Crawford and Dave Clark. Unwittingly, Raymond Chandler became a prime mover in a chain of action whose bloody consequences would later inspire episodes in his fiction.

The lawsuit was filed on October 8, 1929. Three weeks later, on October 29, 1929, the day now known as Black Tuesday, Wall Street crashed. Stocks lost $24 billion in paper value in a single day—ten times the federal budget, more than the government had spent on WWI. "The market went over the edge of Niagara," wrote historian Frederick Lewis Allen. "Orders to sell came in faster than human beings could conceivably record or deal with them." More than 16 million shares were sold in one trading session. The value of major stocks like General Motors and United States Steel was cut by half. Westinghouse fell from 290 to 102. Warning signals had been there, largely ignored. The previous week, bankers at J. P. Morgan and elsewhere had pumped more than $240 million into the market, trying to shore up confidence. Even this desperate remedy failed. Universal prosperity and consumer utopia, as promised by the seemingly unstoppable bull market, were no longer around the corner. Instead the country knew the bitter taste of panic. America's economic structure cracked wide open. Thousands of investors lost all their capital within a day. The hopes of a decade were smashed.

Louis Adamic, the first literary debunker of the golden myth of Los Angeles, was in New York at the time, writing *Dynamite!*, his book about class violence in America. At its center would be a telling of the story of the *Times* building bombing. Adamic was so deep into his writing that he barely noticed the headlines about the Wall Street disaster. But, soon after, he was turning a corner onto Park Avenue when he heard a woman shriek. She stood on the sidewalk, mouth agape and half-hysterical. She'd seen a man leap to his death from the top of an apartment building. "Park Avenue was not safe to walk on any more. There were too many ruined financiers and speculators," Adamic wrote.

At first the crash seemed to many a temporary setback. "Investors may continue to purchase carefully but with the utmost confidence," reported the *New York Times*, while Irving Fisher, economics professor at Yale and the possessor of another cloudy crystal ball, noted that the market was merely "shaking out the lunatic fringe." "WALL ST LAYS AN EGG," said the headline in *Variety*, not exactly fearing the end of the world. We know now that the wipeout of October 29 presaged a wider collapse, the crumbling of American confidence and prosperity, hard times. The shock would be delayed but America's optimism was broken. A cycle of mass thinking was over, and the slide into the Great Depression had begun. The booming L.A. of the 1920s had been a parody of the frontier spirit. Now farce was about to turn into a darker reality.

15

Entrapment of
a News Hound

Photographs of Leontine Johnson, the former secretary to larcenous Julian Pete chairman S. C. Lewis, show an attractive brunette in her late twenties, wearing a cloche hat with her lips thickly rouged. After the collapse of Julian Pete she'd worked for Will Hays in the newly formed film censor's office, and she liked to boast of her references and her integrity. "I have been kind, benevolent and generous. I came from a little Georgia town and have lived a clean, upright, and honorable life," she said. This image of innocence belied the reality of a tough cookie taking care of herself in a city where everybody was on the make. She was another creature of the era, and she at once took center stage in the $15 million lawsuit that Raymond Chandler helped bring on behalf of Joseph Dabney and others. Chandler was present with Dabney's attorneys when Leontine Johnson gave the deposition in which she spoke of the "little gray account book" that was in her possession and the two suitcases stuffed with papers that she'd taken from the Julian Pete offices. These documents, it was supposed, would blow the lid off the entire mess and help secure Dabney victory in the lawsuit. She said that S. C. Lewis had already offered her $30,000 if she'd give this material back. She'd refused, whereupon Lewis increased his offer to $100,000—or so she claimed: Leontine Johnson would soon prove to be a self-serving and crooked witness. Her shenanigans would ensure that the Dabney lawsuit dragged on for years; they would also help usher in the bloody climax of the Julian Pete fiasco.

Proceedings in the lawsuit began in mid-February 1930. The trial's early days were pretty routine for L.A. at this time, which is to say that Leontine Johnson looked a knockout on the stand, then wept, then fainted and had to take a day off while her attorney told the press that she was in a state of nervous collapse. She returned to tell how $10,000 had been paid to bribe a juror in the first Julian Pete trial and how she'd hired a Slavic language instructor to coach S. C. Lewis when, at one point, he'd been planning to flee to the Soviet Union.

This was juicy, but Leontine Johnson was already plotting her big coup. She'd teamed up with *Examiner* reporter Morris Lavine to tell, and sell, her story. In a town filled with tough-mouthed newsmen, Lavine was already something of a legend, a character who might have stepped straight out of Ben Hecht and Charles MacArthur's 1928 newspaper comedy *The Front Page*. Lavine made his first contribution to a paper when he was only fourteen and paid his way through UC Berkeley by writing journalism on the side before joining the *Examiner* in the early 1920s. It had been

Lavine who, in 1922, ventured to Honduras and tracked down hammer murderess Clara "Tiger Woman" Phillips after her escape from jail, inducing her to return to California and face a life sentence. It had been Lavine who had wrung a confession of murder from Herb Wilson, known as the "Preacher Mail Bandit." It had been Lavine who discovered the bloodstains that led to the arrest of William Edward Hickman, and Lavine who had been credited with the first exposé of Julian Pete in 1927. He was a handsome big man, persuasive and confident, not merely a reporter but an action magnet who kicked his stories into another cycle by virtue of his own involvement.

Lavine shut himself away with Leontine Johnson in her apartment at 236 S. Coronado Street, pounding at a type-writer while he doctored her tale. The first installment of "My Three Years with S. C. Lewis, or The Truth about Julian Pete," appeared in the *Examiner* on March 10, offering the titillating information that Lewis had rented three downtown hotel suites a day to conduct business and had "spent money as fast as he got it." The excerpt was presented as a teaser, a taste of deeper and darker revelations to come.

Again, this was all par for the course: an attractive witness in a scandalous trial had sold her story to the press—not exactly praiseworthy, but predictable enough. Then the big twist happened: a plot development of which Leslie White, or even Raymond Chandler, might have been proud.

On the morning of March 10, White was summoned to see his friend Blayney Matthews, the new head of the D.A.'s investigative bureau, Lucien Wheeler having quit (as he'd told Buron Fitts he would) to set up a private detective agency.

"You know Charlie Crawford, I suppose," said Matthews

to White, more of a flat statement than a question.

"Of course," replied White.

Matthews said that a case had come up and he wanted White to get over to Crawford's office right away.

"I won't force you to take this assignment, Les," said Matthews. "There may be political risks. But if you want it . . ."

White, sensing story material, grabbed at the chance.

Crawford's office was in a building he owned at 6665 Sunset Boulevard in Hollywood, a nondescript California bungalow resembling a residence rather than a business. A photographer and a realtor rented some of the space from Crawford. On the porch, ivy trailed down from hanging baskets, and cactus and aloe grew in terracotta planters.

Crawford's lair was at the back, entered either through an interior door or French doors that opened onto a side alley. The room was paneled almost to the ceiling with dark wood and there were hat stands and leather-backed chairs. Light seeped through a skylight, glinting off a big steel safe. There was a fan raised high on a shelf in one corner. A Tiffany lamp stood on the massive desk beside a cigar box and four telephones, one of which, White understood, had been a direct line to the office of the district attorney during the regime of Asa Keyes. This was where Crawford, the Gray Wolf, pulled his strings and did his business.

White was struck by the steel mesh that covered the skylight. Wires ran from the ceiling and from a button on the side of the desk to an alarm bell on the wall. The doors were fitted with special locks and steel bars that could be slid into place. Crawford was either very cautious or very afraid.

Crawford remembered that he'd met White before, in the Hall of Justice, during the Callie Grimes fiasco. Crawford shook White's hand and said he was expecting a visitor any moment. The visitor soon to walk in through the French doors would be Morris Lavine.

White hid himself; it had all been meticulously planned by Crawford.

"When Lavine entered through the French doors, he unsuspectingly dropped into a chair that placed his head less than two feet from where I stood, with only a thin panel intervening," White later wrote.

With his ear pressed to the wall, Leslie White listened while Crawford urged Lavine to talk and Lavine fell for it, asking Crawford if he'd seen the *Examiner*, and warning that unless he "bought" the documents in Leontine Johnson's possession he'd be exposed.

Crawford agreed to pay up.

"Have you got the money?" Lavine asked.

"Now, remember, I don't want to be blasted any more in the paper," Crawford said.

"That's all right, you know me," Lavine said.

"The $50,000 is for you. The rest is for the girl," said Crawford.

White later described how, through the thin partition, he heard the crackling of crisp bills as they were counted out.

"I don't want to be chiseled anymore. I'm just doing this to protect my gray-haired mother," Crawford said, making White, in his hiding place, smile.

Lavine checked that all the money was there and left, only to find Blayney Matthews waiting when he came out through the French doors and stepped into the street. Matthews tapped Lavine on the shoulder, informed him that he was under arrest, and took him back into Crawford's office.

"I jerked open his coat and relieved him of a loaded forty-five Colt automatic pistol, which hung loose in the armhole of his vest. From an inner pocket, I retrieved the seventy-five one thousand dollar bills," wrote White.

The money had been wrapped in newspaper in two separate packages. White checked the serial numbers of the bills and stored them away as evidence while the great Morris Lavine, for once at a loss for words, slumped in a chair.

"This is what happens when you shake down your friends," Crawford said. "It pays to be honest."

Lavine tried to protest: he could explain all this, he said.

"Morrie, you're just a blackmailer," Crawford said.

Leontine Johnson was arrested within the hour. No further portion of her story was ever published in the *Examiner*, and the Dabney lawsuit was left in disarray. Johnson blamed Lavine, swearing she knew nothing about blackmail. Lavine himself said he'd been framed, set up by Crawford to stop the *Examiner* series. Buron Fitts, though, got his hands on the little gray notebook and the two suitcases "stuffed with documentary dynamite," guaranteeing future developments.

On the evening of the two arrests, White left the Hall of Justice and drove with Blayney Matthews and a stenographer back to Hollywood where, in a suite at the Roosevelt Hotel, they took Crawford's formal statement. It came out that Lavine had been to see Crawford the previous day, a step in his plan to extort Crawford and several others who'd been involved in a Julian Pete "ring," including Kent Parrot and California State Securities Commissioner Jack Fried-lander. Through Kent Parrot, Crawford had informed Buron Fitts and the D.A.'s office of the plot, and they'd agreed to entrap Lavine.

Crawford had just used the D.A.'s office as his pawn and he had an amused look in his eye. He rattled the change in his pocket and gave White a wink. He helped himself to whiskey from a decanter, and White gathered that Crawford kept the suite here at the hotel permanently, as a base of operations that he could sometimes use away from his office, his home, and the other real estate he owned around the city.

As the D.A.'s men got ready to leave, Crawford reminded them that they had something of his—the $75,000. White assured him it would be returned at the end of Lavine's trial. In fact, that money, as money often does, assumed its own life and created another story strand. Crawford never saw his $75,000 again. A mild-mannered and hitherto blameless county clerk would abscond with it and go on a stock market spree; by then Charlie Crawford would be dead.

16

Running with the Foxes

Buron Fitts was taking a run at the California governorship. His campaign, and his ambition, added layers to the drama of the Julian Pete. For political reasons Fitts wanted, and needed, further prosecutions associated with the scandal. Documents in the suitcases seized from Leontine Johnson gave him ammunition, suggesting that Jack Friedlander, the state securities commissioner, had been in the pocket of the Julian Pete guys. Friedlander was the appointee of C. C. Young, the present governor, and Fitts's chief rival in the race for the Republican nomination. Young, the documents suggested, had taken a $250,000 campaign contribution to give Friedlander the job.

Here Fitts had a problem: that $250,000 contribution, if indeed it had been made, had come from the pocket of Jake Berman (aka Jack Bennett, by now known to the press as "Immunity Jack") who was prone, according to the *Examiner*, to "prancing about the Hall of Justice with a proprietorial air." Other documents in the Johnson trove provided evidence that Jack Roth, a stockbroker associated with Morris Lavine, had given bribes to Kent Parrot and Charlie Crawford, both of whom had been instrumental in C. C. Young's previous gubernatorial campaign. This was another useful angle for Fitts so he assigned Dave Clark to look into the case. The whole murky stew began to bubble and boil.

Fitts had made an enemy out of the *Examiner* and the paper attacked him for his alliance with the slippery Jake Berman. On March 19, 1930, the *Examiner* published an affidavit that had been sworn out by one of Berman's crew, Carl Vianelli, who had been a bartender and guard at Berman's home. Vianelli alleged that the bribery associated with the first Julian Pete case had been even worse than supposed. Berman, using his dentist as a front, had bought one of the jurors a house and had given another juror $25,000. Fitts worked hard to protect Berman, while hurrying Dave Clark and other assistant D.A.s to line up further indictments.

The Rev. Bob Shuler entered the fray, both in his radio broadcasts and with a self-published pamphlet titled "Julian Thieves," attacking Young and defending Fitts, who, Shuler argued, was "too brave, too splendidly fine" to be made a fool of, even by a "cunning human rat" like Jake Berman. "If he must grant him immunity that the corruption of the community be purged, well and good," wrote Shuler. "Get all you can out of him, Buron, that will help produce justice and vindicate right." Shuler was a partisan, a supporter who believed in Fitts as a transforming agent of reform. In reality Fitts was already sinking deep in the miasma of double-cross and corruption that he had pledged to eradicate.

The *Times* published Berman's grand jury deposition. Fitts had presented the *Times* with this document, in which Berman told of giving Morris Lavine $30,000 so that Lavine would run pro–Julian Pete articles in the rival *Examiner*. Berman also said he'd seen his former partner Lewis present Governor Young with $10,000 cash in a suite at the Biltmore Hotel. Berman, as before, presented himself as a plausible witness, while Fitts took further criticism for manipulating the grand jury for political ends.

Then on the night of April 15, Robert Bursian, a jeweler, was found beneath his totaled Buick at the bottom of a 100-foot embankment off Beverly Boulevard. Apparently he'd been crushed to death. Subsequent investigation, however, revealed that he had "knock-out drops" in his blood and might have been the victim of poisoning. Fitts then made the announcement that Bursian had been an undercover agent working on a "particularly vital phase of the Julian investigation." Fitts stated: "If it is not foul play, it is a remarkable coincidence."

Fitts offered no further details, and ultimately the mystery of Bursian's death would remain unexplained and unsolved, like the death of the chauffeur, found drowned in his car, off the end of the Santa Monica pier in Raymond Chandler's first novel, *The Big Sleep*. When asked who had killed the chauffeur, Chandler replied: "How the hell should I know?" Chandler's fictional story lines, when he came to construct them, would be a lot like the Julian Pete—difficult to follow, full of twists and turns and changing allegiances, reminders of life's potential for chaos and disorder.

For sure, *something* happened to Robert Bursian. On the next day, April 16, Dave Clark appeared in the grand jury room in the Hall of Justice and secured indictments against Charlie Crawford and former securities commissioner Jack Friedlander on charges of bribery and influence peddling. Crawford, according to the allegations made by Jack Roth, had acted as a middleman, shaking down brokers eager to sell Julian Pete stock. These brokers had been required to pay kickbacks, which were delivered to Crawford on fourteen occasions by Roth's friend Morris Lavine. Crawford then passed on a share of the money to Friedlander. Probably Kent Parrot got a slice as well. Morris Lavine had been much more accustomed, apparently, to giving money to Charlie Crawford than taking it from him.

Crawford, furious about this new indictment, refused to cooperate in the prosecutions of Leontine Johnson and Morris Lavine, whose downfall he'd orchestrated. The Lavine/Johnson trial opened on April 29. Crawford, when called to the stand, stood on his right to silence and refused to answer questions. Lawyers on either side argued with such heat that the judge was forced to excuse the jury, whereupon Crawford risked a sly smile.

The case against Lavine and Johnson was in trouble, and great importance was now attached to the testimony of Leslie White, the only witness to the shakedown. White, dressed in a suit and a sober silk tie that he'd bought for the occasion, took the stand. "My palms were sweating," he wrote in his diary. "But I think I did well."

Lavine was represented by Richard Cantillon, one of the city's leading defense attorneys. Cantillon had discovered that White wrote fiction. It was too tempting a line of attack to ignore. "I understand that you are quite accomplished as a writer and as a developer of plots, and that in a current issue of a well-known magazine, under your own name, you published a deep-rooted detective story which even goes so far as to involve and name characters in the office of District Attorney Buron Fitts," said Cantillon.

White admitted that this was the case.

"Maybe your imagination ran away with you and you *invented* the story of the $75,000 in Charlie Crawford's office."

White stuck to his guns, and to his story, and found an ally in the wily Charlie Crawford. Called back to the stand, Crawford poked fun at Cantillon's theory, and Cantillon dropped it. During a recess White caught up with Crawford in a corridor in the Hall of Justice, trying to thank him.

"You don't want to be seen talking to me," Crawford said, warning White off. "I've got a pretty bad name around town. And you're supposed to hate bad men."

"You don't seem like a bad man, Charlie," White said.

Crawford raised an almost rueful eyebrow. "No, I'm not bad," he said in a soft voice, as if talking to himself. "Not like they've painted me. They say I'm the head of the *underworld*, but I don't know what that is. The only underworld I know anything about are the sewers, and I reckon they can't mean those."

White would remember, with some sadness and even a little affection, that moment when Crawford had seemed to bare his soul. He was just "Good-time Charlie," trying to make his way. He had a wife and kids, a family he loved. Why did people want to destroy him?

Then Crawford spotted one of the jurors watching them talk. "Beat it!" he said to White sharply.

Morris Lavine and Leontine Johnson were found guilty and

sent to jail. Meanwhile, on March 30, 1930, Edward L. Doheny stepped off a train in Los Angeles to face a battery of newspaper photographers, movie cameras, and a 500-strong crowd of employees and well-wishers. At his Washington trial he'd been found not guilty of giving the $100,000 bribe that his friend Albert Fall had been convicted of receiving, a verdict that prompted one U.S. senator to remark, "Under this system you cannot convict a man with $100 million." The *Literary Digest* wrote: "The question 'Who bribed Fall?' now passes into American folklore alongside the historic question, 'Who killed Cock Robin?'"

Albert Fall was puzzled. "The *evidence* was the same for both of us," he said, missing the point that he'd made a bad impression in the courtroom, while Doheny, thanks to the efforts of his attorney Frank Hogan, achieved an opposite effect. Hogan once remarked that the best client was "a rich man, scared," and Doheny fit the bill. He took the stand so that Hogan could lead him through a humble retelling of his remarkable and quintessentially American life, a story of poverty suffered, adventure enjoyed, fabulous wealth achieved, and tragedy endured. Pulling a courtroom stunt worthy of Earl Rogers, Hogan sat in a chair and imper-sonated the dead Ned Doheny while tears streamed down his client's face.

In the icy Washington courtroom, a jury of nine men and three women retained their overcoats and fur wraps when they returned after deliberating for only one hour. "Not guilty," said the foreman, and Estelle Doheny threw her arms around her husband's neck and kissed him. She thrust him away to gaze at him then embraced him once more. A stunned Doheny stood immobile but misty-eyed amidst the wild yells of his supporters. Frank Hogan happily handed over crisp $100 bills to reporters who had bet on acquittal. Doheny, grateful and generous, subsequently gave Frank Hogan a Rolls-Royce and an envelope containing a bonus check for $1 million. Rufus B. von KleinSmid, the president of USC, had been among those who testified on Doheny's behalf, and when Doheny secured his acquittal, von KleinSmid got an entirely new campus building, USC's splendid Doheny Memorial Library. Practical politics. Or, as Raymond Chandler would later write: "Law is where you buy it."

Leslie White witnessed Doheny's triumphant return to L.A. He noted in his diary: "Great crowds. Doheny waved in a modest way and seemed pleased."

Dave Clark left the Hall of Justice and headed downtown to the Petroleum Securities Building, to the offices of Wellborn, Wellborn & Wellborn, where spirits were high and champagne was flowing. He chatted for a while with his friend and former boss, Olin Wellborn III, who told Clark that although Doheny was happy to have won the case, he wasn't well. All these years of trials and investigations had worn him out. "The old man needs a rest," Olin Wellborn III said.

Charlie Crawford, though, was more emotional. He knew when a man was under pressure, and he thrilled to the news of Doheny's escape, clapping his hands together, laughing with his wife and saying to her: "The fox outran the hounds."

17

Zig-Zags of Graft

D ave Clark was on the rise, moving toward the center of power. At that time the D.A.'s office was organized into six different departments, and Buron Fitts now made Clark the head of one of them: the complaints department. "Dave Clark is an outstanding attorney and I've come to rely on him," Fitts told the *Times*. In his new role Clark would examine evidence and testimony before deciding which cases should proceed and go to trial. It was a key role at the Hall of Justice and a big promotion for Clark. Eight deputy D.A.s were assigned to work under him, and his salary increased substantially, to $625 a month.

To celebrate, Clark bought a new car, a soft-topped Ford Roadster, bright yellow, with wire wheels and white-walled tires. He took his wife Nancy on a belated honeymoon, the two having married in haste after a whirlwind romance in the spring of 1926. They went south into Mexico and stayed at Agua Caliente where they swam and golfed and sunned themselves. In the evenings they danced in the opulent grandeur of the ballroom and drank at the Gold Bar, before walking outside and strolling arm-in-arm along the resort's torchlit paths to their bungalow. After a few days they drove slowly back up the coast and took a ferry across to Catalina Island. During this trip, Clark, who liked to fish, became friendly with James W. "Jimmie" Jump, a self-made million-aire and self-styled sportsman who held world angling records for swordfish and marlin. Jump took the couple out on his yacht, and the Clarks tasted the leisurely SoCal high life, staying at the Catalina Island Yacht Club, of which Jump was a founder. "I enjoyed meeting you and your wife," Jump later wrote to Clark. "She's a beautiful woman and you're lucky. Look after her."

Nancy—"a fluttering little thing," said the *Daily News*—inspired paternal and protective feelings in many men, though she was tougher and more volatile and experienced in life than her demure appearance suggested. She was of very Irish descent, having been born in New York on January 2, 1905, to a mother whose maiden name was Reilly. Her father, James T. Malone, was a graduate of Harvard Law who became a New York circuit judge, famed for his stands against graft and the corruption of Tammany Hall. Malone was an upright judge and a hard man, "a massive figure in a flowing black silk gown." He suffered a heart attack and died in a restroom in Manhattan's Criminal Courts Building, shortly after having heard the guilty verdict in a murder trial over which he'd been presiding.

That was in 1920, when Nancy was about to turn sixteen, and pregnant. She came to Los Angeles with one of her sisters, to stay with an aunt and have her baby. Life as a single mother took over until she met Dave Clark in 1925. She was passionate, headstrong, hot-tempered, with the baggage of a small child and the bonus of a well-connected legal family. Clark was tall, smart, handsome, close-mouthed, a war hero from a solid background, a young professional with the city apparently at his feet. They fell in love, and a year later Clark became a husband and a stepfather. He called Nancy "sweetheart" and said he loved her and could never love anyone else. Nancy had been around lawyers and the law all her life, yet sometimes found Dave hard to read. Still, she believed she'd found her soul mate and protector.

On returning from the belated honeymoon in Mexico and on Catalina, Clark took up his position as head of the complaints department. He enjoyed the increased power. He spent time further reviewing the Leontine Johnson documents, and Fitts asked him to give special attention to the Charlie Crawford case and other ongoing Julian Pete prosecutions. Soon, though, something very different landed on Clark's desk.

On June 9, 1930, in a pedestrian underpass at Randolph Street and Michigan Avenue in Chicago, a gunman killed journalist Jake Lingle. Harry Chandler, not only the publisher of the *Times* but the president of the American Newspaper Publishers Association, tagged Lingle "a front-line soldier in the fight against crime" and offered a reward of $50,000 for the capture of his murderer. At his funeral, Lingle lay in a silvered bronze casket, behind which marched ranks of policemen and several brass bands. Jake Lingle, martyr, was buried to a muffled roll of drums.

But another angle emerged.

"Ostensibly Lingle was a police reporter on the *Chicago Tribune* earning $65 a week," wrote Herbert Asbury, the great 1920s and 1930s chronicler of the history of American low-life, "but death revealed him in possession of an income of more than $60,000 a year." Lingle drove a big car, gambled heavily, wintered in Florida, and plunged on the stock market. He died wearing a diamond-studded belt buckle that had been given him by Al Capone. He'd been up to his ears in the rackets.

Moments before his death Lingle had bought a racing form. He'd been carrying the newspaper under his arm and smoking a cigar when the killer came up behind him, took out a revolver, leveled it at his head, and coolly pulled the trigger. Lingle pitched forward, dying while still clutching the paper and the glowing cigar. The gun that killed him was traced to Frankie Foster, a lieutenant of Capone, so Foster fled Chicago by train and fetched up in L.A.

Chicago authorities contacted the D.A.'s office. Dave Clark swore out a complaint, and having issued a warrant for Foster's arrest, put Leslie White on the case. On the face of it, this looked like a tricky, not to say dangerous, assignment. White had little trouble finding Foster, who was swaggering about in a suite at the Roosevelt Hotel. Foster and his entourage, though armed, put up no fight when White and two other D.A. investigators made the arrest. They accepted their removal to jail with "an amused tolerance," White said.

Foster made a halfhearted attempt to defeat extradition but was soon slated to return to Chicago. The D.A.'s office surrounded Foster's departure with secrecy, opting to ship him out not from L.A. but from San Bernardino, sixty miles to the east. In the dead of night White drove out to San

Bernardino with Foster handcuffed in the passenger seat, two detectives in the back, and a fleet of armed officers following in cars.

Foster, a sleek and handsome young man of about thirty, laughed at the melodrama. "Why in hell should I try to get away?" he said. "I'll be sprung the minute we hit Chicago."

A surprise awaited Foster, however, and when he got off the train he was taken into custody. Dave Clark once again called Leslie White into his office. Clark was leaning back in his chair, hands clasped behind his head, with his long legs stretched out on his desk, White would recall.

"Do you want to go to Chicago?" Clark asked. "I need somebody to work with the Illinois State Attorney's office. They're getting ready to prosecute Foster. I thought you might be interested."

White, ever eager, jumped at the chance. Chicago, at that time, meant one word: Capone, who dispatched bands of gunmen and sluggers to run his liquor shipments, bomb stores and manufacturing plants, put acid into laundry vats, and kill his enemies. Capone, the one-time New York street hoodlum, now reputed to be worth $30 million. Never had racketeering been developed to such perfection as in Chicago during Capone's overlordship. European journalists traveled thousands of miles to interview him. He received fan mail from China, Japan, and Africa. Sightseeing buses pointed out "Capone" castle, the Hawthorne Inn in the suburb of Cicero. The windy city of skyscrapers and slaughterhouses was in thrall to a plump gangster who lolled on silk cushions and wore a $50,000 diamond ring on his pinkie. Leslie White couldn't wait.

In Chicago detectives vied with each other to prove to

White how corrupt their city was. They showed him judges at the beck and call of mob attorneys. They staged liquor raids that involved plenty of noise and drama but no arrests. He glimpsed Capone, riding (White wrote) in "that infamous seven ton armor-plated car," and heard that Capone was but a figurehead, taking his orders from a syndicate of business-men who kept out of the limelight. White stayed in Chicago several weeks until charges against Foster were inevitably dropped.

Meanwhile White had taken an advanced course in metropolitan politics. "Gangland promoted and fostered vice, and businessmen wanted and promoted it. If you disturbed vice and crime in Chicago, you interfered with high rents, with graft—with *business*," he said.

The more realistic stories in *Black Mask* were often set against the backdrop of a corrupt town. Dashiell Hammett used the theme many times, notably in his first novel, *Red Harvest*, and in his fourth, *The Glass Key*, the early parts of which Leslie White read when they were serialized in the magazine in March 1930. The hero of *The Glass Key* is Ned Beaumont, a gambler whose friend and employer is Paul Madvig, a political boss in an unnamed city (presumably Baltimore) near Washington, D.C. It's an election year, and Madvig has the job of getting his slate of candidates elected. Beaumont is paid to help Madvig get this done, not an easy task when Madvig is suspected of murder.

"For a novel in which political power plays so great a part, 'The Glass Key' is remarkably apolitical," writes Richard Layman, one of Hammett's biographers. That's because Hammett is writing, not about ideals and the public face of politics, but about the grimy, slippery, insidery, practical politics that thrived in Charlie Crawford's fiefdom. Hammett's fiction challenges the idea that traditional, and basically turn-of-the-century, civic institutions could govern a swiftly growing modern city in a way that wasn't corrupt. In Los Angeles successive waves of reformers came in promising to clean house. Somehow the corruption stayed put, and the reformers either got out or became a part of it. "The word 'progressive' means something different here," Hammett wrote when he came to L.A. in 1930. "It means graft progresses everywhere and all the way."

White had been reading Hammett but also making a study of Lincoln Steffens, whose 1904 classic of muckraking reportage *The Shame of the Cities* had laid out for the first time how corruption actually worked in local politics. "The uniformed police were in cahoots with certain politicians and associations of liquor dealers, gamblers, and other law-breakers," said Steffens. In a succession of articles that Steffens wrote for *McClure's* (pieces that formed the basis of his book), he found this pattern repeated in St. Louis, Pittsburgh, Minneapolis, Philadelphia, and Cincinnati. He saw capitalists, workingmen, politicians, citizens—all breaking the law, or letting it be broken. "Politics is business," he wrote. "In America politics is an arm of business and the aim of business is to make money without care for the law, because politics, controlled by business, can change or buy the law. Politics is interested in profit, not municipal prosperity or civic pride. The spirit of graft and lawlessness is the American spirit."

Each of the cities that Steffens researched was governed by an open alliance with crime, and at the center of that alliance always stood a "boss," "easier to deal with than the people's representatives," a manipulator connecting crime, business, and politics.

White knew that Charlie Crawford had been such a figure—delivering votes, raking off cash, pulling strings, fixing politics—but behind the scenes, running the discreet L.A. System. But what White saw in Chicago shocked him. It was "an astonishing spectacle," he wrote, a city turned upside down where gangsters quite openly ran the show, and on his return, he saw Los Angeles differently. The city would soon be like Chicago, he concluded, run openly, and much more violently, by the gang interests. "Big business had long used gangsters to suppress strikes and to intimidate workmen, but now small business began to use gangsters to fix prices, eradicate competition, and to force demands they could not force by process of law," he wrote. Crime and malignancy were starting to run amok. Within days of White's arrival back in town, movie theater owners hired gangsters to blow out the fronts of properties belonging to rivals, machine-guns rattled on Hollywood Boulevard, and a bomb went off at the Clover Club on Sunset Boulevard. "It was a short step for businessmen to use gangsters in their private quarrels, and we began to enjoy unsolvable murders. Witnesses began to act, in Los Angeles, like they did in Chicago. They vamoosed," White wrote.

L.A. was falling into the hands of the underworld in a way that seemed like anarchy, or as one journalist noted, "terroristic." Charlie Crawford's hold had slackened with the election of Mayor Porter; other racketeers, including some of his former allies, or Italians with Eastern mob connections like John Rosselli, looked to gain control of the gambling, prostitution, and bootlegging now that the power of the L.A. System seemed to have crumbled.

A gang war was in the offing, and seemingly to save his skin, Crawford made a big display of quitting "politics." He joined a church. On Sunday, June 29, 1930, at St. Paul's Presbyterian on South La Brea Avenue, along with twenty-five others, he was baptized with water specially imported from the River Jordan. Onto the collection plate Crawford dropped a ring set with two large diamonds, later valued at $3,500. He said that the ring, a treasure from his days in Seattle, meant more to him than anything in the world except his family. Accompanying the ring was a note addressed to the pastor of the church, Reverend Gustav Briegleb: "Please sell this ring and use it for the building of the parish house Sunday school," the note said.

Briegleb was a graduate of Yale and a one-time lieutenant of "Fighting Bob" Shuler. He had grizzled hair and a frowning arrogant face. He dressed well but lacked Shuler's oratorical gift. He and Shuler had parted ways soon after Mayor Porter's election, with Shuler accusing his former ally of sucking up to the rich. "As I see it, his trouble is that the 'big boys' can feed him stuff," Shuler said.

Crawford and his mother had been attending Briegleb's church for some weeks. "I think Mr. Crawford is entitled to a great deal of credit for taking this step," said Briegleb of the Gray Wolf's sudden turn toward the Lord. "Especially in view of his mature years."

The L.A. press took up the story with the kind of relish that these days might greet some flaky celebrity's involvement with Scientology or rehab. "CHURCH JOINED BY CRAWFORD," said the *Times*, while the *Examiner* greeted the move as Crawford himself would have wished: "CRAWFORD DONATES DIAMOND, QUITS POLITICS."

On the morning of July 14, 1930, Frank Keaton, a disabled and unbalanced machinist, rose at dawn. He dressed hastily and headed downtown to City Hall where the banker Motley Flint was slated to give evidence in a civil trial. Keaton, dour and ordinary, had lost his savings when Julian Pete collapsed. He was one of the herd whose dreams L.A. had shattered. On the other hand, Flint, the suave brother of a former senator, had made millions out of the scam through a privileged investor pool. Perhaps the first banker to see the future in Hollywood and a backer of Warner Bros., Flint was a booster, a player in the drama of making the city happen, a prophet of the golden days that he said would be L.A.'s future in perpetuity. Flint had in the pockets of his slick suit $63,000 cash. Keaton had ten cents, a pack of cigarettes, a copy of Bob Shuler's pamphlet "Julian Thieves," and a .38 caliber nickel-plated hammerless revolver. "It felt big as a cannon," Keaton later said.

Keaton sat in the spectator section while Flint, cool and poised, gave his evidence on behalf of a young motion picture executive named David O. Selznick. By the end of the decade Selznick would produce *Gone With the Wind*. Motley Flint, on the other hand, was about to meet his doom.

Frank Keaton wasn't a well man. He'd recently been struck by a falling electric cable. Sitting in the courtroom, he felt his eyes begin to sting and a pain in his head grow sharp. As Flint left the witness stand and got ready to depart the court, pausing only to chat with David Selznick's mother, Florence

Selznick, Keaton sprang to his feet, drawing the .38 from his pocket and firing three times. Motley Flint was dead before he hit the floor. Keaton made no attempt to escape. Instead he slumped in a chair, saying, "Oh God, why did I do it?" Keaton's trial was a formality; he was found guilty on September 5, sentenced to hang, and the Julian Pete had claimed two more victims.

The murder of Motley Flint was another fatal collision of have and have-not. It was a tragic climax, for the gusher of Julian Pete scandal blew itself once and for all when Dave Clark, acting in his new capacity as head of the complaints department, went to see Buron Fitts and reported that there was insufficient evidence to proceed with the bribery and influence peddling charges against Charlie Crawford and Jack Friedlander. This meeting took place in Fitts's office, high in the Hall of Justice. From his window Fitts had a view of City Hall with its high white tower. On his desk was a small American flag, in a case were medals he'd won in France, and the walls were lined with shelves of law books. Later Fitts said he was surprised by what Clark told him, and asked Clark if he was really sure.

Clark replied that he'd reviewed all the paperwork, and spoken to Jack Roth and other witnesses; there just wasn't enough to go on. "I wish we could get Crawford. I wish it as much as you, Buron. But it can't be done," he said.

Fitts gave Clark a sharp look but then shrugged, and the two discussed other business. On October 30, 1930, both the *Examiner* and the *Times* reported that the charges had indeed been dropped. Within days the statute of limitations on potential Julian Pete prosecutions expired. That was it: there could be no further indictments or grand jury inquisitions. Fitts didn't like this outcome, but there was nothing he could do about it. Later, it would come out that in the weeks prior to the dropping of these charges, Dave Clark had dined twice at Charlie Crawford's house in Beverly Hills and visited Crawford's Sunset Boulevard office several times; and it would be alleged that Crawford gave Clark $50,000 to fix things. Clark would laugh at this allegation, but by then he would be on trial for murder, his golden aura in ruins.

In the clear, Charlie Crawford felt free to show his hand. He had big ideas, having donated a further $30,000 to Gustav Briegleb, who used the money to build a grand church, white-walled with rough-hewn rafters. In the basement of the church was a soundproof room intended for the radio station Briegleb planned to use to attack his former captain Bob Shuler over the airwaves while furthering the interests of Charlie Crawford, his new patron. Crawford invested in a magazine, *The Critic of Critics*, using it as another instrument for propaganda and self-promotion. In 1932 the Olympic Games would arrive in L.A. Crawford's plan was that by then he would have taken back control of the grand jury and he and Kent Parrot would have orchestrated the defeat of Mayor Porter and once again put their own man in office. "I'll run things the way they've never been run before," Crawford promised.

The little play with the diamond ring had been a feint to throw off his enemies until Crawford judged the time as right. His wife, Ella, pleaded with him to stay out of politics for good, but that had never been his intention. Ella suffered from bad dreams and bleak daytime thoughts about what could happen to her husband. Crawford was canny and knew he was vulnerable. Hence the security precautions and devices that Leslie White had seen in his office—the locks, the bars on the windows, the steel bars that fell across the doors. These were measures of a man who knew himself to be at risk.

But all his life Crawford had been around violence without resorting to it or having it done to him. He was cautious and clever and, like E. L. Doheny, a sly old fox. Crawford believed in himself as a player and believed, too, that he would ride out the attempted underworld coups and impose the L.A. System on his rivals again. The System, after all, was of proven value, both in terms of profit and viability within the workings of City Hall. The System allowed the rackets to flourish in an orderly way; it was good strategy, good business, how things had always been done. The Gray Wolf, armed now with more modern political weapons, aimed to climb back in the saddle and stay there. He was signing his death warrant.

18

Red Hot Bow

Buron Fitts failed in his gubernatorial run, but his strong showing in Southern California destroyed the chances of the incumbent C. C. Young, instead gifting the Republican nomination and the governorship to Mayor Sunny James Rolph, Jr., of San Francisco. L.A. had shown its increased electoral muscle in a statewide contest, and Fitts was already starting to look like a political fixture. He had his detractors. "Fitts is an incurable exhibitionist; utterly lacking the legal acumen, ethical conformity and mental balance essential in a competent prosecutor," wrote local newspaperman Guy Finney. "He is constantly on the hunt for sensations in which he can pose as the hero; thinks of himself as a legal D'Artagnan. He is theatrically intemperate."

Guy Finney was a hater of Fitts and had an axe to grind, though he was right that Fitts liked publicity and had quickly learned its value. Hollywood, a bottomless well of high-profile crime and scandal, was useful in this regard but had to be handled carefully. No master in court, Fitts nonetheless led the prosecution of theater-chain owner Alexander Pantages, accused of raping Eunice Pringle, a lithe and lovely seventeen-year-old high-school dropout. It was a great show, generating weeks of headlines; the young Jerry Giesler, having already bested Dave Clark, furthered his reputation by securing Pantages's acquittal on appeal. Buron Fitts was once more displeased, but generally he knew where his bread was buttered. He tended to side with, and not against, men like Pantages, the new Medicis of L.A.

"To put it bluntly, the studios owned Buron Fitts," wrote Budd Schulberg in his autobiography. Schulberg, author of the legendary Hollywood satire *What Makes Sammy Run?*, came of age in L.A. in the 1920s, growing up a "Hollywood prince," as he put it. He was the son of B. P. Schulberg, one of the early moguls and by 1930 head of production at Paramount. "This was in the post-Desmond Taylor and Arbuckle days, when scandals that might have destroyed the reputations of valuable movie stars could be hushed up by the hear-no-evil-see-no-evil approach of the D.A.'s office," Budd Schulberg wrote. "This was Cover-up, Hollywood style, in the days when the film capital was a self-sufficient oligarchy, sunny and benevolent on the surface but hard and vindictive at the core."

In the late summer of 1930, B. P. Schulberg called Fitts about his biggest star, Clara Bow. While visiting her boyfriend at Lake Tahoe, Bow played blackjack with what she was told were fifty-cent chips. It was a shake-down, and those fifty-cent chips actually turned out to be worth $100 apiece. To cover the debt, Bow wrote a $20,000 check she later cancelled. Within days two tough customers came to her Beverly Hills home on North Bedford Drive, demanding the money in terms that came straight from a Warner Bros. gangster story. "Either you make that check good tomorrow or you'll get acid all over your pretty puss. Instead of the It Girl, you'll be the Ain't Girl," one of them said. Jimmy Cagney couldn't have put it better. Terrified, Bow called B. P. Schulberg, who turned to Fitts, and the two hashed out a plan. Next day, when the goons came to Schulberg to complete the extortion, D.A. investigators sprang out from behind a curtain, pistols at the ready, and arrested them. Chalk one up for Leslie White and his colleagues.

Clara Bow was a gum-chewing beauty whose childhood in a Brooklyn tenement had been poor and hellish. Her father raped her. Her schizophrenic mother beat her and hovered over her bed at night, threatening to slit her throat. But Bow was ambitious and fated to rise. She won a beauty contest, and by 1922 B. P. Schulberg had discovered her and put her in silent films. Huge-eyed, with flaming red hair, she was effervescent, voluptuous, reckless, damaged, and in eight years had made more than forty-five films, notable among them *Kiss Me Again*, *Wings*, *Mantrap*, *Dancing Mothers*, and, of course, *It*, Eleanor Glyn's story of a lingerie salesgirl on the make that associated Bow forever with sex appeal and the Jazz Age. In *It* Bow was outrageous, flirtatious, and often only half-dressed. "She didn't need *It*, she had THOSE," said Dorothy Parker.

In *Free to Love* Bow descended a gigantic staircase, leading six tuxedoed men by a leash. In *Hula* she lived on an island "where volcanoes are often active and maidens always are." She was having an affair with a young actor, Gary

Cooper, and gave him his first big break in *Children of Divorce*. Cooper, she told reporters, was "hung like a horse." After making a score of quota-quickies, Bow worked with top directors—Victor Fleming, Ernst Lubitsch, Wesley Ruggles, and William Wellman. Her lack of self-consciousness and even her lack of control made her performances particularly emblematic. She was the queen of the flappers, "hotcha," "hotsy," a playful sexual aggressor and Scott Fitzgerald's "girl of the year, the real thing, someone to stir every pulse in the nation." On screen Bow had an astonishing spontaneous vibrancy and life. She was the first mass-market love-goddess "communicating with sex," said Budd Schulberg, "because she had little other vocabulary." She was a personality and an underrated actress, the Marilyn Monroe or Madonna of her time—a massive star.

In 1930 Bow was Hollywood's top box-office draw, the recipient of more than 30,000 fan letters a month. Even so, her career was in big trouble. The 1928 release of *The Jazz Singer* led to an immediate infatuation with the talkie and killed the pantomime art form for which Bow had an instinctive genius. For a while it seemed she might negotiate the switch from silence, though sound stages and looming overhead microphones terrified her and inhibited her natural effervescence. In 1929 she looked fabulous in *The Wild Party*, and according to the *New York Times*, her voice was "better than the material, not overly melodious in delivery but suiting her perfectly." Her second talkie, *Dangerous Curves*, directed by Lubitsch, was better still.

She might have survived the crashing of the age she had symbolized, but her personal life was a mess. She spoke without a care to reporters and couldn't keep scandal away.

She wasn't surrounded by minders or agents who protected her. She roared around L.A. in a fire-red Packard, ridding herself of chauffeurs who refused to drive fast enough. Hollywood's self-appointed aristocracy—Chaplin, Mary Pickford, Douglas Fairbanks, Irving Thalberg, Norma Shearer—snubbed her because she was low class. B. P. Schulberg took to calling her "Crisis-A-Day Clara" and got tired of the fireball who'd brought him a fortune. Bow made movie after movie, was unfailingly generous, and felt stifled and tortured. "I always wanna cry," she told *Photoplay*. "I could cry any minute. Had no childhood. Worked like a dog all my life. Really my nerves is shot."

With a history of insanity in her family, Bow feared that she'd end up in the madhouse. Maybe all she needed was a rest. After a visit to New York, where she hobnobbed with boxer Jack Dempsey, socialite Jack Whitney, and gangster Dutch Schultz, she announced that she was returning to L.A. because she wanted to have her nervous breakdown "in the proper surroundings." The girl from the slums had wit. These days such a career would be taken in hand and helped by powers determined to preserve its economic value; but in the fall of 1930, Clara Bow was about to be swept away, another victim of changing times.

The final crisis arose from her friendship with Daisy DeVoe (born DeBoe), a tall, smart, no-nonsense blonde who'd been Bow's on-set hairdresser during the shooting of *It*. The two young women became pals, and DeVoe decided to sort out the star's messed-up life. "She figured Clara needed a strong-armed dame to take charge," said Paramount publicist Teete Carl. "So she appointed herself."

DeVoe cleaned up the Beverly Hills house and kept at bay

the hangers-on who were bleeding Bow dry. "I worked 24 hours a day for her and if there were 48 hours in a day I would have worked 48. I didn't kick because I had her best interests at heart," DeVoe said. She went on doing Clara's hair and nails, and helped her dress. She took charge of the checkbooks, got the mortgage paid off, and set up a trust fund. "I pulled Clara out of plenty of messes and saved her plenty," she said.

Trouble started when Bow found a new boyfriend, stuntman and cowboy actor Rex Bell. DeVoe couldn't stand him, and the two fought for Clara's attention, for control of the whirlwind. Bell got DeVoe fired, whereupon DeVoe emptied a filing cabinet in Clara's office, taking away checkbooks, business papers, letters, and telegrams, and transferring them to her own safety deposit box in a Hollywood bank. She did this, she told biographer David Stenn decades later, to keep the stuff out of Rex Bell's hands. Bell struck back, telling Clara that DeVoe had robbed her and had been stealing from her for years.

"I wrote her checks, but he slept with her," DeVoe said. "He had the real power."

The tiff spiraled out of control, and toward the law. Despairing over getting her job back, having been locked out of the Beverly Hills house and seemingly out of Clara's life, DeVoe resorted to blackmail. She went to Clara's attorney, W. I. Gilbert, and demanded $125,000, otherwise she'd turn the explosive letters and telegrams over to the press. "One more slam and Clara's through in pictures," DeVoe said.

Gilbert, an Oklahoma attorney who'd come to L.A. in 1913, didn't fall for it. Down the years he cleaned up messes for

Chaplin, Cagney, Gable, Kate Hepburn, and a dozen or more other stars. He got on the phone, telling Clara of DeVoe's demands. DeVoe went to the Beverly Hills house that night, pleading for her job back. Clara was incredulous. "Didn't you just go to Gilbert and tell him you wanted $125,000?" The matter passed into the hands of Buron Fitts, who had DeVoe's safety deposit box opened on suspicion of grand larceny. Items of jewelry were recovered, along with the checkbooks and letters and cash that she'd allegedly stolen. On November 6, Daisy DeVoe was arrested and taken to the Hall of Justice where, she later claimed, she was grilled for twenty-seven hours straight without food or the chance to call a lawyer.

Do we believe her? Leslie White offered a much less threatening picture of how the D.A.'s men conducted their interrogations. "We seldom permitted more than one or two people in the room and one detective did the talking. In a casual, conversational tone, we began our questioning," he wrote. This doesn't sound like strong-arm stuff. But James H. Richardson, for years the city editor of the *Examiner* and a one-time friend of Buron Fitts who later became the troubled D.A.'s fixed enemy, described an incident that occurred in the Hall of Justice at about this time:

There was no one in sight. The long halls were bare and empty. I walked along the corridor, my footsteps echoing against the marble walls. It was eerie, all right, but I liked it that way at night. Then I turned a corner and something hit me in the stomach.

It was a gun. A big, .45 caliber, blue steel revolver. I saw the finger trembling on the trigger before I looked up.

He was one of Buron's investigators and he was red-eyed drunk. He was shaking all over. "I'm going to blow your guts out," he said.

Richardson was an old-school newsman, a drunk with a nose for a story. His description of this incident, written more than twenty years after the event and published in his autobiography *For the Life of Me*, may be shaded by the tough-guy conventions that came to be applied to the time, but he's getting at a truth. At some point in the early 1930s the D.A.'s investigative unit, or a part of it, stopped being a small unit of policing reform and became a part of the disease it had set out to cure, another aspect of the darkness of the time.

Leslie White knew this, even if he didn't write about it or indulge in the third-degree himself. His feelings about what the D.A.'s office was doing, and what it had failed to achieve, would lead ultimately to his departure from the Hall of Justice. Maybe Daisy DeVoe was indeed "grilled for 27 hours straight." Fitts was now playing a rough game. He announced that DeVoe had signed a thirty-five-page statement confessing to the theft of more than $35,000 in cash and property. DeVoe's lawyer, Nathan Freedman, brought a countersuit, claiming that she hadn't signed the statement and charging false arrest. Fitts went to the grand jury, and on November 25, 1930, an indictment for thirty-seven counts of grand theft was handed down against DeVoe. Each count carried a possible one- to ten-year sentence.

David O. Selznick, B. P. Schulberg's boy-wonder assistant, was meanwhile arguing that Clara Bow's career could be saved and made to flourish again by casting her in a quality project. Having read *Red Harvest* and *The Maltese Falcon*, Selznick hired Dashiell Hammett and brought him out to Hollywood to write an original story. The result, *City Streets*, in which the daughter of a racketeer falls for a carnival worker, was to be Bow's next picture. Selznick argued that the charges against DeVoe should be dropped. No possible good would come of a trial, he knew. Bow agreed with Selznick. The prospect of court frightened her. "She didn't want her fans to see her this way. She was afraid of the reporters and the photographers who would hound her," writes Budd Schulberg. But B. P. Schulberg did nothing, and Fitts proceeded to trial, appointing his star deputy Dave Clark to lead the prosecution.

Dave Clark had asked for the case. He'd been missing the action while running the complaints department and he wanted to be in court, knowing that, whatever the result, the publicity would be good for his career. It's possible, too, that he and Buron Fitts had already agreed to part company; Fitts would later suggest as much, saying he'd wanted Dave Clark to have his final hurrah as a servant of the D.A.'s office. "Dave Clark asked for the Bow trial. He was a great performer in court and he knew it would be a big deal. Do I regret that decision? No, not in any way," Fitts would say, sounding unconvinced.

19

The Gutting of Clara

Before the trial, Dave Clark flew down to Mexico to enjoy the luxuries of Agua Caliente. Nancy stayed at home while Clark swam, played golf, bathed in the sun to top up his tan, and ate and drank well. A friend of Clark's, an LAPD detective, saw him in The Gold Room, looking bronzed and relaxed, clicking a couple of chips together, standing alone with his back held straight. Clark always carried himself with a military bearing—it was almost the first thing that Leslie White had noticed about him.

The detective joked, "Are you going to buy me dinner with your winnings?"

Clark shrugged and offered a somewhat wintry smile. "I'm not even gambling," he said.

The detective asked Clark how he expected the DeVoe trial to go.

"I expect to win," Clark said with offhand nonchalance. "It's an open and shut case."

Some people saw Dave Clark as a bit of a playboy, and maybe he himself agreed. There was a tension in him between his father's upright work ethic and the promise of quick wealth and transformative fame that had always been in the air around him in Los Angeles. He was very much a part of the city: he knew its institutions and was familiar with the humdrum ladders to success that were available to insiders; but he was seduced, too, by L.A.'s fancier and more dangerous dreams. He could be dogged, but he was also impatient.

W. I. Gilbert, Clara Bow's attorney, came down while Clark was in Agua Caliente, and the two spent time going over documents and hashing out strategy for the trial. A professional relationship developed that would soon become very important for Clark. And he had a second visitor, June Taylor, whose hair was sometimes blonde and sometimes brunette, a beautiful woman whose soft eyes belied a worldly toughness. June Taylor was a businesswoman; she ran a downtown hotel that had been owned by Albert Marco where she kept a brothel. She'd been Dave Clark's friend for a couple of years by now—ever since the Marco trials. A part of Clark lived for excitement and risk; he found both in his affair with the lovely June Taylor. He was heading for trouble.

People v. DeVoe got under way on Monday, January 12, 1931. The first day was routine. Opening statements were made, and Clark introduced into the record hundreds of cancelled checks that had been written by DeVoe in Clara Bow's name. A jury was selected. When the court session was done, Clara herself came to the Hall of Justice, wearing a movie star's watch-me idea of disguise: a scarlet coat, a cloche hat pulled down around her face, and dark glasses with huge frames. For an hour Clark conferred with her about the evidence she'd give. He noticed a small V-shaped scar on her cheek, the result of a minor operation to remove a mole.

Next day the carnival began in earnest. Crowds mobbed Judge William Doran's courtroom and spilled into the corridors of the Hall of Justice. Hundreds waited outside, cheering and jostling when Clara arrived, "an entrancing study in ivory gray," said the *Examiner*, "from her modish pumps to her chic hat, gloves and purse." A *Times* photograph, running beneath the headline "REAL DRAMA AND NO CAMERA GRINDING," showed a beauty with a white patch on her left cheek, covering the scar that Clark had noticed the day before. Nervous, clinging to boyfriend Rex Bell's arm, Bow had nonetheless dressed like a flapper on some fabulous F. Scott Fitzgerald spree. A silence fell when she took the witness stand.

"What is your name?" asked Clark.

"Clara Bow."

"And your occupation?"

"Acting in motion pictures."

Clark knew he had a clear-cut case. DeVoe's attorney, Nathan Freedman, promised "a strange, fascinating tale of two young and lovely girls, a blonde and a redhead, who traveled a path strewn with the pleasures and excitement which money and fame can buy." Freedman's strategy was to shift the emphasis from DeVoe's alleged theft onto Bow's presumed behavior. And here lay Dave Clark's big problem: much of the stuff that DeVoe had taken, and therefore the evidence he would produce, was intimate and revealing. For instance: the sheaf of telegrams that had been removed from the Beverly Hills house and found in DeVoe's safety deposit box gave more than a glimpse of the unmarried Clara's impassioned friendships with various men. "CLARA BOW LOVE NOTES REVEALED!" said the *Examiner*, describing how Bow, "at times in vexatious tears, at others in explosive anger and then in dazzling smiles," was forced to share the limelight with these messages. "There were more than a dozen of them. They had come to the 'It' girl over a period of two years. Chiefly, they came humming their promises of love . . ."

Clara Bow, the world's most famous movie actress, liked men, and liked to sleep with lots of them; the information, though not surprising, would provide even today's media with a field day, and in 1931 every newspaper in the country seized upon those "humming" love telegrams. "Night-time and insomnia may not be for long. Wire me darling, Earl," ran one. Let's forget about her fans. In the men she actually knew—directors, producers, other stars, other women's husbands—Clara Bow inspired lust and adulation.

The following day served up more scandal as Clark read into the court record the thirty-five-page statement, the "confession" that DeVoe had made in the D.A.'s office back in November. The statement told of the expensive gifts Clara gave to her boyfriends, of the diamond-studded vanity case she let her dogs play with, of visits from the bootlegger, of drunkenness and all-night poker sessions, of dresser drawers stuffed full of love letters from Gary Cooper, letters so explicit that DeVoe had felt compelled to burn them. DeVoe had told, too, of her visit to W. I. Gilbert and the extortion attempt, and had stated her motive. "It's hard to see a girl like Clara with everything and no respect for anything," she'd said.

The dynamic recalls that which led to the deaths of Hugh Plunkett and Ned Doheny, Jr. A put-upon and humiliated servant was finally drawing the line. But DeVoe, "a cookie baked hard," said the *Examiner*, used slur and innuendo to assault her employer. Clara Bow listened to this recitation, dressed in a different outfit this day, but with Rex Bell still at her side. A *Times* photograph shows the two huddled close together in the courtroom, aware of the camera and playing for it, a gorgeous couple.

Dave Clark called upon Bow and W. I. Gilbert to give their versions of the attempted extortion. Gilbert, the famous attorney, under oath, described matter-of-factly how DeVoe came to his office late one afternoon and put on the squeeze. "I said to her, 'How much do you want?' And she said, '$125,000 and not a nickel less,'" Gilbert testified. Few could doubt his word; DeVoe had been intent on blackmail, had taken the letters and telegrams for that purpose, and was, by implication, capable of scheming and systematic theft.

Clara, dazzling in black, took the stand to tell of her final meeting with DeVoe. She spoke calmly at first, but then with emotions rocketing dangerously. "She said, 'I've got some letters and telegrams that won't do you any good at all if I turn them over to the papers,'" Bow told Clark. At this point she burst into tears and couldn't resume her testimony for several minutes. Finally she managed to control herself, though her words came slowly and were still punctuated by sobs. "I asked Daisy—I asked, 'You're not kidding me? You went to Gilbert and said I had to pay you $125,000? Isn't it true Daisy? You're trying to shake me down for $125,000?'"

Clara sobbed openly again, blurting out an apology to the

packed courtroom. "She was my friend—my best friend—my best friend in the world. I'm sorry to be crying but I can't help it. I can't help it," she said.

Dave Clark was stunned. This wasn't acting. A star, a beauty, the most famous young woman in the world, was cracking up right before his eyes.

The breakdown proved too much for B. P. Schulberg; or maybe it gave him the excuse he'd been looking for. Next day he and Paramount announced that Clara Bow would not be starring alongside Gary Cooper in Dashiell Hammett's story *City Streets*. She'd been dropped and her part given to Sylvia Sidney, a fresh persona for a more sober time. Sidney, only twenty, was a product of the Theater Guild School and already a brilliant actress on the New York stage. Her waif-like appearance was a better fit for the beginning Depression than Bow's brazen Jazz Age sex appeal. Sidney, far from coincidentally, was also B. P. Schulberg's new mistress, sharing his bed just as Clara Bow had back in her ingénue days. All of which is fascinating, "hard and vindictive" indeed, and in no way surprising: a new star was being burnished even while another whose luster was fading was cast roughly aside.

Clara Bow's travails were only beginning; Daisy DeVoe had yet to take the stand in her own defense, and she'd promised to tell a juicy tale. Press and public waited while Dave Clark laid out the rest of the prosecution's case. He called Leslie White to the stand, and White, who was gaining experience in court, presented evidence confidently, laying out photographs he'd taken of the diamonds and jewels that DeVoe was alleged to have stolen. The moment was significant—not for this case, although White could scarcely believe that he was standing only feet away from Clara Bow and breathing the same courtroom air as her, but because of what happened later. White would remember: "The trial involving Daisy DeVoe and Clara was another big show, and I played a small part in it. Dave Clark was a leading performer that day, and maybe he always was, though the next time I saw him in court the circumstances were different."

Marjorie Fairchild, the first woman on Fitts's investigative team, testified about DeVoe's confession and the opening of the safety deposit box. Fairchild said that DeVoe, far from being ill-treated, had thanked her for her consideration. Clark called the manager of the Hollywood bank where the "Clara Bow Special Account" had been set up, and went through the laborious process of identifying the checks DeVoe had written in Bow's name and the cashier's checks she'd taken.

The trial went on, intermingling tedium with vivid flashes of excitement, until DeVoe took the stand late on Friday afternoon. Led by Nathan Freedman, she unveiled more stories about poker, liquor, and Clara Bow's men. "There were so many of them I can't remember," DeVoe said. Part of her job, she claimed, had been to inform Bow's lovers when their services were no longer required. She threw her barbs with a free and eager hand. "Shopping annoyed Clara so I did all that," she said, a point that also went to the nub of her defense. Every check she'd written had been to pay for something of Clara's, she argued. She'd hidden the jewels to look after them and taken the letters and telegrams so they wouldn't fall into the wrong hands. She talked too about her childhood and her father, a railway brakeman.

Dave Clark kept jumping to his feet to protest the relevance of all this, but damage was done. Next day was a Saturday. With a nice sense of drama, DeVoe held an impromptu press conference in Judge Doran's empty courtroom on the eighth floor of the Hall of Justice, posing for cameras in the witness box. Meanwhile, across town, buried beneath blankets, swathed in towels, Clara Bow spoke to reporters from the *Examiner* in her bedroom. She made no effort to control her weeping. "I shall never trust anyone again," she said. "Daisy talks about me dyeing my hair. She wants people to believe my hair isn't red. It's always been red."

It was funny, it was sad; she was clinging to the shreds of her identity. The *Daily News* listed her boyfriends: "Victor Fleming, John Gilbert, Gary Cooper, Fredric March, Howard Hughes, and others." The *Evening Record* noted drily that the coach of the USC football team had declared Bow's house off-limits to his players, one of whom, Marion Morrison (later John Wayne), was known to have been Clara's particular pal.

"It seems to me we ought to take check of just exactly who we are trying here. Daisy DeVoe is the defendant and not someone else and the issues are clear cut. The question is: did she steal this money?" said Judge Doran, trying to stop the slaughter when proceedings resumed. Nathan Freedman had lined up maids, dressmakers, and cleaners to report on the frantic comings and goings in the Bow household. Doran kept their testimonies short. In his cross-examination of De-Voe, Clark went back to her reputed confession, reading sections to her and asking whether she'd said these things or not. DeVoe denied making the approach to Gilbert, denied that she'd admitted stealing Clara's money and telegrams.

Summing up, Clark said the issue was therefore simple: either DeVoe had just committed perjury, or every other witness he'd called to the stand was lying. This was Clark's big moment. The weather was chilly in L.A. that day, and many court spectators still wore their coats. Clark had bought a new suit. He'd been to the barber that morning. Groomed and relaxed, he spoke to the jury:

Miss Bow was no business woman. She did not pretend to be one. She is an artist. That is why she wanted someone to take this burden off her hands. You may think her foolish, but, as I have said before, Miss Bow does not pretend to be a business woman. She is simply an artist.

Miss Bow trusted this defendant. She trusted her as a close friend and as her confidante. She took her with her every place and she placed utter trust in this defendant. In everything, including her finances.

And the defendant, how did she repay this trust? She betrayed it callously and deliberately, stealing close to $1,000 a month. She not only betrayed the friend who trusted her, but I charge that she deliberately perjured herself in this trial, time and time again.

She was authorized to buy everything that Miss Bow wanted and needed, but she was never authorized to transfer Miss Bow's money to her own private account.

She was not authorized to take Miss Bow's private letters and telegrams and later to use them to extort $125,000 from the generous girl who had befriended her.

Actually she was stealing from her employer right and left, as the evidence shows.

Clark's performance was calm, measured, clear. He stood close by the jury box, not raising his voice, with his hands clasped behind his back. He saw no need for theatrics.

He'd judged the progress of the trial and felt confident.

The case went to jury at 3:25 P.M., Wednesday, January 21, and the jurors spent several hours in argument before they were sequestered for the night in a downtown hotel. They spent the entire next day deadlocked, returning to Judge Doran to receive more instructions before being shut away in the hotel again. Two male jury members, the *Examiner* reported, had been fistfighting, and one of them said there was no chance of a verdict. DeVoe, who was waiting in court, surrounded by family and friends, visibly brightened. "I'll sleep better tonight," she said. She spoke too soon. Next day, after more than forty-eight hours of deliberation, the jury came in, finding DeVoe guilty—but on only one count.

Now it was DeVoe's turn to break down. She lost her hitherto remarkable self-control and pitched face forward on the counsel table, her sobs sounding through the otherwise silent court. As a bailiff escorted her to the stairs leading to the county jail, she stumbled. "I can't stand it, I can't stand it," she said, at the point of collapse, hanging in the arms of the bailiff and a newspaperwoman. "If they were going to convict me at all, why didn't they convict me of everything?"

That was a good question. Various jurors seized their own moment in the limelight, telling the press that the verdict had been a compromise—a punishment not only of DeVoe's theft, but of Clara Bow's celebrity and lifestyle. A submerged but ever-present theme of life in L.A. came to the surface: class warfare.

Before the sentencing, Buron Fitts received a letter from Clara Bow, pleading for leniency for her former friend. "It is my hope that mercy will be shown," she wrote. Judge Doran was firm, however, handing DeVoe eighteen months in county jail and telling her flat out that she was an embezzler. "From a position of trust you conducted systematic raids and the jury was generous," he said. "The evidence was sufficient to convict you on all counts."

DeVoe stood rigid before the bench and was led away by a jail matron.

Clark's job was done, but the torture of Clara Bow went on. Frederic Girnau, publisher of the *Pacific Coast Reporter*, another "political weekly," jumped in with the "facts of the blushless love life of Clara Bow." " 'IT' GIRL EXPOSED!" ran the headline. Girnau asserted that Bow had seduced her chauffeur, her cousin, and a pet koala bear. According to him, she'd slept with Duke, one of her dogs, a Great Dane. In Agua Caliente she'd initiated a whorehouse orgy while another of her lovers, a Mexican croupier, watched. The croupier subsequently murdered his wife before turning a gun on himself. Girnau accused Bow of incest and lesbianism. She had venereal disease, drank highballs before breakfast, and was hooked on morphine. "You know, Clara, you'd be better off killing yourself," he wrote. In time Girnau was prosecuted for criminal libel and sent to prison for eight years for publishing this filth. By then, though, Clara Bow had checked into a mental asylum in Glendale and her Paramount contract was terminated by mutual consent. Her career was over, and she was only twenty-five.

People v. DeVoe could scarcely have worked out worse for Clara Bow, and it's hard to escape the suspicion that B. P. Schulberg had engineered her downfall. His son, Budd Schulberg, thought so—but then Budd, the jaded insider, had his own grudge, his father having deserted his mother for

Bow's replacement, Sylvia Sidney. Certainly B. P. Schulberg jumped on the chance to dump a tempestuous star who had become troublesome freight. Buron Fitts was the tool with which B. P. Schulberg achieved a desired end, and Fitts had turned loose Dave Clark, who then did his job.

Clark had scaled a peak. He'd been the star performer in another of L.A.'s great goldfish bowl trials, where crime and celebrity mingle and swim around together, weirdly magnified. Three days after the sentencing of Daisy DeVoe, Clark quit the D.A.'s office, rejoined Wellborn, Wellborn & Wellborn, and announced that he was running for a judgeship. He set up his campaign in a suite at the Alexandria, then the swankiest downtown hotel, and soon he was standing before the Republican Women's Study League in Van Nuys, giving a campaign speech in which he spoke darkly of "the head of vice in Los Angeles," saying that this man was tied into the D.A.'s office and the LAPD. He meant Charlie Crawford.

A story in the *Van Nuys Tribune* was headlined: "CRIME-BUSTING ATTORNEY RUNS FOR JUDGE." The story reported Clark's speech, in which he attacked "the underworld of Los Angeles, its narcotic, gambling and prostitution branches," and praised "the dashing and handsome Clark, a beacon of virtue in our community, a foe of the underworld, the man who brought down Albert Marco." Clark, cashing in the chip that the DeVoe trial gave him, envisioned a future involving more money and prestige, greater power. Was he really interested in virtue? Probably not. After he was elected judge, he planned to move into politics in some substantial way. With his adoring wife Nancy on his arm, the sky was the limit.

20

Hard Times in Lotus-Land

Clara Bow had been Hollywood's biggest box-office draw of 1930. Charlie Chaplin was still probably the most famous being on the planet, though his future, too, was uncertain. His most recent film, *The Gold Rush*, had been released way back in 1928, before *The Jazz Singer* and America's infatuation with sound. Chaplin—the purist, the perfectionist—defied the trend and spent the next two years making another silent film, *City Lights*. Actually *City Lights* wasn't completely silent: Chaplin included sound effects that mocked the talking fad.

On January 30, 1931, only days after *People v. DeVoe* wrapped up, Chaplin's film premiered at the 2,200-seat Los Angeles Theater, downtown on Broadway. Like *City Lights*, the Los Angeles Theater had been begun with grand expectations at the height of the boom and finished, barely, at the Depression's onset. Chaplin himself had to put up the money to complete the building so his premiere could go ahead. In his autobiography, he confessed that he was worried: "Would the public accept a silent picture?" Nobody was sure. *City Lights*, as history knows, proved a triumph, a critical and box-office smash, regarded by many as the summit of Chaplin's art.

In the middle of the film Chaplin's tramp and his sometimes friend, the millionaire (it's a running gag that the millionaire, when drunk, recognizes the tramp, only to forget him again when sober), return home in the millionaire's car after a night-club binge. A studio shot of the car pulling away from a curb cuts into location footage of the same car hurtling through the deserted pre-dawn streets of downtown L.A. The car careens around another car, jumps on the side-walk, and almost turns over. "Be careful how you're driving," reads the tramp's line on the dialogue card. The millionaire replies: "Am I driving?" The sequence provides, in the back-ground, startling views of what downtown Los Angeles looked like: the freshly-built buildings are spotless, unblemished, and dense tangles of streetcar wires run high over the streets. The streetcar wires are now long gone, and the little dialogue exchange feels like the socialist Chaplin's comment on America's economic disaster. Nobody had been driving.

Chaplin attended the premiere with Albert Einstein and his wife. The new age of celebrity waved its wand at some surprising figures, and Einstein was one of them. The ship bringing him to the West Coast on December 31 had been besieged by dozens of reporters, a comical scene evoked by reporter Gene Coughlin. "Two of our number fell off the Jacob's ladder of the liner *Belgenland* and pitched into the ocean," he wrote. Coughlin usually covered the crime beat and prepared for his interview with the great scientist by consulting with a professor of physics at UCLA and trying to bone up on the subject of relativity. The physics professor told Coughlin he himself couldn't understand it, so Coughlin came away none the wiser. Instead, notebook in hand on the deck of the *Belgenland*, he asked Einstein a single question: "Is there a God?" Einstein just smiled, and Coughlin had his story.

Einstein headed north to Los Angeles, where he at once announced his desire to meet Chaplin. Lunch was arranged, and the two men became friends. Now, dressed in tuxedoes and walking arm-in-arm, they posed for the press photographers and the newsreel cameramen in the high-ceilinged, walnut-paneled, and gold-leaf decorated lobby of the Los Angeles Theater. "They cheer me because they all understand me and they cheer you because nobody understands you," Chaplin said to his new friend. Chaplin, like Einstein, was no mug.

Outside the theater searchlights fingered the cool of the night sky while limousines continued to disgorge celebrities and pandemonium reigned. The premiere was one of the biggest in Hollywood's history. UPI reported that 400 policemen tried to keep in order a crowd of 50,000 that mingled with the downtown bread lines. Soon celebration and curiosity turned into anger and a chaotic rampage. The mob tore up chunks of the sidewalk and smashed store windows. The LAPD responded with tear gas and clubs. More than 100 arrests were made—this was a riot.

L.A. had been magicked into existence and the Depression in no way fitted with the city's unswerving onward and upward view of itself, and affronted especially the politicians and businessmen who had worked so hard to pump full the balloon of civic optimism. "The situation is remarkably good and not at all alarming" said Mayor Porter, leading the way in denial, adding, "You have nothing to worry about." The *Times*, the bullhorn of the boosters, noted: "The Depression is mostly psychological." But reality set in, as reality will. Businesses kept failing and jobs kept being lost. A human river of the displaced and the dispossessed poured into the city from all over America. People loaded everything they had into their cars and took their families and their failed lives in the direction of California. In 1931 a total of 876,000 automobiles entered the state.

The economy had fallen off a cliff and even in California people were starving. Yet crops of citrus and wheat were being destroyed in dumps to keep prices up. Dorothy Comingore, the actress who would star in *Citizen Kane*, recalled: "I saw heaps of oranges covered with gasoline and set on fire and men who tried to take one orange shot to death." The situation certainly wasn't "remarkably good," and hard times would get harder, conjuring not belief and hope in the limitless future but a desperate mood of fear and bewilderment. The L.A. Chamber of Commerce took out ads in the *Saturday Evening Post* and *Collier's* and *The New Yorker*, the "slicks," saying that although the city was still a place to visit, people shouldn't come looking to work. They did more than just warn people away. For a while the authorities tried to seal off the borders against transients bound for the city. The LAPD's anti-Red squad was becoming a success, much more so than its anti-gang squad, though Leslie White wrote that "most of the so-called 'Reds' weren't communists but unemployed men and women beaten down to the danger line."

Wealthy men were targets for extortion plots. *Times* publisher Harry Chandler received an anonymous letter threatening to blow up his home unless money was paid. Leslie White was put on a twenty-four-hour detail, standing outside the Los Feliz mansion in the rain because Chandler didn't want "any damn flat-feet" messing up the carpets inside.

More seriously, White became part of a "gangbusting" unit, assigned to track down Ralph Sheldon, a famed Irish gangster out of Chicago and an associate of Capone's, who popped up in L.A. in January 1931. Sheldon and his crew kidnapped gambler Ezekiel "Zeke" Caress, one of the owners of the racetrack down in Agua Caliente. While making the snatch, Sheldon shot and nearly killed an LAPD cop. Facing mobsterism on this serious scale, White visited a friend in Ventura and returned to L.A. with a Thompson submachine-gun and tear-gas grenades wrapped in towels on the backseat of his car. He also acquired an "auto-riot gun," a double-barreled shotgun with a fifteen-inch barrel and a snug pistol grip. "It was called an auto-riot gun because one blast fired into an automobile would kill everyone in the car," he said, clearly expecting life-threatening thrills and spills.

He and other investigators interrogated informers. They raided a house in Glendale without any luck and spent days staking out a lonely cottage in Hermosa Beach, accidentally taking potshots at each other in the dark before learning that the gangsters were being tipped off and had split up. Afterward White laughed, saying how lucky he'd been not to be killed during this little escapade, most likely by one of his own colleagues. Everybody, White included, had been determined that there should be a shoot-out and the fearsome "auto-riot" gun brought into play. But the danger passed; one-by-one, and without further gunplay, Sheldon and his gang were brought in.

White was selling more stories and meeting other writers. As his horizons began to broaden, he ceased to foster any illusions about the invincibility of justice. He was tired of jaded old detectives telling him, "You'll learn, kid." He fretted about the uselessness of his daily work; but, with the Depression tightening its grip, he was happy to be employed. The incident that would provoke his exit from the D.A.'s office began harmlessly enough when Blayney Matthews summoned him in. Matthews opened a drawer in his desk and tossed White a small black book.

"In that offhand gesture, he started one of the most sensational cases in the court annals of California, a case that cost millions of dollars and changed the pattern of many lives," White said. On the outside of the little black book was stamped a single word: "MILESTONES."

"It's the five-year diary of a prostitute," Matthews said. He had the idea this material might be useful for White's fiction. "Maybe you'll get a yarn out of it."

The diary had been written by a woman named Olive Day, and delivered to the D.A.'s office by the man in whose house she'd left some of her belongings. The man had found the diary strange, but Matthews had barely glanced at it. White took the diary home, started to read it, and found himself stepping into a remarkable story.

On September 10, 1930, Olive Day had written: "Camilla to lunch. Decided to risk taking her to M's. There is a good profit if she will get drunk enough." The entry for September 14 was: "Bill and I started out leaving Rita in charge. We picked up Camilla and drove pleasantly through to San Diego. The house was waiting for us, but I am nervous about Camilla's actions." And for September 15: "Camilla got drunk and proved a tip-over, but Mills is satisfied. I'm convinced he is a terrible bull-thrower. We had a weary drive home. The trip cost fourteen dollars, meals and all."

White gathered that girls, aged as young as twelve and fourteen, were being sold to wealthy men around Southern California. Having pieced this together, he went back to Blayney Matthews who then sanctioned an investigation. Together with female investigator Marjorie Fairchild, White set out on a search for Olive Day, finally finding her in a cheap hotel on 6th Street.

Day, who had "oily skin and large clear eyes," was hostile at first but agreed to make a statement. She'd been a prostitute in Los Angeles, Reno, and San Francisco. Exhausted by the game, she'd gone into business with her partner, William Jobelman, procuring young women for rich clients who didn't like to think they were being served professional whores but wanted "good girls," like their sisters and daughters. Day told of one man to whom she'd delivered a virgin every week, a multimillionaire realtor named John P. Mills. White found Jobelman, then he and Fairchild scoured Hollywood for girls involved in the case, some of whom had been taken from orphanages and children's homes. Before long they had enough evidence to go to Buron Fitts, who summoned the press and ordered the arrest of Mills.

White had heard that Mills drove a V16 Cadillac, one of the

most distinctive and exclusive cars then being made, so he waited in the parking lot outside Mills's downtown office until the big car rolled up. "Mills paled, but took it standing," White said, and soon Mills was down at the Hall of Justice and the presses were thundering. "L.A. 'LOVE MART' SECRETS BARED IN DIARY OF GIRL," said the headline in the *News*.

White had never before arrested twenty million dollars, and he was interested to see what would happen. He got his answers quickly. Within the hour Mills was out on bail and his attorneys had hired a private detective to help prepare his defense. White's heart sank when he heard the news, for the private eye was none other than his old boss, Lucien Wheeler.

"In Wheeler, I recognized a grim investigative enemy. He was one of the cleverest detectives I had ever met, and I knew I was no match for him in the struggle," White wrote. "The rigid boundaries of the law clipped my claws, whereas the defense, with their clever detectives and brilliant lawyers, were only bound by their own ethics." And he no longer had any illusion about those.

21

Double Death
on Sunset

B ig news," said Blayney Matthews, late in the afternoon of Wednesday, May 20, 1931, and this had nothing to do with the approaching Love Mart trial. Matthews, usually so calm and genial, was scarcely able to contain himself. "Charlie Crawford's been shot."

White, amazed, stared at Matthews for a moment. "Is he dead?"

"No."

Crawford, badly wounded but still conscious, was in an ambulance on the way to a hospital. A journalist, Herbert Spencer, who had been with Crawford at the time, had been shot too, and *was* already dead. Spencer was the editor and co-owner of *The Critic of Critics*, the political weekly that Crawford was backing. All this had happened in Crawford's office at 6665 Sunset Boulevard, inches from the door through which White had heard Morris Lavine extort

Crawford the previous year. The gunman had fled the scene. None of Crawford's numerous alarms had sounded.

"I want you to get over there," Matthews said. White started to gather together his forensics gear.

"I knew at once this was dynamite," White later wrote.

All over town phone lines buzzed. Newsmen grabbed their hats and cops dropped what they were doing. Within minutes two LAPD men arrived at Crawford's office. They'd been cruising in their patrol car on Sunset Boulevard when the call came in and had narrowly missed catching the perpetrator.

Lucille Fisher, Crawford's young receptionist, said that a man—dressed in a blue suit, fair-complexioned, obviously an American—had arrived at 6665 Sunset Boulevard at around 3 P.M. She hadn't known this man, but Crawford had greeted him at the doorway to his office, smiling and saying pleasantly, "How are you? How have you been? Come on in." A little while later, Fisher said, at about 3:30 P.M., Herbert Spencer had arrived. He, too, had looked friendly and calm, and there was still no sign of trouble. At about 4 P.M., Fisher took a call from Spencer's wife, knocked on the door of Crawford's office, and went in with the message. "They were sitting there at ease, talking," Fisher said. Spencer came out and spoke to his wife, assuring her that he'd be home soon, before returning to the inner office. Thirty minutes later, a chair scraped back, a heavy fist seemed to pound a tabletop, and voices were raised; then there was scuffling, and the shooting started.

Herbert Spencer, mortally wounded, staggered out of the office. At the front of the building he stopped to steady himself against the signboard advertising a photographer's studio; then he collapsed, spilling his blood, bright-red

201

against the sidewalk on Sunset Boulevard. "I saw him fall," Lucille Fisher said. "We carried him in and I held his head." George Copeland, a realtor who leased an office from Crawford, went to the cooler for a glass of water, but Spencer was dead before he had the chance to drink it. The fatal bullet had torn off the tip of his right index finger before plowing through his heart.

Roger Fowler, the owner of the photographer's studio at the front of the small building, said he heard two shots and saw a man walking out the side door, buttoning the jacket of his neatly tailored blue suit. "He walked erectly and didn't seem disturbed," Fowler said.

Mildred "Billie" Rohrback, Fowler's assistant, also heard the shot and described the man: slender, straight-backed. Rohrback, dark-haired and stunning, would become a photographers' favorite in the coming weeks, and would parlay the fame the case gave her into a screen test and bit parts in pictures. She added the details that the suit the man wore was double-breasted, and he'd been carrying a straw skimmer hat. Neither she nor Fowler had known him.

George Crawford, Charlie's brother, came forward with his story. At 3 P.M. he'd been sitting in his car on Sunset Boulevard, gun at the ready. For months he'd been acting as Charlie's bodyguard. Through the rearview mirror George saw an expensive sedan draw up at the curb. His eyes focused on the gorgeous woman, "a bejeweled blonde," who was behind the wheel. Beside her was a man "dapperly dressed in a dark blue suit," who paused for a moment and smiled at the woman before getting out and going into Crawford's office. George, evidently not much of a bodyguard, reckoned there was no threat. Hungry, he started up his car and drove to a drugstore at the junction of Sunset and Highland. He was eating a steak when Copeland rushed in to tell him about the shooting.

Leslie White, having been in Crawford's office before, was familiar with the layout and quickly set to work. He took photographs of the desk, the upturned chair, and the blood on the floor where Crawford had fallen. On the wall, newly added since White had been in the room, was a framed photograph of the Reverend Gustav Brieg leb, whose new church—with the empty room ready for a radio station in the basement—Crawford had paid for. In a box on top of the large safe were back issues of *The Critic of Critics*. An empty whiskey bottle was in the trash, suggesting the three men had been drinking, although when White took his photos, only one glass stood on the desk. In a daybook Crawford had recorded the income from his brothels and other businesses. Another entry spoke of his anxiety that he was about to be "taken for a ride." White examined the room for fingerprints and found many. He also found a spent bullet slammed into the wall.

Mike Schindler, co-editor of *The Critic of Critics*, reported that Spencer, too, had been threatened. Anonymous callers had warned him to "lay off." "Go see the motion picture *The Finger Points*," a mysterious voice had said, referring to a Warner Bros. film based on the Jake Lingle affair, starring Clark Gable and Fay Wray. "You will find out what happens to newspapermen who know and print too much." Only a few days before, *The Critic of Critics* had carried this:

"TO WHOM IT MAY CONCERN—A few days ago one Guy McAfee, who lords it over certain phases of the Los Angeles nether regions, informed a member of the staff of *The Critic of Critics* that unless this publication 'got wise to itself' he would see to it that we were 'taken apart.' That, we suppose, is the 'take 'em for a ride' threat in the Los Angeles manner . . . If any member of the staff of this publication is molested in any way it will be the signal for the opening by the authorities—and a certain daily newspaper—of a well-filled safe deposit box now reposing in the vaults of a certain bank. In that bank, among other things, are described the names, addresses, haunts, and habits of all those who would be closing the mouth of the editor."

The magazine had been in business for a year. It was small, only pamphlet-sized, but neatly laid out and well written, mixing local politics with showbiz news. Its announced aim was "to rid the city of such persons as Mayor Porter and Rev. Robert Shuler and show up other long hairs who try for fame or money by limiting personal liberty of Americans." It sounded good. In fact the magazine, with a circulation of 15,000, pitted one set of vested interests against others, siding with its backer Crawford and slamming his enemies, attacking the efforts of eastern and rival racketeers who were gaining a foothold in the city.

A recent article, headlined "Guy McAfee—'Capone' of L.A.," had exposed the alleged activities of former police captain McAfee. Back in the early 1920s McAfee had been head of the LAPD vice squad. He married a woman who ran one of Albert Marco's brothels, left the police, and went into business with Marco and Crawford. But with the election of Mayor Porter, the rise of Bob Shuler, and the apparent dwindling of Crawford's power, McAfee had assumed more control. The *Examiner*, the *Times*, and the *Daily News* called Mc-Afee "a gambler," and it's true that he owned the

Johanna Smith, the gambling ship moored off Long Beach, and the swanky Clover Club, just above Sunset Boulevard at La Cienega.

The Clover Club, situated at the end of a long driveway so that McAfee's men could see the cops coming, was a haven for the movie crowd (it was here that director Howard Hawks met his glamorous second wife, Nancy "Slim" Hawks, the inspiration for the droll, tough-talking persona that Lauren Bacall would adopt in various Hawks pictures, including his adaptation of Raymond Chandler's first novel, *The Big Sleep)* and for high-rollers who sometimes lost tens of thousands in an evening and were escorted from their cars by security men armed with machine-guns. McAfee wanted his patrons to lose their money inside, not in the parking lot. The Clover Club was fitted with tables that could be flipped over and hidden during raids, details that Chandler would use in *The Big Sleep*, whose smooth mobster Eddie Mars is modeled after Guy McAfee.

At the time he was shot, Crawford had been feuding for months with McAfee. Along with the incendiary article, *The Critic of Critics* had published a cartoon featuring Guy McAfee as an octopus, sitting at the back of the Jeffries Bar on Spring Street, his tentacles stretching into every one of L.A.'s criminal and civic pies. He was more than just a "gambler," in the same way Crawford had been no mere "politician."

"I know who killed my husband," Herbert Spencer's widow, Frances, told the *Examiner* reporter who sped to the Spencer house in Los Feliz, arriving ahead of the cops. At first Mrs. Spencer, usually known as "Frankie," refused to believe what the reporter was saying. Then, heartbroken, she collapsed on a divan with her weeping son in her arms. "Daddy's gone, dear—those terrible, bad men finally got him," she said. Sympathetic neighbors told the reporter he must leave. He didn't. Other newsmen and photographers were already piling out of their cars, dispatched in a hurry by their city editors, and soon the grieving Frankie Spencer held an impromptu press conference for an audience of fifty.

"You know who killed Herbert as well as I do. He knew they were after him. He was telling the truth in his magazine about the gang that keeps this town wide open," she said. "My husband had only one enemy in the world. That man controls the saloons and casinos in Los Angeles. Herbert was telling things he knew about this man and the crooked officials who let him operate."

Frankie Spencer recalled the times when her husband had been a top man on the *Evening Express*, covering stories as a reporter. He'd call her and say, "Gee, Frankie, do we have a beautiful murder . . . it's a natural . . . don't wait up, honey . . . no telling when I'll get home with this story breaking . . ."

Thinking of this, Frankie Spencer broke down. "Beautiful murder! Oh God, I can't stand it. That phrase rings in my ears. It's haunting me. It all seems a nightmare. I just can't believe he won't walk in the door any minute or call me."

She prayed for vengeance. If she'd been there, she said, the man who killed her husband would have been forced to kill her too, otherwise she'd have killed him. "I'm going to see that justice is done in this terrible case if I have to fight the gangs who are fattening on this city alone. Herbert knew the word had gone out on him. He told me a few days ago, 'Honey, if they ever find me dead, you know who did it—or, rather, had it done, because he's too yellow and cunning to do it himself.' So I tell you now—go ask Guy McAfee who did it."

The cops—both the LAPD and Buron Fitts's men—had precisely the same idea. McAfee was the top suspect. But at the time of the shootings he'd been nowhere near Crawford's office on Sunset Boulevard. He'd been downtown in the Hall of Justice, the possessor of an iron-clad and nose-thumbing alibi. McAfee was only too glad to let himself be taken into custody.

In conversation with reporters McAfee agreed that he and his former boss had been engaged in bitter "political" fights. "Everybody knows that," he said. "But here is something that is not generally known—Charlie Crawford and I buried our chief differences at a meeting last Monday night."

Subsequent investigation revealed this last part to be false, a blatant lie. A meeting had indeed taken place that Monday night but had ended in an argument, with both men shouting abuse and threats. Now McAfee was almost laughably measured and thoughtful:

I figure it this way. The man who did the shooting had called on Crawford to discuss some problem—some business matter in which both were interested and in which it was necessary for them to reach some agreement. They couldn't reach an agreement and Herb Spencer was sent for, or entered the office by chance, and became a sort of arbitrator. Probably the argument reached a point where there were hot and angry words. Possibly Crawford sided with Spencer against the unknown man. The unknown, enraged by this, either pulled his own gun and shot Crawford and Spencer, or else picked up Crawford's gun, which was supposed to be in his desk. I don't think it was in any way planned or premeditated. No-one who plotted a murder would pick out that tiny little office, where there is scarcely room for three men.

As analysis, this seems reasonable, even plausible—given the oddity that the Los Angeles press corps was encouraging a racketeer and suspect to hold forth expertly like Sherlock Holmes or Hercule Poirot. In the LAPD McAfee's badge number had been 396. He had a big handsome face with stick-out ears, and he was tall: his nicknames were "Slats" and "Stringbean." He was also known as "The Whistler" because, while still a cop, he'd whistled down the phone line to warn his friends of upcoming raids. A much later photograph, taken in the late 1940s, shows a laughing man, rocking back on his heels, face creased and transformed by glee. His performance here, talking to the men from the *Times*, the *News*, and the *Examiner*, seems similarly self-amused, almost too cute, as if he wished to shine a spotlight on his smarts and sense of growing power.

Charlie Crawford, the man who could answer many questions, lay on an operating table at downtown's Georgia Street Receiving Hospital. Cops and reporters surrounded him. His gray hair fell back from his forehead. The skin on his face, filmed with sweat, kept changing color—first pale, then livid blue as the burly frame of his body fought for oxygen. He called for his wife and two little daughters. "I want to see them. Tell them I'm all right, but I want to see them," he said.

Crawford's brother, George, was at his side, holding his hand. "I've sent for them, Charlie," George said.

Joe Taylor, the LAPD's chief of detectives, came into the room. "Hello, Charlie," he said.

Crawford turned his head, looking through half-open eyes. "Hello, Joe. I know you."

"What's up, Charlie? How are you?"

"Fine," said Crawford, smiling.

Taylor glanced down. A doctor swabbed the wound in Crawford's belly, preparing for surgery.

"Who did it, Charlie?"

Crawford shook his head.

"You'd better tell us now while you can."

"I don't know. Ask Spencer—he knows."

"Spencer's dead, Charlie."

Crawford smiled faintly and shut his eyes; even as he was about to go under the knife, he adhered to the code of his world: he wasn't about to rat out anybody to a cop.

"Call the Reverend Briegleb right away," Taylor said to one of his uniformed LAPD men. "Maybe he'll tell him who did it."

The doors of the white-walled operating theater opened and Crawford was wheeled beneath the big lamps. "Has she come? Has my wife? Has she come?" he said in a whisper.

"She's on her way," a nurse told him.

A doctor applied ether to Crawford's face. Sweet fumes wafted into the nostrils of cops and reporters. Crawford had already lost consciousness when his wife, Ella, did arrive. A slight and slender woman in her late thirties with sad blue eyes, she rushed down the hallway holding a Bible. "I want to see him," she said. "I'm in trouble and I want to pray. He's my husband . . . God, help me!"

The nurse led Ella Crawford into a small adjoining room,

where she fell to her knees and wept. Gustav Briegleb swept in, smartly dressed as always, in flannel pants and blazer, his arrogant face even more frowning than usual. "There's nothing I can say," he told reporters. "Only that Charlie has joined my church and is right with God."

From down the hall came the sound of Ella Crawford, weeping and crying out. Briegleb went to join her, and soon the two, suited in surgical gowns with masks covering their faces, were allowed into the operating room. Doctors gave Crawford transfusions of blood; they cut him open, tried to fix his wrecked insides, and sewed him back up again. "Mrs. Crawford stood there like a Trojan and only the tears that rolled from her eyes bespoke the surge of emotions that engulfed her," wrote the *Examiner*.

At 7:45 P.M. orderlies wheeled Charlie Crawford out of the operating theater. "We can only hope," one of the surgeons said. Ella Crawford waited with her sister and Charlie's brother, George. The Crawford family doctor arrived from Beverly Hills and did his best to comfort them and offer hope. Gustav Briegleb led them in prayers. An agonizing hour crawled by before an intern came with the news. He didn't need to say anything; they read the surgery's outcome in the expression on his face. At 8:32 P.M. Charlie Crawford had passed away. The Gray Wolf was gone. That elaborate security system in the office at 6665 Sunset Boulevard had been installed in vain. Crawford had died as he feared he would, violently and by a bullet.

22

The Ballad of Dave Clark

Leslie White was finishing up his work on Sunset Boulevard when news came through of Crawford's death. He felt a pang, remembering how Crawford had saved him from further embarrassment during the Callie Grimes trial. Had Crawford really been such a bad man? There'd been something very human and sympathetic about him, White thought. Few others in the D.A.'s office mourned Crawford's passing, however. "Good riddance," pronounced Buron Fitts. It was more surprising, perhaps, that the death of Herbert Spencer provoked little outrage. He'd been a newspaperman, after all. It quickly emerged, though, that Spencer had milked the rackets. The Los Feliz house that he owned was worth $25,000. He drove a $4,000 Lincoln. His grieving widow dressed in fur. Herb Spencer resembled Jake Lingle in the wrong sorts of ways.

Next morning, White was at the Hall of Justice, talking

with colleagues in his small cubbyhole of an office, wondering who, if not Guy McAfee, might have committed the murders, when Blayney Mat-thews burst in and astonished them with the news. The man they were looking for was Dave Clark.

White refused to believe it at first, but then Matthews told him that Crawford had mentioned Clark's name moments before he died. Or so the Reverend Gustav Briegleb was claiming. Briegleb's story was that he'd held Crawford's hand and asked who did it. Crawford had whispered "Dave" before passing away.

Matthews agreed that Briegleb was self-important and self-dramatizing, but there were other witnesses. George Crawford, Charlie's brother, had recognized Clark all along, it seemed, but had waited to tell Briegleb rather than the authorities. The lovely Billie Rohrback, shown Clark's photograph, had confirmed that he was the man she'd seen leaving Crawford's office, walking slowly at first, buttoning his jacket, then hurrying and donning his straw skimmer. LAPD detectives had already checked Clark's bank account. On Tuesday morning, the day before the shootings, he'd bought a .38 Colt and fifty copper-coated bullets from a downtown sporting goods store. He'd paid with a $27 check that bounced.

"Where is he now?"

Matthews believed that Clark had crossed the border into Mexico and was holed up in Agua Caliente. "I want you to go down there and check," he said. "Make sure you're armed. He might be dangerous."

White spent the next three hours in his car, heading south toward San Diego and Tijuana. He wore a holstered Colt beneath his arm and beside him on the seat was the magnificent "auto-riot" gun that he'd fetched from Ventura. In his diary he recorded that he felt "pretty silly" with this weaponry. After all, "it was only Dave." Then again, White realized, perhaps he didn't know Dave Clark. Was the cool and debonair fellow with whom he'd worked, and with whom he'd chatted on the steps of the Hall of Justice, really a murderer? Much had changed for Leslie White since his arrival in L.A., but this seemed the most bizarre development of all. On arriving at Agua Caliente, White talked to the manager of the resort who told him that Clark was a frequent and respected guest. The manager checked the reservation book, confirming that Clark had spent the previous Saturday and Sunday nights at Agua Caliente but wasn't there now.

White was relieved. "I didn't care about the wasted time and gasoline," he said. "Whatever Dave Clark had done, and wherever he was, I wouldn't have to arrest him or threaten him with a gun."

The mystery of Dave Clark's whereabouts perplexed the LAPD and the men of the D.A.'s office for the better part of a day. It would transpire that Clark had indeed been at 6665 Sunset Boulevard at the time of the shootings, but he hadn't fled to Mexico.

On leaving Crawford's office, Dave Clark walked down Sunset Boulevard toward Los Palmas and got into his car, the yellow Ford Roadster with the wire-rimmed wheels and the white-walled tires. He drove the entire winding length of Sunset, about fifteen miles, through Hollywood and Beverly Hills, past UCLA, through Brentwood and Pacific Palisades, all the way to the beach. He drove up the coast, as if heading for San Francisco, then turned and came back to Santa Monica, where he parked in the Palisades looking out over the ocean. He sat in his car, apparently thinking, for about two hours before driving back downtown, another twenty miles or so, and left the Ford in a parking garage. He checked into the Stowell, a luxurious hotel crammed into a narrow downtown lot, registering under the name Dave Coleman. Next morning he rose early and drove to the beach again. By this time he knew that Crawford and Spencer were both dead. Again, he went up the coast, past Malibu, and walked for hours. He'd panicked, and now, with the surf pounding in his ears, he figured out what to do. He felt oddly calm, but then he was known to perform well in a crisis; he hashed out a plan, a strategy for survival.

Having not seen her husband since Tuesday morning, when he'd kissed her on the cheek and promised to be back for dinner, Nancy Clark had called the police and reported him missing. Now investigators called at the Clark house on North Detroit Avenue in Hancock Park, asking if she knew where he was. She didn't. She told them that yes, Dave had been under strain recently, because of his run at the judgeship. But he hadn't been complaining. He was, she said, "close-mouthed." She told them he couldn't possibly be connected in any way with the shootings. Nancy Clark, frantic and frightened, said that her husband must be in San Francisco, talking politics with the governor. Such was her hope—desperate and rather sad.

Another bulletin went out over the police radios and the teletype machines. "Arrest and hold for investigation in the case of the Crawford-Spencer murders—David H. Clark, former Deputy District Attorney, well known to all peace officers—American, 33 years of age, 6 feet and ••• inch tall, 175 pounds; medium complexion, small moustache. Wearing dark gray Oxford suit, green tie. White sailor straw hat. Very neat dresser. Very erect." The bulletins gave details of Clark's Ford, then warned: "This man is armed with a .38 caliber revolver No. 576025."

Clark was on the Santa Monica pier when he saw the *Examiner*'s evening "extra" with its headline: "DAVE CLARK SOUGHT IN SHOOTING." It was about ten o'clock. He collected his car and drove east along the empty stretches of Pico Boulevard, stopping at a little roadside diner to call the D.A.'s office. Fitts wasn't there, so he spoke to Blayney Matthews and said, "Blayney, this is Dave Clark. I'm coming in." Thirty minutes later he left the Ford in a downtown parking lot. He was haggard, with deep circles under his eyes. "He fairly ran past the gauntlet of popping gleaming flashlights and the array of cameras," said the *Evening Express*.

The night's drama wasn't done. Roger Fowler, Billie Rohrback, and George Crawford, the witnesses from 6665 Sunset, were brought to the Hall of Justice and asked to identify Clark in a lineup. Buron Fitts, Blayney Matthews, and detectives from the LAPD grilled him for hours. Clark refused to explain himself. He said nothing, leaving Fitts no option but to charge him with double murder. "I understand what you have to do, Buron," Clark said. The morning found him sitting in his shirtsleeves on a bed in the hospital at the L.A. County jail, waiting for a psychiatric evaluation. His jacket hung in a nearby closet. From the lapel he'd removed the Royal Flying Corps pin he customarily wore with such pride.

Talking to reporters, Clark said something remarkable in its sangfroid. "I'm here as an accused man and I know that many cases I won as a prosecutor came because a defendant talked too much. So I have nothing to say." The balance of his mind was scarcely in doubt. He had a plan. At one point he buried his head in his hands. "There were the three of us there together. But I'll talk from the witness stand, not before," he said, admitting something that Fitts by now knew from other witnesses—namely, that he'd been in the murder room. He also said that he went to Crawford's office alone, denying that he'd been driven there by any "beautiful bejeweled blonde." The mystery deepened—or maybe this was Clark starting in on what would be a big part of his strategy: putting up blocks, throwing interference.

"LOVE FRAME-UP SUSPECTED IN DOUBLE MURDER"; "GANGLAND GUNS BARK"; "GAMBLING CZAR ARRESTED IN MURDER PROBE"; "GREED FOR GOLD PROMPTS FIGHT OF RACKETEERS." Already the press was having a ball: banner headlines, pages of photographs, witness interviews, crime scene diagrams, reconstructions, and reams of copy. The intimacy of the coverage startles. Celebrities reckon they have a hard time these days, but the L.A. press of the 1920s was a ravenous pack. Reporters barged right into the swiftly changing story, peeking over the partition of the operating theater when the scalpel made its incision, offering handkerchiefs while they counted the grieving widow's tears, making gleeful note of the beads of sweat on Charlie Crawford's forehead as he gave up the ghost. The *Examiner* ran a cartoon strip in which the first cell showed a man with a smoking gun in his hand, blasting another man who sat behind a desk; in the second cell, Dave Clark was seen glumly reading the *Examiner* edition which named his name; in the third, wearing the straw skimmer, he waved from behind the wheel of his car, surrendering himself at the Hall of Justice; in the fourth, tagged "FINAL EPISODE," there was "the candidate for judge lodged behind bars, accused of murder."

The style of the strip recalls the illustrations then appearing in *Black Mask*. People were thinking about Clark like a character from a novel or film. They wanted to know his motives. What interplay of hidden forces had propelled his fall from grace? The theories that began to emerge call to mind the flashlit, close-up moments of the great American street photographer Weegee and, perhaps more surprisingly, the archetype of "A Rake's Progress" as depicted by eighteenth-century London artist William Hogarth. This was a tale both classic and contemporary. Clark was no career crook, but an apparently upright and regular guy, an ambitious working professional trapped by ambience, fate, and his own character flaws.

But what were the specifics? Clark was keeping his mouth shut, so the D.A.'s investigators pursued their own theories. Blayney Matthews had one in particular. "Find the blonde," he said, referring to the woman George Crawford said he'd seen in Clark's car, the woman whose existence Clark had been at pains to deny. "And we might get some answers."

Matthews believed the woman was either Mrs. M. Donovan, aka June Taylor, who'd worked for Albert Marco and was known to be a friend of Clark's, or Elizabeth Wren, a pal of Taylor's. "The case was red hot and I streaked for

New York," wrote Beverly Davis, the young woman who, with much sexual swagger, had been running Crawford's ritzy brothel in Hancock Park, and had been his mistress and spy. "I knew too much to keep my health in Los Angeles."

Nothing about a murder suspect's private life remains secret for long. His or her every past action is examined, or reexamined in a new light, and Matthews recalled a rumor that had been flying around back in 1928, when Clark had led Marco's prosecution. This had been before Leslie White joined the D.A.'s office, so Matthews filled him in on the details. The story went that, in between Albert Marco's first and second trials, Clark had been invited to a party at a downtown club and oiled with booze before a woman lured him into the inevitable "compromising situation." Flashlights boomed, pictures were taken. Clark was then given the names of three prospective jurors favorable to Marco and told to ensure that they wound up on the final panel. At first Clark went along with this blackmail, but then defiantly sent Marco to San Quentin. After this, the incriminating photographs were gathered by Charlie Crawford, who kept them in the safe in his office, waiting until now, when Clark was running for judge, to use them.

According to this theory, either June Taylor or Elizabeth Wren had delivered Clark to Sunset Boulevard to hear Crawford's terms. Then there'd been an argument and the shootings, and Clark had escaped with the photographs. Or perhaps it had been his intention all along to kill Crawford and steal the photographs. In which case Taylor's—or Wren's—role might have been different. Either way, Herb Spencer had been killed because he happened to be in the wrong place at the wrong time.

Judge William Doran supported this idea of the Marco trial connection. Doran recalled how he'd known something was fishy about the jury and that Dave Clark had said, "If you're smart, Judge, you'll dismiss that jury panel right now," almost out of the blue, as if making up his mind on the spur of the moment. A Hollywood detective gave further credence to Blayney Matthews's blackmail theory, telling how Clark had shown up at his precinct the day before the shootings. Clark had said, "I've got a story to tell," but had left without telling it.

Frederic Girnau, publisher of the *Pacific Coast Reporter*, already in trouble for the trash he'd published about Clara Bow, pointed out that he'd run a story months back about the wild parties Dave Clark was in the habit of attending. In an April issue, Girnau had addressed himself to Dave Clark directly, concerning Clark's candidacy for the judgeship: "You are the candidate of Guy McAfee and Helen Werner. The underworld is 100 per cent in back of you. We have no personal animosity against you, but we contend you are not the man to sit on the municipal bench. Get out of the race pronto, Dave. You know what I mean, don't you? And stop sending people to my office to try to bribe me with money. I don't play that way, Dave."

Had Clark really sought to bribe Girnau? It seems more likely that Girnau was taking a swipe at Clark because of Clark's work on behalf of Clara Bow. But everybody jumped in with their opinion about the killings. The Reverend Bob Shuler swiftly devoted an entire issue of his magazine to the story. Shuler had Buron Fitts as a source, and Fitts was already busy trying to rewrite history—claiming that he'd known for months, even years, that Clark had been corrupted. "Fitts has reason to believe that Albert Marco was convicted in spite of Dave Clark not because of him," Shuler wrote. "Fitts believes that Dave Clark is the fair-haired boy of the Guy McAfee gambling control and that he was running for the judgeship, as many men do all over the nation, so that the racket might have one more friend in court."

Titled "The Strange Death of Charlie Crawford," Shuler's sixty-four-page pamphlet weaves together a sketchy telling of Crawford's early career history in Seattle with a persuasive analysis of the struggle for power that led to his death. Buron Fitts was in no doubt that Clark had pulled the trigger. Shuler wrote:

Just what was the immediate cause he does not know. That Dave was getting over a jag might have entered in. That the three men consumed a bottle of whiskey during their conference, evidently Crawford and Clark getting the lion's share, might partially explain. Crawford might have been putting the screws to Clark, to get at McAfee. They might have sent for Clark to put him on the spot. On the other hand, Clark might have gone to Crawford for some more campaign money and Spencer butted in just in time to provoke a couple of murders. Or Clark might have gone over to persuade Crawford to make up with McAfee after Monday's quarrel. Or yet again, Clark may have been told by McAfee that Crawford was going to withdraw his support, muddy the waters and defeat him. In which case he might have gone over for a showdown.

Dave Clark, the man with a multitude of possible motives, was in a jail cell in the Hall of Justice. Without any great effort on his part, while there he gathered 67,000 votes in his run for the judgeship—not enough to secure the seat (the winner polled 71,000 votes) but an amazing showing. A then-current *Times* photograph shows him behind bars, looking suave and elegant in his shirtsleeves, sitting on the ground playing cards with a bunch of other prisoners, black and white, who look at him with a mixture of curiosity and almost hero-worship. He cut a remarkable figure. A *Times* editorial attacked not Clark's nerve, but his refusal to come straight out and tell his story. This smacked of opportunism and determination to survive at all costs, the *Times* said, sounding an unreasonably high moral note. Clark was worried, even if he was too stoic and self-assured to show it. Writing on yellow scrap paper, the only material available to him, he sent a note to his wife: "Nancy, sweetheart: Believe in me."

"I *do* believe in him," Nancy told the *Examiner*. She'd recovered her composure. In the photograph that ran with the interview she stared into the camera with her chin resting on a leather-gloved hand, poised and pretty and defiant—once again her tough father's daughter. "I don't know what happened. I don't know who committed those awful murders. But it wasn't David." (She was the only one who called him that; everybody else knew him as "Dave.") She'd never heard of any trouble between her husband and Crawford or Spencer. "He sometimes spoke of them, but just as he spoke of dozens of other people he knew." Nancy took comfort from her husband's brief message. She read it repeatedly, tucked it under her pillow, and lay down and went to sleep for the first time since his arrest.

"She's a little brick," Clark said. "She believes in me and

that's all I care about." Clark rose at 6:30 A.M., breakfasted on coffee, toast, and oatmeal, and attended services conducted by the prison chaplain. Nancy started visiting him two or three times a day. "I can stand everything else so long as she doesn't desert me, which I know she never will," he said.

For Buron Fitts, Clark's situation was more than an embarrassment. With his tendency to self-pity, Fitts took the matter as a personal attack. Furious, he withdrew every remark he'd made about the brilliance of Dave Clark. "There were three racketeers in that room," he said, claiming to have firm evidence that Clark was acting for McAfee. "The murders were nothing more than the result of Crawford's attempts to gain back power he lost two years ago. Racketeers met racketeers and there was murder."

To lead his defense, Dave Clark turned to W. I. Gilbert, whom he already knew well from the Clara Bow trial. Now he got to know him even better. Gilbert had an easy manner and a wit that could be biting or genial. His memory was phenomenal and he had the great trial lawyer's gift: in his examination of a witness, he never hammered a question without driving it all the way and getting an answer; and he never hammered unless he knew where the inquiry would lead. He was tough too; in Oklahoma, where he'd had his training, "to be dressed" meant to carry a gun. "I can see him slowly and deliberately walking along the railing of the jury box calling each man juror by his name as though he had known the juror a lifetime. The southern courtesy he showed the women jurors made the deepest impression on them," recalled Los Angeles Superior Court Judge Charles Haas. "No-one could anticipate his courtroom tactics. He often turned coups to his advantage."

Clark knew he was in good hands: Gilbert had never had a client convicted and executed for murder. Backing up Gilbert would be Leonard Wilson, a friend of Clark's and a former judge.

At his arraignment Clark was mobbed by reporters and a crowd eager to glimpse the suave and newly notorious figure. The murder complaint had been sworn out by Assistant D.A. Tom Menzies, an old friend of Clark's. Llewellyn Moses, another friend, handled these formal proceedings for the prosecution. The presiding judge, William S. Baird, had known Clark since childhood and couldn't meet his eye, while the court reporter, Sam Coulter, a classmate from USC, shook Clark's hand and told him, "I know you'll come out of this okay."

Small wonder, then, that Fitts looked to an outside lawyer to take charge of the prosecution. "It's just too difficult for anyone at present on my staff to handle this," he said. He picked W. Joseph Ford, a veteran who, back in 1911, had been part of the team that prosecuted the McNamara brothers for dynamiting the *Times* building. Subsequently, Ford had squared up against the great Clarence Darrow in Darrow's trial for bribery, and the two lawyers had grown to hate each other. Ford remained convinced that Darrow had been guilty. On leaving the D.A.'s office in 1914, Ford became a criminal defense lawyer, then the first dean of the law school at Loyola Marymount University. He was already an aging man but his integrity was beyond doubt, or at least as unimpugnable as anybody's could be in L.A. at that time. He'd known Fitts for years, having been his senior officer in the National Guard. Ford wore his gray hair long. Round, thick-lensed glasses made his eyes look big and black. Plunging into his task, he moved into an office suite in the Hall of Justice. "I expect to go into every gangland and racketeering ramification of the case," he told the *Evening Herald.* "It's not just the blind prosecution of Clark, but the tracking down of whoever else was behind these cold-blooded killings."

Ford summoned back all the witnesses, interviewing them personally. He learned that four days before the shootings Charlie Crawford had withdrawn $7,000 from one of his accounts—a massive sum of which only $500 had been accounted for. Had Clark stolen the rest, taken it from somewhere in the office, or from Crawford himself as Crawford lay dying? Clark was known to be strapped for cash. Here was another possible wrinkle. Those secret strongboxes and safes that had belonged to Crawford and Spencer were scattered all over town. Located and opened by the D.A.'s men, the boxes disclosed lots more money, but none of the hoped-for clues or dope about the underworld. June Taylor popped up, not in Los Angeles but across the bay from San Francisco, at San Quentin where, amazingly, she paid a visit to Albert Marco. The LAPD posted men at local railroad stations to look for Taylor, should she return to L.A.

Charlie Crawford lay in state. For a day continuous lines of men and women paid their respects, gazing at the faintly smiling face of the slaughtered boss through a pane of beveled glass set in the lid of a $15,000 silver and bronze casket, the most expensive available in L.A. The funeral service took place close by USC, at Briegleb's spanking new St. Paul's Presbyterian, the church built with Crawford's money. More than 2,000 people assembled. Those who couldn't get in jammed the sidewalks and streets outside. Crawford's two little girls sent a single rose with the message, "For Daddy." Guy McAfee sent a wreath that was six feet high and in the shape of a heart. "For my old friend—gone now!" said the note. Still, nobody came away with the idea that McAfee was very sorry. Boy Scouts in uniform occupied the front pew, marking Crawford's many contributions to their troop. The choir, almost obscured by banks of flowers, sang two of Crawford's favorite hymns—"Safe in the Arms of Jesus" and "Jesus Loves Even Me."

At the center of this orgy of sanctimony was the stocky and grizzled figure of Briegleb himself, standing beside a furled American flag with a gold spike on the top and eulogizing in a voice choked by sobs. "I knew the real Charlie Crawford, not as the world knew him. He has gone from the land of life. And how he loved life. To be near him was to feel the radiance of living," he said. "He has gone into the land of explanation, where all enigmas are made clear. He knows the answer to the question we are asking: 'Why should this have happened?'"

Briegleb praised the good Crawford had done, the donations he'd made: the $25,000 to pay for the church; the famed $3,500 diamond ring, slipped on top of a card on which was written, "Use this for the children."

"He said to me: 'Next to my family, that ring means more to me than anything else. I want to give it to the church because it will be a real sacrifice,'" said Briegleb.

Later, Briegleb delivered a sermon on "The Crawford Tragedy's Lessons and Revelations." Again his church was packed, the congregation hanging on his words. Briegleb spoke of Crawford's frequently expressed fear that he would be assassinated. Chicago gangsters had been trailing Crawford for days, plotting to kidnap him for a $150,000 ransom, Briegleb claimed. Beneath Briegleb's feet, in the church basement, was the soundproofed room that was to house the radio station Charlie Crawford had paid for. Maybe Briegleb's broadcasts could have indeed put him on a par with Bob Shuler, and Crawford back in charge of L.A. But the room would remain empty, never to be used.

23

They Can Hang You

"All trials are for one's life," said Oscar Wilde, and for Dave Clark this was literally true. Buron Fitts and W. Joseph Ford sought the death penalty when proceedings began at ten o'clock on the morning of Monday, August 3, 1930. "A milling mob fought deputy sheriffs for seats in the tiny courtroom," wrote the *Times*. Squads of extra police and bailiffs were on duty to control the crowds. A temporary high-walled chamber had been erected outside the court-room door, through which entrance was gained one by one. People greeted Clark from all sides as he entered the court with Nancy on his arm. They thumped him on the back and shook his hand, wishing him all the best while he spoke with them casually, appearing more confident and relaxed than he must have felt on the inside. But who knows? Dave Clark was ice-cool. He'd spent the weekend on Catalina Island as a guest of his friend Jimmy Jump, the millionaire sportsman.

"A little relaxation before the battle," he told reporters. He'd golfed, fished, and played tennis in between going over the details of his defense with his attorneys. As usual, he'd worked on his tan. He was groomed and ready, dressed in a suit of dark blue that, in the past, had brought him luck.

"Today the columnesque young man with a rancher's bronzed skin and a faro dealer's frigid eyes will begin the battle of his life for a scant dozen votes," wrote Gene Coughlin, returned from the adventures with Albert Einstein to his more usual beat of juicy murder and purple prose. In the years since the Marco trials, the tempestuous, hard-drinking Coughlin had fallen out with *News* owner Manchester Boddy and revolved through the doors of almost every other newsroom in town. But now Boddy, forgiving and smart, had hired Coughlin again, knowing that the Clark trial would be the perfect showcase for Coughlin's writerly gifts. Coughlin knew Clark and pointed out Clark's great advantage: "He was a prosecutor and he knows what to expect from the prosecution."

However, he did not know what to expect from the judge. The presiding judge of the Los Angeles Superior Court was William Doran, who had handled the Marco case, the Bow/DeVoe case, and numerous others that Clark had prosecuted. Obviously Doran couldn't preside over this one. He gave the trial to an out-of-towner, Stanley Murray, who journeyed down to L.A. from Madera County in central California, close by Yosemite. Murray, the son of a pioneer settler, had grown up in the shadow of the Sierras and had earned his law degree in San Francisco; he'd worked for the Southern Pacific Railroad before returning to his roots in the country. Not much crime happened in Madera County, but in 1923 Murray had sentenced a murderer to hang, a robber who shot and killed a traffic cop—a typically modern crime intruding into the California wilderness. Murray was fifty years old, solid and reliable, an outsider with no special interests to protect. Dave Clark could expect no mercy or favors from him.

Most of the trial's first day, and the second, was consumed by jury selection, a ritual whose importance is often ignored but had been emphasized by Earl Rogers and was well appreciated by Clark. Each time, before issuing a challenge on a prospective juror—for instance, a man who'd been a fellow churchman of Charlie Crawford—the defense attorneys W. I. Gilbert and Leonard Wilson deferred to their client, huddling with him and paying heed to his shrewdness. Clark knew who he wanted on the jury. He wanted women, and in this first key battle he emerged victorious. Women outnumbered men on the final panel seven to five.

Trials are self-contained, and like novels and films, they have themes. *People v. DeVoe* had been, at heart, about class and envy. *People v. David Harris Clark* would be about not only the violent deaths that had happened in a Hollywood office, but a sexual atmosphere that crackled through the courtroom. "Decked out in pure white and capped with a tiny blue turban from which her golden hair peeped at the forehead and neck Mrs. Nancy Clark occupied a front seat as the trial got under way and with wide open eyes examined the jury as they filed into the box," said the *Times*.

"Let me stand by my husband and you can have all the pictures you want," Nancy told photographers.

Clark knew very well his wife's effect; one way or another, she meant votes. He understood, too, that perhaps the central question confronting the jury would be this: Could a man as plausible, upright, and attractive as he knew himself to be really have committed cold-blooded murder? Dave Clark, so suave and athletic, had never underestimated his own best qualities, and he played them well.

Prosecutor Joseph Ford also knew how to milk a court. "Look out for Uncle Joe Ford," warned Gilbert. "He's a crafty old codger." Ford would play for time when he needed it, by complaining about his false teeth. He walked slowly with a pained stoop. The horn-rimmed glasses that jutted from his narrow, creased face gave him a disconcerting stare. A Catholic, he had ten children, and in prosecuting Clark played the role of the stern father, saddened by the necessity of bringing to task a gifted young man whose derailed life had caused tragedy. At the front of the court Ford put up a blackboard, on which he pinned a detailed plan of the maze-like interior of 6665 Sunset Boulevard. Wielding a schoolroom pointer, he made his opening statement, speaking in a measured voice and pausing to dramatize certain moments as he ushered the jury through the events of May 20. "There were two shots fired in that conference room of Crawford's office," he said. "The first shot was fired to kill Crawford. The second shot was fired to kill Spencer, the only living witness to the first murder." Ford waggled the pointer. "Then Clark came out, with his characteristically jaunty manner, buttoning up his coat."

"Clark, lolling in his chair at counsel table, chuckled at this reference to his erect carriage and his military walk," wrote Gene Coughlin for the *News*, though Clark may have been grinning with relief. Ford was pinning the prosecution's case on placing Clark in Crawford's office and proving that nobody else could have fired the shots. After weeks of investigation, the D.A.'s office had no real clue about Clark's motive. Blayney Matthews and Leslie White had failed to pin down the mystery blonde, whether she'd been June Taylor or June Taylor's pal. "Guy McAfee and his underworld associates brought down the shutters," White wrote. "But that woman vanished as if she was part of a trick by Houdini. The department searched everywhere, to no avail. We were frustrated."

Fitts and Ford still didn't know *why* Clark had been in that room. Their case, even at this early stage, was looking incomplete.

"We will not be able to show you the revolver used by David H. Clark because the defendant has never produced the weapon," said Ford, and Gilbert jumped to his feet with the court in uproar. "Well, anyway," continued Ford above the hubbub, "we have never seen the revolver."

Gilbert, when it was his turn, spoke to the jury: "If it should be proved that there were four men in that room and that two of them were dead and one on trial here and the other missing, then would you give the benefit of doubt to the defendant?" he asked, hinting at a possible tactic that would invoke the presence of an unknown assailant, a fourth man.

Next day, the trial's third day, Clark suffered setbacks. First, Judge Murray rescinded the bail that Gilbert had managed to secure for Clark. This meant Clark would be once again committed to jail when court adjourned. Murray then denied a key motion from Gilbert, a strenuously argued attempt to force the state to try the two shootings simultaneously. A fight about this had been ongoing for all the weeks during which Clark had been maintaining his uncanny sphinx-like silence. As the trial began, Ford had no idea whether or not Clark would testify in his own defense. He had no inkling what Clark's defense might be. Therefore he and Fitts had been pressing for two separate trials: the first for Spencer's killing, the next for Crawford's. Thus, in the second, they'd be armed with full knowledge of Clark's story, should he be acquitted in the first.

The Dave Clark trial would happen very differently if held today. But California legal procedure still had one foot in frontier times, and this is how it played out back then. Judge Murray took the prosecution's side, settling that Dave Clark would be tried for his life not once, but twice. For crafty Joe Ford, this was a big victory, and for Clark a crushing blow. On hearing the decision, Nancy Clark bowed her head and wept. The nightmare wouldn't be over anytime soon.

The trial transcripts and newspaper reports give a sense of how drama heightened and tightened as the case progressed. Surgeons described the autopsies they'd conducted, telling in detail how the bullets had wrecked the bodies of the two men, killing both. It was a big moment, when the grisly reality hit the court. Then Leslie White was called to the stand. "I was forced to forget how much I liked the man," White later wrote, confirming that for everybody in the D.A.'s office this was a strange situation. Some, like Fitts, responded with anger; but White felt bewildered and sad. He avoided Clark's eyes, testifying about the crime scene photographs he'd taken, images that were then shown to the jury.

"And finally, the white, strained faces of the women bereaved gave a lasting touch of stark, aching tragedy to the picture," wrote Gene Coughlin for the *News*, describing how first Frankie Spencer and then Ella Crawford took the stand, identifying their respective husbands from White's pictures, and stating that both men had been unarmed on the day of their deaths.

Charlie Crawford had owned five guns, all duly laid out on the evidence table, but his widow Ella swore that he'd been carrying none of them.

"How do you know he wasn't armed?" Ford asked.

"He hugged me when he left home," Ella Crawford said. "He always did and if he'd been wearing a revolver I would have felt it."

It was an emotional moment, and for Joseph Ford effective, introducing a gentle side of Charlie Crawford and the love he'd felt for his family. Frankie Spencer, though grief-stricken, came off sounding worldly and hardboiled. "I've had some pretty hard knocks boys," she told reporters, "and I don't want you to take my picture now that Herb is dead." Frankie, it was clear, had full knowledge of the dangers of her husband's professional and political involvements. Ella Crawford struck a different figure. "Widows reeds rustled through Judge Stanley Murray's courtroom and swept all light informality from the case," wrote the irrepressible Coughlin. "Last night the debonair defendant went to sleep with the full realization that he is on trial for MURDER."

A prosecutor can take nothing for granted. A trial is supposed to start as if from nothing, in terms of the information given the jury about the alleged crime. Big cases, of course, can't work that way because of media coverage; but that's the theory. Ford had to show that two men had died, describe who those men were, and establish how they died, and when and where they died. After four days he'd done all that, and his focus began to narrow. He sought to show that Dave Clark had been with them in that small inner office. In his testimony George Crawford put Clark at 6665 Sunset Boulevard. Lucille Fisher, decked out with all the care and glamor that Clara Bow had brought to her courtroom appearances, did the same. Fisher wore a low-cut, short-sleeved suit with soft gauntlet gloves that stretched up her bare arms. She was "blonde and willowy, Crawford's voluptuous private secretary and human repository for the political and underworld secrets of the 'Lone Gray Wolf,'" wrote Coughlin, smacking his chops. Fisher's lips were rouged, her hair freshly done, but her nerves showed. She flubbed her lines at first but finally put Clark in the office, alone with Crawford and Spencer up to the moment the shots were fired.

Then it was Mildred Rohrback's turn; she, too, was a wow. "Dressed in a two-piece sports dress of rose crepe, trimmed with beige and with a bolero jacket that matched her dress, the witness was a cynosure of all eyes as she took the stand, her testimony having been anticipated as a high spot in the trial," wrote the *Times*.

Rohrback said: "I heard two shots and then a man groaned. I ran to the front porch and the first thing I noticed was blood spots. Then I noticed a man walking along the path that leads from Mr. Crawford's office."

"Did you get a good opportunity to look at him?" asked Ford.

"He was tall and dark, but his face was pale and calm."

"Have you seen him since?"

"He's sitting right there," Rohrback said, pointing at Clark while the court gasped. "It was the defendant."

She described how she'd gone back into Crawford's office, and had seen Crawford, bleeding, on the floor but leaning back against his chair, sprawled and semi-conscious, with a cigar still clutched between two fingers of his right hand.

None of this was good for Clark, though Gilbert had successfully filibustered so that Rohrback's persuasive testimony was delivered first thing one morning rather than at the conclusion of the previous day, as Ford had hoped. Then it would have had maximum effect, giving the jury a chance to sleep on what she'd said. Such nuances, Gilbert knew from experience, might prove decisive.

Ford called Leslie White to the stand once more. This time White testified about ballistics, another area of his expertise. He told the court that the bullet shot at Crawford had passed straight through his body. White himself had dug out the bullet from the splintered plaster of a wall at 6665 Sunset Boulevard. On the bullet were traces of a special kind of grease used by Colt, indicating that it had been the first fired from a brand new revolver. Attached to the bullet, when it came out of the wall, had been a small piece of fabric, part of Crawford's shirt. Ford introduced the rest of the shirt as evidence, giving it to the jury to handle.

White was no more comfortable than he'd been before. He didn't like Ford's melodramatic stunt with the shirt, and stole a glance in Dave Clark's direction. "Dave was expressionless, calm and cool," he wrote. "He'd always been difficult to read. In court, at that moment, he was brave, and even harder to understand. Was he guilty? I wanted him to be innocent, but I didn't know. I couldn't help but remember the times when I'd seen him as a prosecutor, hectoring and working a defendant. Now Joe Ford did the same to him."

The trial obsessed and perplexed L.A. People flocked to buy new editions of the papers as they hit the streets and argued openly about whether or not Clark had murdered the two men. A local radio station put out dramatized reenactments of the trial as though they were real, thrilling and confusing listeners in the same way that Orson Welles would with his 1938 Mercury Theater broadcast of *War of the Worlds.* Judge Murray ordered a stop to the broadcasts, whereupon the radio sponsors asked to put microphones in the courtroom so they could air the actual events. Murray nixed that too. "Description of the Clark murder trial," wrote Harry Carr in his *Times* column "The Lancer," ridiculing the fever to which the city gleefully submitted: "Miss Tweety-tum wore baby blue adorned with pink spots . . . Mrs. Clark kissed her husband twice, the last shot landing under the ear . . . A mysterious woman in black winked at the District Attorney and took two digestive tablets . . . Eldridge Pulp, the well-known author, says that this is serious and Los Angeles had better watch out . . ."

Meanwhile, as the trial's first week went on, E. L. Doheny, acquitted but in disgrace, had a stroke and was said to be close to death. The violinist Jascha Heifetz gave a concert at the Hollywood Bowl to benefit unemployed musicians. A Los Angeles mother, unable to feed her family of eleven, tried to gas herself. Another woman threw her baby from the Colorado Street Bridge in Pasadena and then jumped herself. A man shot himself in the head as he leaped from the same bridge, making doubly sure of his death. A plumber, his business failing, placed the muzzle of a shotgun beneath his heart and pulled the trigger. In Oklahoma, the oil fields were declared under martial law by a state government striking at magnate Harry Sinclair, Doheny's fellow-indictee in Teapot Dome. In Washington, the Wickersham Commission (a federal inquiry into the functioning, indeed the feasibility, of law enforcement during Prohibition) was attacking police brutality, the "third degree" that appeared to be endemic in cells and squad rooms across the nation, notably in Los Angeles. Earthquakes shook Kansas, Texas, New Mexico, and Nova Scotia. America's tectonic plates were shifting.

24

Telling It All

By midway through the trial's second week, Joseph Ford had laid out an unbreakable chain of evidence showing that only Dave Clark could have killed the two men. Ford hadn't shown why and hadn't tried to. He'd failed to produce a motive and he'd failed to produce a murder weapon. But he'd proved beyond doubt that Clark had been in a room with two living men and had left behind two dead ones. This hadn't happened by magic. The onus now passed to the defense.

"I'm going to tell it all," Dave Clark told the press when court adjourned on the afternoon of Wednesday, August 12, 1931. Maybe we all have a fantasy of setting the world right about our actions and our characters, but for a defendant to take the stand in his or her own defense is rarely a good idea. Defense lawyers encourage the move only as a last resort. In the history of criminal law many famous defendants have secured acquittal without taking the risk of exposing themselves to a prosecutor's merciless attack: O. J. Simpson, for instance, and Madeleine Smith, the seductive Scottish angel of arsenic, to name but two.

"The actual happenings within the little room where the lives of two men were snuffed out may never be known," wrote Bob Shuler. "It is not to be believed that Clark will tell the truth about these happenings. It is his task to save his own life. He is an astute lawyer and will know exactly what to tell and what not to tell."

Shuler made a nerve-shredding task sound simple, but people of L.A. knew better and anticipated great theater. The news that Dave Clark was about to go public went into the papers and out over the airwaves. The next morning a crowd of more than 3,000 flocked to the Hall of Justice, milling in the streets outside, galloping through the corridors, fighting each other and the fifty bailiffs who tried to keep order. Buron Fitts was knocked to the ground in the rush. Reporters and cameramen and Joseph Ford himself fought through the scrum. An exiled Russian general, Theodor Lodijensky, had been hoping to attend another trial, that of His Imperial Highness Michael Romanoff, aka Harry Gerguson, the Brooklyn-born con man. Years later Romanoff would become a famed Hollywood restaurateur and friend to the stars. In the early months of 1931 he had swept through L.A., showering bad checks like confetti before being arrested. But now, on the morning of his trial, Romanoff had skipped town, and the puzzled Lodijensky was swept along with the mob that tried to break down the barricades outside Judge Murray's court. The mayhem continued inside, as the *Times* made vivid: "Every available seat was taken, including many makeshift chairs. Others sat on the floor. The aisles of the courtroom were clogged. Lawyers, motion-picture celebrities, wealthy businessmen and society women sat squeezed in the smallest space they could wedge into. Outside the courtroom the din was terrific, and all the doors and windows had to be closed so that testimony could be heard."

Clark wore his lucky dark blue suit and a blue and white dotted silk tie. After several days in jail he'd lost some of his tan. He was nervous but left his seat with swift strides when his name was called. It was a warm and sultry summer day, with the temperature rising into the eighties. A chandelier, hanging from the courtroom ceiling, swung to and fro in the breeze made by spinning fans.

Gilbert asked: "What is your name?"

"David Harris Clark."

"How old are you?"

"Thirty-three."

"How long have you lived here?"

"All my life."

"You were born here?"

"Yes, I was born in Los Angeles."

Gilbert stood at a distance, encouraging Clark to speak up so the jury could hear him. They'd rehearsed this moment, and Clark had been planning for it ever since he left 6665 Sunset Boulevard on that fatal afternoon. He'd had months to prepare. First, Gilbert led Clark through the story of his relationship with Herbert Spencer. "I met him first about the latter part of January or the first part of February this year," Clark said. He explained how, soon after launching his campaign for the judgeship, he'd run into Spencer in the lobby of the Alexandria Hotel. They'd talked politics, of course, and Clark had angled for Spencer's support. Some weeks later, though, Spencer had ordered Clark to stop running his campaign on an anti-vice angle. "Cut it out," Spencer had said, and started to make threats.

"He said that one night, and soon, I'd pull into my driveway and someone would be waiting and I'd never get out of my car," Clark told the court. He'd been frightened, and had tried to borrow a gun. Failing in that, he'd gone to the sporting goods store and bought a .38 caliber Colt revolver and some bullets.

Here, sensationally, Gilbert produced the Colt and introduced it as evidence, together with four bullets and two empty shell cases. This was the weapon that Joseph Ford had been demanding to see the previous week.

"Where did you go after you bought the gun?" Gilbert asked.

"To my office in the Petroleum Securities building, and I stayed there until about five-thirty or six o'clock, then I went to Venice and checked into a hotel."

"And did you stay there all night?"

"Yes, I did."

"Why, Mr. Clark, didn't you go home?"

"I was afraid to."

Was it possible to believe that the tall and strapping Clark had been so frightened by Herbert Spencer that he'd fled to a hotel and stayed there all night without telling anybody? That was his story. "As he talked, Clark gripped his hands in a prayer-like clasp and the knuckles stood out white and trembling," wrote Gene Coughlin in the *News*. "He looked neither to the right, where his wife, Nancy, sat huddled in a chair at counsel table, nor to the left where the jury seemed curiously apathetic to the drama of the occasion. His eyes remained fixed on the portly figure of attorney Gilbert, who is a general physical replica of the slain Crawford."

Gilbert asked what Clark did the next day, after he left the Venice hotel.

"I returned to the city and called Mr. Crawford and made an appointment with him for three o'clock," Clark said.

"When you went in, what occurred?"

"I asked Mr. Crawford if he had any information about the threats which had been made against me, and he said he'd been working on that all week and that he thought it would turn out all right. He said it was lucky I came to him, because of serious consequences for me if I hadn't."

"What else?"

"I thanked him because I thought it was fine of him and I asked him about Mr. Briegleb's support."

Clark's manner was calm and unruffled, his gaze candid as he came to the crux of his tale. He proceeded to paint a picture of Charlie Crawford as a big politico and fixer. Crawford had bragged that he would control the next grand jury and the D.A.'s office was powerless to stop him. He'd shown Clark sample blue and pink ballot papers which Lucille Fisher would send out and would be worth 100,000 votes. He'd said, "I'm going to run things as they've never been run before."

It was at this point in the meeting that Herbert Spencer had arrived, Clark said. And soon after, Crawford had made his proposal, naming the price Clark would have to pay in order to be elected judge.

"Then Crawford turned to me and said, 'Listen, I've done a lot for you and now you have to do something for us. I want you to take Dick Steckel down to a certain place in Santa Monica and I'll give you the details in a couple of days,'" Clark said.

Dick Steckel, Clark's friend, was still chief of the LAPD; but he'd hold the job for only a few more months before another mayor came in, with another police commission, and the pistol champion and red-baiting J. Edgar Davis was brought back.

Clark went on, "Well, I had been leaning up against the table in the room and I stood up and I faced Crawford and I said, 'You want me to frame my best friend, you damned dirty dog, you low-down skunk. You were just indicted for framing Councilman Jacobson. Now you get me out here and want me to frame my friend Dick Steckel. You join the church and throw a diamond ring on the plate and now this is what you propose. I'm going to go out and get on the platform and preach to the world everything that's happened in this room.' Then Crawford turned to me and said 'No —— can talk to me like that.' At the same time he pulled a gun out of his belt."

Gilbert: "Which hand did he have it in?"

"In his right hand."

"Did you hear the statement of the young lady the other day about the cigar being in Crawford's hand? Did he have any cigar? Was he smoking?"

"I didn't see any cigar. He whipped out the gun and turns it on me and I grabbed his right hand with my left hand and held the gun parallel between us."

Gilbert, the wily and experienced litigator, got Clark down from the stand. He retrieved Clark's revolver, the Colt, Exhibit 84, from the evidence table, and handed it to him. He seized Exhibit 3, one of Crawford's guns, a Colt automatic, and gave it to Leonard Wilson.

Seeing that one of Gilbert's famous courtroom coups was about to be foisted upon him, Joe Ford jumped to his feet to object. He'd called witnesses and spent considerable time trying to show that Crawford had been unarmed on the day of the shooting. Judge Murray overruled, saying that Clark must be allowed to give his version, and the reenactment went ahead on the floor of the court, as Gilbert had been hoping, with Clark taking his own part and Wilson and Gilbert playing Crawford and Spencer respectively.

"The minute that gun came out I grabbed Crawford's wrist," Clark said, and now he took Leonard Wilson's wrist, struggling with him, showing how he'd tried to hold Crawford's gun away from his body. "With his left hand he caught me by the throat and said: 'Get him, Herb.' I pulled out my gun and I shot Crawford right in there."

Pointing with the barrel of the Colt, Clark indicated a spot in Leonard Wilson's belly. "And then I saw Spencer come across the room. He was leaning over, and I pointed my gun at him and shot him."

A gasp went around the courtroom. There was a split second of silence then bailiffs called for order as pandemonium threatened to break loose. Once order was re-established, the only sound was that of Nancy Clark sobbing convulsively, crying for the first time since the trial began, her cheeks running with tears she didn't bother to wipe away. The other three hundred spectators, jammed into a space provided for 125, sat breathlessly and on the edge of their seats. "Juror No. 4 fanned himself complacently, his eyes wandering over the high ceiling of the room. Juror No. 5 probed a molar with his thumb and gave it a tentative tug," wrote Gene Coughlin, capturing another angle from the movie of the trial he seemed to be shooting at his typewriter.

Gilbert asked Clark to place Wilson's hand where Spencer's had been.

"He was moving in my direction. It seemed to me that he was stooped over, closing in, like this . . ."

"All right. Place your hand there."

"Up here." Clark pointed to his own chest. "I don't know the exact place."

"He had his thumb—well, you heard the description of the wound, didn't you?" said Gilbert, leading Clark to be as precise as possible so his testimony would jibe with the known fact that the top of Spencer's index finger on his right hand had been ripped off by the bullet.

"What happened then?" asked Gilbert.

"The minute I fired Spencer went out the side door onto the porch. I walked to the door to see where he was. I saw some blood spots and I knew I hit him. I took my gun, put it in my belt, and I left."

Now the world knew—Gilbert's "fourth man" theory had only been a feint. The plan all along had been that Clark would plead self-defense. A problem here, in terms of his credibility, concerned what had happened after the gunplay. Why, if the shootings had been justified, had he fled and driven around town and holed up in a hotel and gone walkabout? Gilbert swiftly led Clark through a telling of this, including the story of what had happened to his gun. Before finally turning himself in at the Hall of Justice, Clark had wrapped the Colt in newspaper and hidden it in bushes on a vacant lot off Pico Boulevard. It didn't seem like the action of an innocent man.

Clark told his story in less than two hours. Then he had to withstand more than nine hours of cross-examination, an interrogation that would span three courtroom days. Ford quickly hinted that gambling boss Guy McAfee had been behind Clark's run for the judgeship. He established that Clark had enjoyed "champagne dinners" with McAfee and that Clark had known Charlie Crawford far better than Clark had wished to admit at first. Ford had learned of Clark's visits to Crawford's house, and to Crawford's office, during the period before the final Julian Pete charges against Crawford were dropped.

"As a matter of fact, Mr. Clark, last October didn't you go out there to arrange with Crawford that you would get the charge against him dismissed, for the sum of $50,000?" asked Ford, an allegation that drew a laugh and a rueful smile from Clark and brought Gilbert soaring from his seat like an angry bird.

Ford asserted that Clark, far from "defying the under-world," had been seduced by it, had become a part of it—a pawn and a player in gangland politics—and that he'd been at Crawford's office on the day of the slayings not because he'd been threatened, but because he'd been sent there by McAfee to help fix "the magazine beef" that McAfee had with *The Critic of Critics.*

"I'm not vindictive but I want to see justice done. Frankly I don't believe Dave Clark's story," said Frankie Spencer, who appeared in court again in her widow's weeds and wearing more black eyeliner than the vamp actress Theda Bara. She looked goth and had perhaps gone a little mad, though she merely echoed what many felt. "I know that my husband never made any threats against him," Frankie Spencer said. "The story just doesn't ring true. That's all."

"Through the minds of women in the courtroom ran this question: 'Justifiable or not justifiable—would I be afraid to be alone with Dave Clark?'" wrote Eleanor Barnes of the *Daily News*, catching the trial's strange sexual tingle. "Courtroom fans scrutinizing the defendant closely wondered whether those sharp grey eyes could soften. Does the taking of another man's life do things to a man psychologically? Nancy Clark— if she wanted to—could record any changes in her husband's demeanor since May 20."

Nancy herself was showing the strain. Lines stood out around her eyes, though she remained defiant: "I still believe in him," she said. "Dave wouldn't murder two men in cold blood."

A remarkable *Daily News* photograph shows Nancy standing outside a cell in county jail, seen in half-profile, wearing a black cloche hat and black gloves with a purse tucked under the short sleeve of her dress. She gazes into the eyes of her husband who stands barely a foot away, his fists gripping the iron bars that separate them. The right half of Clark's face is in shadow, but we see that he returns the intensity of Nancy's look. They have eyes only for each other. This immensely powerful photograph looks unposed, like a snapshot or a still from a movie. The voyeuristic snatching of such intimate action was, in 1931, still relatively new, even in the Los Angeles press. This wasn't because of any previous scruple, but because newspaper photography had recently been revolutionized by the arrival of the lightweight Speed Graphic, a version of the camera that would be standard for decades due to swifter shutter speed, faster film, and a flashgun attachment that was much easier to use. Arthur Fellig, better known as Weegee, would make this camera famous through the 1930s and 1940s, capturing action-packed images of people and the streets and what violence did. In this picture of Dave and Nancy, we see the beginning of the age of tabloid noir.

Nancy was in court every minute of every day of the trial. She grew tense if Dave hesitated, relaxed if he answered well. She twisted in her chair as though every one of Joe Ford's questions was hurled at her. During one lunch break she was standing in the corridor of the eighth floor of the Hall of Justice waiting for the elevator, when an older woman she'd never seen before pressed a note into her hand. "Mr. Clark," the note began. "Watch out for a man, rather stout with a light suit, straw hat. He carries a gun. *You will understand.*" By this time the Clarks had been subjected to many death threats, and there was the possibility that the note was the stunt of a reporter, fishing for the next lead. Remembering what had happened to Motley Flint, however, Nancy was worried. She passed the note to Gilbert, who showed it to Judge Murray. Thereafter bailiffs searched everybody, further delaying and entangling the process of gaining entry to the courtroom.

Ford kept hammering away with his questions. He got Clark down from the witness box and handed him his revolver and made him tell the story of the shootings again and again, trying to break him down. "Is it not a fact," Ford asked, "that after you had shot Crawford and Spencer you rushed to Crawford's desk and searched it with the idea in mind that you would find there a revolver and that you intended to fire a couple of shots and then claim self-defense?"

Over the roar of Gilbert's objections, but before Judge

Murray could rule, Clark denied that he ever rifled the desk and denied that he'd searched anywhere for a weapon.

"Did you even look at Crawford after you shot him?" Ford asked.

"I don't know if I did or not," Clark said. As the cross-examination entered its third day, he told reporters, "I can stand it as long as Joe Ford can," though the struggle for his life left him pale and haggard. Each night, back in his cell, he studied the trial transcript, which was now approaching 542,000 words and 2,000 pages in length. "I know that Joe Ford can almost make white look like black but I feel that a careful analysis of the testimony will show that he hasn't caused me to change my testimony on any material point," he said, cool-headed and analytical, a remark that testifies to the chilling powers of his lawyerly judgment. He was under incomprehensible pressure but his self-control wasn't about to crack. He understood that the trial was all about how he projected his personality. He was convincing and didn't overplay his hand. He knew how to work the court without appearing to work it. People, especially women, didn't want to believe that he was guilty.

"Judging from the panting anxiety of all the women I know for the acquittal of David H. Clark, I think he is wasting time on the law," wrote Harry Carr in his *Times* column. "He ought to go into the movies. He is slightly John-Barrymoreish at that. To flappers of all ages it doesn't seem to matter so much what you have done as what you look like."

Joe Ford returned to the attack, going for Clark's jugular one more time. "As you went past the office, after the shooting, did you see Mr. Spencer?" he asked.

"Yes, out in front—I thought he was still alive," said Clark.

"But you went past him—even if you did think he was armed?"

"Yes."

"You weren't afraid of Spencer then, is that it?"

Clark paused a moment before replying. "I don't know, Mr. Ford."

Judge Murray interrupted here. "At any time, Mr. Clark, did you see a weapon on Spencer?" he asked.

"I did not," Clark said.

This was a key admission, and Ford let it sink in for a few seconds before asking Clark why, if he'd shot the two men in self-defense as he claimed, he then fled and hid his own gun rather than call the authorities.

Again Clark paused. "I don't know, Mr. Ford," he said. "I panicked. I behaved like a ten-year-old kid."

After more than eleven hours of fierce cross-examination, Ford finally let Dave Clark down from the stand. Clark later said he'd never been so glad to see anything finished in his life. Exhausted, he wobbled a little as he walked toward the counsel table. Then he turned to Nancy and she fell into his arms. "He clung for an unusually long minute to his wife," wrote Gene Coughlin.

"You know, I feel sorry for Mrs. Clark," said Joe Ford, musing out loud. "You needn't be," Nancy shot back, with the court in uproar and tears of anger and grief filling her eyes.

25

Verdicts

Judge Stanley Murray gave the case to the jury at 3:15 P.M. on Thursday, August 20, 1931. His instructions seemed to lean toward the prosecution, emphasizing that when it came to a plea of self-defense, "The law will not tolerate the killing of one person by another unless such killing is necessary for the preservation of life." And, once the fact of the killings had been admitted, the onus of proving their "absolute necessity" passed to the defense. "Motive becomes unimportant if you believe the defendant guilty beyond a reasonable doubt," he said.

The jurors filed out of the court and, with bailiffs clearing a way through the crowds, walked up a flight of stairs to the jury room on the floor above. There, with the court exhibits assembled in front of them, they began their deliberations. The small stuffy jury room was connected to the court below by a buzzer with which the jury signaled that, for instance, a

251

verdict had been reached, or one or more of the jurors required something. At 5:45 P.M. the buzzer rang for the first time, bringing bailiff Richard Gilmore to his feet. Gilmore raced up to the ninth floor to see what was required. Reporters and spectators crowded back into the courtroom, rushing and jostling and overturning chairs. "Women were shoved aside," the *Times* noted, shaking its editorial head. For a few minutes the atmosphere was tense while everybody anticipated the verdict. Bailiff Gilmore burst back in with the news: "The jury wants to know, when do they eat?"

Judge Murray agreed that the jury could leave the building for dinner. They were loaded onto a bus and taken to a nearby hotel with teams of reporters in pursuit. Dave Clark had been hoping for a swift acquittal and his confidence appeared to fade. A tearful Nancy did her best to keep up his spirits. "In the courtroom, in the adjoining corridors, and in front of the Hall of Justice, a human tide swirled and laughed and wagered on the verdict," wrote Gene Coughlin. "While the men and women who must decide his future were handling the blood-stained clothing of the men he killed, Clark and his wife, Nancy, held hands in the attorney room of the county jail, and tried bravely to laugh and chat of other things, of happier evenings."

The jury, having taken dinner, returned to their deliberations. A little before 9 P.M. the raucous buzzer sounded for a second time. Again, Bailiff Gilmore sprang to his feet and scurried upstairs. Again the courtroom, lit now by the electric bulbs in the chandelier, filled with eager spectators. Gilmore, who seemed to have been assigned the sort of comic-relief role that Shakespeare gave the porter at the castle gates in *Macbeth*, came back this time with the message: "One of the ladies has indigestion and wants some bicarbonate of soda. They ate heavy."

A pattern was set. Hours of mounting emotion and tension were relieved or punctured by moments of frank human absurdity. After thirty-one hours of debate, the jury was deadlocked. One juror asked if, on the next day (which happened to be a Sunday), he and his comrades could go see a movie. Murray denied the request, and rumors filtering from the smoky confines of the jury room suggested that tempers ran high. "They're beginning to hate each other," said one observer. "Anything is liable to happen."

Four of the exhibits, the four remaining bullets from Dave Clark's Colt, were taken and hidden in a restroom by juror Judd Wilson, who was worried that one of the others might be taken with the idea of putting the bullets back in the gun for purposes of more efficient persuasion. Occasionally the buzzer rang downstairs, snapping everybody to attention, but it would be one of the twelve, calling for ice water or some other refreshment. At mealtimes the jurors trooped out, got into the bus, and went to the hotel where reporters, controlled by Gilmore and the other bailiffs, were allowed to watch them from a distance of fifty feet, studying their faces and trying to read their minds. Who was the holdout? Was it Juror No. 5? Or more likely, Juror No. 8, the stout old man with the moon-like face who sat apart from the others? "The signature tune of this jury," wrote Coughlin, "is 'WE WANT TO EAT.'" Time dragged on, while the late-August temperatures soared above 100 degrees and the city sweltered through its worst heat wave in five years. When Juror John Langdale collapsed from stress and exhaustion, an ambulance rushed him to the Georgia Street Receiving Hospital, scene of Crawford's death.

The crowds never lessened in number. Thousands came every day, swarming in the corridors. The case made the pages of the distant *New York Times* every day that week, sandwiched between stories about Charles Lindbergh's flying to Japan, Al Capone facing arrest in Chicago, and the call being made by Franklin Delano Roosevelt, then the governor of New York but already touted as a presidential candidate, to tax high-income earners and so provide $20 million in nationwide unemployment relief. In Los Angeles, Coughlin and his friends and rivals raced and scrambled for fresh angles on the Dave Clark story. Waiting drove people half-mad with anticipation, anxiety, and boredom. It was hot, and Coughlin sat in the press room at the Hall of Justice, picking his teeth and fanning himself. The bailiffs tried to persuade some of the mob to go to another court, where a man was about to be sentenced to hang. Somehow that murder didn't catch the imagination the way this one did. Everybody wanted a glimpse of Dave Clark, or his lovely wife Nancy, or Clark's mother and father who were showing their support, or the top lawyer Gilbert, or crafty old Joe Ford, or the jurors—some of them red-eyed and shambling like zombies from lack of sleep.

"This was a cold-blooded murder or it was a shooting in self-defense," Gilbert had said in his final argument, gambling because he thought his case was strong. "Manslaughter or second degree murder cannot be the verdict. Hang Dave Clark or free him." Gilbert had referred frequently to Spencer and Crawford as "habitual gun-toters." He'd said the prosecution was asking the jury to believe the extraordinary coincidence that neither of these men had been armed on May 20, the day of the shootings. The fact that no weapon had been found on either was easily explicable, Gilbert claimed—Crawford had been "dressed" alright, but his weapons had been removed by one of his flunkies and hidden before the police arrived.

Joe Ford had scoffed at this. He'd scorned, too, the notion that because Crawford had been "king of the underworld," it had been somehow acceptable to kill him. "Murder is murder," he'd said in his closing argument, an oratorical performance that filled four hours and fifteen minutes, not counting the time-outs Ford called when he needed to fix his teeth, his "artificial grinders," as the *Times* called them. Ford declared flatly that Dave Clark was a liar. "Look at me, I'm fifty-four years old, Charlie Crawford's exact age," he said, playing up his own infirmities to emphasize the improbability of Crawford having been able to put up much of a struggle against the athletic Clark. "He has been calm and collected, always—too calm and collected," said the prosecutor, assessing the defendant. "He's shown no sign of nerves or perturbation. I tell you, friends, that he shot Herbert Spencer because Spencer was the only living witness to the murder of Crawford—and for no other reason."

Clark's story may well have seemed a little too pat and prepared, but Ford hadn't been able to put a dent in it. After months of investigation the D.A.'s office could offer no persuasive and coherent alternative version of what had happened. Rather, Ford and Fitts were still awash with possibilities. Had blackmail been involved, and scandalous photographs dating back to Clark's prosecution of Albert Marco? Was Guy McAfee behind it all? Had Clark been *planning* to kill Crawford and Spencer, hence arriving with the gun in the waistband of his pants, or had he drunk whiskey with them and killed them in a blind rage during some argument about campaign funds or another electoral issue?

"Dave Clark killed those two men and only he knew why and he never told anybody," Leslie White wrote. "I don't think he was bad all along. I think he was a decent man who got mixed up in the rackets and yanked into situations he couldn't control. Maybe his friend June Taylor knew what happened—and maybe she didn't. I'll never know."

Judge Murray said that, from the strict point of the law, motive wasn't really at issue here; but in people's minds, it mattered—if Clark wasn't telling the truth, then what *was* the truth?

In the end the trial came down to a stark and fascinating question: Who was Dave Clark? Was he "a fine and upright young man," as Gilbert argued, or, in Joe Ford's words, "cruel and cold, a calculating killer"? The *Times* compared Clark not only to John Barrymore but to Clark Gable, who in the very weeks that the trial unfolded was becoming a major star. "GABLE FEVER SOARS HIGHER. GABLE MADNESS!" said the *Times*. Was Dave Clark really like Gable—confident, a little dangerous while being essentially good-hearted, an image of manly cool? Or did devils wrestle inside him? The ultimate unknowability of events that had occurred in a small back room reflected a still darker mystery, that of a man's character.

"The truth is that none of us would show to advantage in the dock. It is a trying situation in which nobody looks their best," wrote William Roughead, the Scottish lawyer and gourmet of murder. Oddly, Clark *had* looked his best. During Joe Ford's final argument, when Ford subjected him to savage attack, Clark kept his eyes not on the ground or the ceiling or on Ford, but on the jury—a reaction, or performance, that impressed reporters and spectators with its apparent openness and honesty.

It was eleven o'clock on Sunday morning when the buzzer sounded yet again and this time the jurors did appear, filing into the jury box they'd left on Thursday afternoon. "Have you reached a verdict?" asked Judge Murray.

"We have not, Your Honor," said Alice Thomas, the jury forewoman. After fifteen ballots the jury was deadlocked, eleven for acquittal, one for guilty.

"Do you believe you can reach agreement?" said Murray.

"I do not," said Thomas.

Each juror was then asked individually if there was any chance of agreement, and each said "no." Murray had no choice but to dismiss the jury and abort proceedings.

Joe Ford, nettled and apparently a little dazed, at once called for a retrial, saying: "I am unable to imagine eleven normal minds arriving at such a ridiculous conclusion."

Nancy Clark, on the other hand, said: "It's tragic, a travesty of justice. It's almost unbelievable that one man, and one man alone, could do this to us."

Eagerly talkative jurors spilled their stories to the hungry press. All the women, it turned out, had been in favor of acquittal from the very first ballot. Indeed, most of them said their minds had been made up before the trial began. "You played me like a piano," one juror said to Gilbert; "I loved you from the first moment," another told Nancy Clark.

"Shucks, fellows, Clark isn't any Sunday school boy," said William Weller, the lone holdout, a seventy-three-year-old former Midwesterner whose no-nonsense puritan values were scarcely softened by his folksy air.

During jury selection Nancy Clark had apparently said, "I

don't trust that mean old man," but Dave had waved aside her fears.

"Oh, those women on the jury! You should have heard them," Weller said. "They didn't want to talk about the evidence. It was, 'Clark was a clean-cut boy. He'd been a flyer. He had a nice family.' Rot! Shucks, I just voted the way I saw it. I never believed him to be innocent. I've never seen a guiltier man."

Somebody got mad, or wanted to get even, and threw a bomb at Weller's house on Carmelina Avenue in West L.A. Weller and his wife were lucky. "INFERNAL MACHINE TOSSED AT HOUSE FAILS TO EXPLODE," said the *Santa Monica Outlook*.

Clark deplored the incident, saying he admired any man who stood by his beliefs. Clark faced retrial but was now granted freedom on bail of $30,000. As he stepped outside County Jail, Nancy reached up and fixed both the treasured Royal Flying Corps pin and a pert pink rose on his lapel. "He's never coming back," she told reporters, and she was right. Clark never did go back, not to that jail anyway.

The second trial fizzled, even though Joe Ford was armed with exact knowledge of Clark's story. Ford didn't look well. He'd lost weight and was ghostly pale. The frailty no longer seemed like a performance to woo the jury, and though he tripped up Clark on a couple of minor inconsistencies, he himself made mistakes, misremembering names and situations. In other ways, too, life's way of just happening conspired to swipe the prosecution. Star witness Mildred Rohrback, now an actress, had during the course of the first trial met and fallen in love with Ed Dudley, an investigator from the D.A.'s office and a colleague of Leslie White's. She and Dudley had married, giving the wily Gilbert an easy handle that he seized to destroy the credibility of Rohrback's testimony. The outcome of this second trial was never in doubt, and the jury acquitted Clark after only a few hours' deliberation. Clark, the brilliant prosecutor, had known that trials can turn into tests of endurance, and he crossed the finish line of this marathon a victor.

"Nancy, the defendant's pretty wife, became almost hysterical with joy, throwing her arms around his neck," wrote the *Times*.

"It certainly is a grand and glorious feeling," Clark told reporters. Not for Joe Ford, who made a point of turning away when Clark offered his hand. Ford resigned immediately as special prosecutor and Buron Fitts saw no point in pursuing the case any further. Clark was never again tried for the killing of Crawford.

Soon after, Joe Ford was at home in Glendale when he was struck down by a heart attack and died. He'd been much loved; this was never more clear than when rich and poor, high and low, office holders and people from the poorer sections of the city crowded St. Vibiana's Cathedral downtown on the occasion of his requiem mass. Dave and Nancy Clark, meanwhile, were out of town, getting away from it all, camping in Yosemite.

Clark shot Crawford and Spencer on May 20, 1931, and by the middle of October he was a free man. His arrest and trial were book-ended by the release of *The Public Enemy* and *Scarface*, two classic Warner Bros. films that were ripped from the headlines. Both are downbeat and brutal films set in the Jazz Age but reflective of the gathering gloom of the Depression. *The Public Enemy* made a star of James Cagney, who shoved a cut grapefruit in his moll's face and whose dangerous, natural, and graceful performance pushed film-acting in a whole new direction. These films still shock even today, though their moral straightforwardness—charting the gangster's rise from the streets and his inevitable downfall—was perhaps even then starting to become outmoded. *The Public Enemy* features an Irish saloon-keeper and "political" boss and big-time bootlegger named Paddy Ryan—in other words a character in some ways like Charlie Crawford. Crawford was readily comprehensible in terms of the violent but simple worlds of *The Public Enemy* and *Scarface.* Dave Clark, whose story offered multiple layers of ambiguity and unknown motive, wasn't at all comprehensible. He was a hero, or a villain, for the coming time—not for the boom era whose funeral rites these early mob films enacted.

Trials that catch the public imagination respond, like movies, to a public need. Los Angeles, in that hot and dark summer of 1931, needed Dave Clark to walk. He had enormous charisma and in those months became a vehicle of people's longing for glamor and integrity. They wanted to believe in his looks, his tan, his family, his wife, his basic decency, the possibilities in his future. He didn't look like a murderer so the city's nascent and embattled Midwestern values raised their heads one more time, calling for him to be innocent. An odd swoon of the zeitgeist ensured his acquittal.

"He is one of our finest Americans," said Alice Thomas, who'd been forewoman of the jury in the first trial and attended the final day of the second, to embrace Dave and Nancy Clark and talk to the press once more. "I think he's grand."

26

A Hooker's Tale

I see they acquitted Dave. It was in the cards. A lot of people don't believe his story but I wish him the best," Leslie White recorded in his diary on October 27, 1931. By then, however, White had more on his mind than Dave Clark's welfare. He, too, faced a crisis, a defining moment.

In the thirty or so months since joining the D.A.'s office, White had worked on more than 200 cases, a couple of which, like the murder/suicide at Greystone and the Crawford/Spencer shootings, had shaken the city. But no previous case consumed him like the Love Mart trial, featuring as it did White's gut hatred of the millionaire John P. Mills and his growing respect for the prostitute Olive P. Day, the witness he'd found and was determined to protect. The dismay that swept over him crystallized as he watched events unfold and contemplated operations of the justice system in which he had a tiny part.

On March 31, 1931, the case against Mills was continued until April 30. On April 30, it was continued until June 18. On June 18, it was continued until July 1. On July 1, it was continued until September 15. This was unusual back then, when trials happened fast. Leslie White's reading of Olive Day's diary had triggered the investigation two months before Clark killed Crawford and Spencer; and now that Clark had been acquitted, Love Mart was still dragging on. Buron Fitts himself agreed to the continuances sought by Mills's defense, puzzling White and making Olive Day nervous. She liked White but didn't trust the D.A.'s office and felt that, some way or another, she'd end up holding the bag. Such had been her experience in life and the world, growing up as a hooker on the streets of Hollywood. White sought to reassure her. He'd been given a free hand in the case so far, and reckoned his superiors would support the promises and choices he made. He told Day everything would be fine.

Then, in the middle of the night, Leslie White got another of those phone calls. An operator down in Long Beach asked if he'd accept reverse charges. Puzzled, White agreed, and moments later found himself talking to Olive Day. Now he was astounded because Day should have been in her cell on the eleventh floor of the Hall of Justice. She begged him to come see her as soon as possible in Long Beach and made him swear not to reveal her whereabouts to anyone.

Next day, on arriving at work, White found himself in the midst of a hue and cry. Olive Day had vanished, he heard. Nobody knew where she was. Apparently goons from Mills's defense team had gotten to her and spirited her away, another example of the kind of witness tampering and removal that Joe Ford reckoned had influenced the Clark trial, especially with regard to June Taylor. White kept quiet, but slipped from the Hall of Justice as soon as he could, got into his car, and sped down to Long Beach.

He found Olive Day hiding in a storeroom, scared out of her wits. She said she'd been awakened around midnight the previous night. It had been the jail matron, telling her that her bail had been posted and she was free to go. Olive Day at once feared a trap. She said she didn't want to leave, but the matron ordered her out. The Hall of Justice was hushed and empty. She rode down in the elevator and was walking through the marbled vault of the lobby when a man stepped from the shadows and asked if she was Olive Day. "No," Day replied, and ran. She got out into the street and jumped in a cab, telling the driver to take her as far toward Long Beach as the two dollars she had in her purse would allow. When the cabbie dumped her, she thumbed a ride on a milk truck, got the rest of the way to Long Beach, and found this hiding place. "I called you, Mr. White, because you've shot square with me," she said. "I honestly believe I'll be killed if the other side gets hold of me."

Had White played by the book, he would have taken Olive Day back to the Hall of Justice. Instead, believing her fear, he made arrangements to hide her, taking her first to a hotel in Glendale. That night he introduced Day to his wife, and the three went to dinner and to a movie. They talked, not about the Love Mart case, but about politics, the weather. Afterward Day burst into tears, telling White she was unused to being treated with such courtesy or respect. The next day White drove this troubled woman to Ventura County and checked her into a small hot springs hotel where he knew she'd be safe. Lucien Wheeler's men were still scouring Los

Angeles for her, and White waited a few days before telling Fitts that he knew where the now-celebrated witness was. A surprised Fitts agreed that Olive Day should be placed under protective guard out in Ventura County, and nodded when White said the D.A.'s office should meet Day's expenses. Thereafter White spent a lot of time with Olive Day, hearing of her plans to help the young girls she'd served up to John P. Mills. There was one who could get work as a beautician, she said—another who was quick and might become a stenographer. White was impressed. "The sulphur springs had cleared her complexion and as she practically lived in a bathing suit on the edge of the swimming pool, she looked well, talked well, and thought well," he said.

On September 15, 1931, the Love Mart trial began. This time the defense sought no continuance. Instead Buron Fitts appeared personally in court and asked that the case against Mills be dismissed, declaring he intended to use Mills as a witness against Jobelman and Day under a separate charge. The judge denied the motion. Fitts then produced a letter from one of the young girls in the case, Clarice Tauber, who had married a few weeks ago and was trying to create a new life for herself. In the letter she'd begged not to be called upon to testify, Fitts said, waving the piece of paper while being careful not to let anybody actually see it. Fitts pleaded that this little girl, now age seventeen, this new bride, should be spared the indignity of having her name in the headlines again.

Again, the judge was unimpressed. He refused to dismiss the case, and Fitts stormed to no avail. The judge ordered him to call his witnesses.

"I have no witnesses," Fitts said. "The girl refuses to testify."

Leslie White, sitting in court, was both furious and mystified. What game was Fitts playing? Later White would observe that this was the moment when the light bulb went on at last and he realized that Buron Fitts had joined the "citywide carousel of graft" and it was "utterly impossible to work in the D.A.'s office and retain any semblance of personal integrity."

The judge was angry, too, but had no choice but to discharge all three defendants on this particular charge. Mills, Jobelman, and Olive Day walked out of the court, apparently free. John P. Mills stepped on out of the Hall of Justice, into his V16 Cadillac, and back into his life, while Jobelman and Day were arrested again at the door. Jobelman promptly turned state's witness so only Day was prosecuted. Within a month she'd been found guilty and was sentenced to five years, indeed left holding the bag as she'd suspected she would all along.

"Don't talk to me about justice. Don't talk to me at all," she told Leslie White. "I should have known better than to trust a cop."

She called him Judas, and White squirmed.

A few weeks later a colleague of Gene Coughlin's on the *Daily News*, a reporter named Charles "Brick" Garrigues, lifted the lid on a stink that would linger around Buron Fitts for the rest of his life. Shortly after being hired by John P. Mills, Lucien Wheeler, Buron Fitts's friend, the former head of the D.A.'s investigative unit and one time presidential bodyguard, had taken $18,000 from Mills and used it to buy a plot of land in Claremont, a seven-acre orange grove valued at $9,000. The title of the orange grove belonged to Buron Fitts's sister. It had been while the sale was being finalized that Fitts had agreed to the numerous trial continuances, and after the sale had been completed that he had sought dismissal of the charges against Mills.

Fitts had taken a bribe. He'd spend the next three years fending off charges, using his investigators as thugs to intimidate his increasing number of enemies, turning his office into an embattled fiefdom while he slogged through trials, never being convicted, but never clearing his name either.

It was a dark time, and an ironic retrospective triumph for Charlie Crawford. After the brief interruption of Mayor Porter's regime, the L.A. System came back in force, working in just the same way as before, though Guy McAfee had supplanted Crawford as the chief who connected City Hall to the underworld. Kent Parrot helped put in place a new mayor, Frank Shaw, who rode in with the customary promises of reform and quickly outdid his predecessors in political and police corruption. Shaw's brother, Joe Shaw, openly sold favors and jobs from City Hall. An LAPD captaincy could be had for $500; unsurprisingly, the department was still riddled with officers owned by the rackets. A secret political police squad was set up to harass, spy upon, and kick around people who dared to indicate they didn't like what was going on. Phones were tapped; wires installed. Gambling and prostitution flourished as never before.

"Big time establishments were about as secret as the Washington Monument," wrote George Creel in an article titled "Unholy City" for *Collier's*, counting 600 brothels by the decade's end, plus 300 casinos running full blast, and 1,800 bookies. Clubs were furnished with the glitz and elegance of movie sets. Crime went on seamlessly pervading L.A.'s body politic, and much of what Charlie Crawford predicted came to pass, in terms of the underworld "running things as they've never been run before."

Crawford got one crucial detail wrong, of course: he was no longer around to pull the strings and run the show. Whether with direct intent or not, Dave Clark played the role of king-making assassin, guaranteeing that power passed conclusively, if temporarily, to his friend and patron Guy McAfee.

"This isn't a city, this is a conspiracy," George Creel wrote, a situation that only started to change when the boodling Shaw brothers were finally handed their hats late in 1938, and Guy McAfee was forced to depart for new pastures.

27

Music of the City

It was Orson Welles who called Los Angeles "a bright and guilty place." In his 1948 film *Lady from Shanghai* the heroine, who is also the villain, a classic *femme fatale*, played by Welles's ex-wife Rita Hayworth, says to the bewildered hero, played of course by Welles himself: "Everything's bad, Michael. Everything. You can't escape it or fight. You've got to get along with it, make terms."

The Love Mart case embittered Leslie White, and the fraying rope of his idealism snapped for good. Some of his friends—like Casey Shawhan, the reporter—regarded the civic structure as a gigantic farce and the public as suckers. "But while they jeered, they paid taxes and did not recognize the public as a collective group of which they were a part," White wrote. "The reformers, 'we,' rode into office like a roaring lion and cast out . . . *individuals*. We did not alter the structure which made these individuals crooked."

White talked things over with his wife, then went to see Buron Fitts and quit. "I liked the work, most of it," he said to Fitts. "But I hate politics."

Fitts asked why.

"You can't stay in it and be honest," White said. "You've got to barter in politics, and that's the beginning of corruption. Sooner or later you get jammed up. You know that, better than I do."

Buron Fitts went red in the face.

White was lucky and didn't have to "make terms." Writing gave him another option. He went to New York, met with editors, and was soon cranking out more for the pulps: "Dynamite Molls" and "Lucky Crash" for *Detective Story Magazine,* "The Phantom Killer" for *Far East Adventure Stories,* and "C.I.D.: Secret Inks" for *Detective Action Stories* were all published in the final months of 1931. He created tough, honest cops who treated their job like a religion. In "The Last Wayne," published in the *Saturday Evening Post,* he wrote: "Big Terry Wayne went into a basement hideout after several mugs of the Ritter mob. Since there were only five of the gang present, Big Terry barged in alone. Ordinarily, that would have been alright, but one of these five guys was carrying a load of cocaine when Big Terry pushed his foot through the door panel. And when a rodman is high, even a Wayne doesn't look impregnable, so the snowbird went for his gun and managed to sink a slug through Big Terry's ribs."

This is pretty silly writing, but not without gusto. White, tireless, turned his hand to nonfiction too. He wrote a series of articles for *Better Homes and Gardens* about the buying, training, and caring for Scottish terriers. "I'm getting along in years now; not old, you understand, but I've sure seen a lot of doggy friends come and go," ran one piece, written from the point of view of Sandy, White's own dog. He covered flying, deep-sea diving, forensics, and the investigative process for the *Saturday Evening Post*. "The average American citizen regards the work of the police as a major sporting proposition, akin to baseball. He views it objectively, as though it were of no personal concern," he wrote, though he himself was no longer an average citizen and knew that the effects of police work were not akin to those of sport. White studied his markets with care and made good as a writer. He missed the adventure of investigation, but earned more money now. Called upon to address Rotary Clubs, he trotted out stories of derring-do. He moved out of Los Angeles, heading north to Santa Cruz where he bought a place and named it "Mystery Ranch."

White's life changed further when he began visiting the aging Lincoln Steffens in Carmel; theirs turned into an important friendship. "Leslie White, former detective, cultural troglodyte, and Red-baiter, drove down frequently from his ranch near Santa Cruz," wrote Justin Kaplan in his 1974 biography of Steffens, a funny if somewhat unfair snapshot. "White underwent a complete transformation, found himself radicalized and considerably heightened in awareness, perception and self-confidence."

Steffens lived a hundred yards from the ocean in a house with a wild, irregular garden; it was in this house that he'd written his already famous *Autobiography*, published in 1931. White had read this book that, in its questioning of wealth and power, turned many leftward during the Depression. Steffens gave context to White's dissatisfactions.

He told him: "You can commit any crime, break any rule of etiquette, violate any custom, but they will never forgive you for using your head, for thinking." Steffens listened to White's stories and suggested that he write a book about his time in law enforcement. He fixed up White with his own publisher—Harcourt, Brace—and even gave White a title for the book.

White's memoir, *Me, Detective*, was published by Harcourt, Brace in 1935. It's easily his best work, a jazzy account of his experiences in Ventura County and with the D.A.'s office. White grappled with his growing disillusion and drew admiration from Carey McWilliams, as well as others. The memoir did well, prompting Harcourt, Brace to commission two novels, *Harness Bull* and *Homicide*, which White wrote quickly, although with more thought than his pulp stories. These books were published in 1936 and 1937 respectively, and like *Me, Detective* still await a reprint. They're early police procedurals, notable for neat and clever construction.

Harness Bull takes place in a day, a night, another day. It's prefaced by a glossary, a guide to cop and lowlife vernacular, "S'Language," as White calls it. Thus: "fish" = prisoner; "bindle" = small quantity of narcotics; "croaker" = physician; "typewriter" = machine-gun; "foreign talent" = crooks from other cities; "noble" = boss strike-breaker; "show-up" = parade of prisoners for observation; "yegg" = tough character; "whips and jingles" = case of nerves. The action concerns the routine of a police captain, Barnaby, and the pressures he's under.

"The constant attendance at the shrine of politics was starting to wear on his nerves," White writes. "A machine-appointed mayor put in a police commissioner whom he could control and who in turn commanded the police department." Barnaby's cases involve a jewelry heist, a bank-job, the attempt to enroll police support to break a strike. "Everything was confused and intricate in its workings, plain in its manifestations," White notes, and he knows this world; he's describing the L.A. System, even though he never names the city and the writing sometimes makes us feel it through cotton wool, if not blocks of wood. "It was her very earnest-ness that caused her to assume that air of almost maternal protectiveness and in the four years that she had been his secretary, Jenny had made herself indispensable," goes one passage. "Chuckling softly, he wondered how Mrs. Kenner would react to the square-hulled sergeant."

Homicide is cast in the form of a documentary of an investigation, with crime scene reports, witness interviews, trial transcripts, radio bulletins, newspaper clippings, and autopsy details. All these are framed in a series of letters from a fictional detective, Steve Muttersbach, who writes in a vaguely Runyonesque style. The letters, and all the other materials, are presented as if sent to Leslie White himself on his Mystery Ranch at Santa Cruz. "The defense fought like hell to get a lot of middle-aged dames on the jury, on the theory that a motherly dame would not order the hemp for a pretty looking boy," notes Muttersbach, and White was remembering Dave Clark. The form of the book was original for the time and, like all White's stuff, gallops along.

Writers don't really write what they know; they write what they can. White had a quick, agile mind and an undauntable temperament. He didn't look too deep but moved restlessly on. He was thorough and inquisitive, capable of making himself expert in whatever caught his imagination; but his fiction brings with it no feeling of danger and no whiff of the physical presence of Los Angeles whatsoever. *Harness Bull* and *Homicide* made almost no use of the notorious cases in which White had been involved. Nor do they show any interest in scene or place or mood. It was as if, having escaped L.A., White refused to let the city again affect or infect him.

Others, though, soon caught the disease. With the development of talking pictures, and the onset of the Depression, writers from all over the English-speaking world swarmed to L.A. Hoping to work for the studios, they found themselves assailed by the city's color, flora, and climate—its unique atmosphere. A few, such as Daniel Fuchs, extolled California's "happy, lazy days." Most found their material in the shadows. Charles G. Booth arrived from the north of England, yet his 1933 *Black Mask* story "Stag Party" is a direct reflection of the struggle for control of the rackets that involved Guy McAfee and Charlie Crawford, right down to the names of the characters. Paul Cain drew upon this same background in "Fast One," depicting a savage hardboiled world of racketeers, molls, losers, blighted buildings, political infighting, and gambling ships.

Horace McCoy came to L.A. from Texas in 1931, hoping for a career as an actor. By then he'd been a flyer and had already published a number of stories in *Black Mask*, action-packed shoot-'em-ups about a Texas Air Ranger named Jerry Frost. In L.A. his acting career amounted to only a few bit parts, but he landed a job as a contract writer for RKO, then one of the big studios, and a new wife—his third—Helen Vinmont, the daughter of a wealthy oil man. The existential absurdities of low- and high-life in Los Angeles then became his subject. He began a short story, "Marathon Dance," later expanded to novella length and retitled *They Shoot Horses, Don't They?*, featuring a pair of Hollywood wannabes who starve and degrade themselves through the hundreds of hours of a dance marathon, such contests being a grisly symptom of the Depression. The contest takes place in a barn-like hall at the end of the Santa Monica pier while the surf rolls and crashes beneath. "It's peculiar to me," says Gloria, the heroine, "that everybody pays so much attention to living and so little to dying." She wants to commit suicide but doesn't have the guts, so the exhausted hero does the job for her, shooting her in the head with a revolver he pitches into the oblivious depths of the Pacific.

They Shoot Horses, Don't They? was published in 1935, and Charlie Chaplin wanted to film it at once. The material was too bleak, however, too closely representative of its time, showing a society traumatized by unemployment yet still driven by bogus myths of success and freedom. It reads with the intensity and inevitability of a nightmare, written in a stark simplicity and despair that in no way resembles McCoy's earlier writing, as if what McCoy saw and felt in the first months after his arrival in L.A. acted on him like a blow to the head.

The historian Carey McWilliams said he had to keep pinching himself as a reminder to get down on paper the city's abnormal world, but he could never break out of the trance long enough to do it. The shock of arrival, the newness and strangeness of what struck them, stirred writers like McCoy. Others were impressed, released almost, by what they heard—the sound of California, the direct, accentless, and immediate way people spoke. James M. Cain, a former managing editor of *The New Yorker*, a womanizer and a drunk, arrived, like McCoy, in 1931. In his pocket he had a Paramount contract, though he would never achieve much as a screenwriter. Instead he unexpectedly found his fictional voice. The loose energy of Southern California's language and the intensity of its psychic geography released Cain's fascination with tabloid murder into the urgent first-person confessionals of *The Postman Always Rings Twice* (1934), *Double Indemnity* (1936), and *Serenade* (1937). The later and slightly different *Mildred Pierce* (1941) actually opens in 1931, the year Cain rolled into town, with a guy clipping his hedge in Glendale, unable to accept that he's been wiped out in the crash and still dreaming of the "vast deeds he would do when things got a little better." Cain's stories are driven by frustration, disappointment, and a bluntly amoral lust for transformative cash that seems very particular to L.A., both then and perhaps still. Murder might just be a necessary step along the way.

28

Black Mask
Merry-Go-Round

The greatest single chronicler of L.A.'s gathering malaise, its sunlit moods of loss and hopelessness, had been here all along, or since 1912 anyway. I mean Raymond Chandler who, like Leslie White, switched careers at the height of the Depression. In Chandler's case, the move was involuntary. He lost his high-paying job as an executive in the oil business, fired by Joseph Dabney in 1932.

Quite likely, Dabney was looking to cut loose employees and restructure his business at that point, and Chandler's skirt-chasing and lost weekends provided an easy excuse. Chandler, drunk most of the time, was abusing the lawyers he had hired and Dabney paid for. An envious colleague, John Abrams, drove all the way from L.A. to Dabney's cabin at Big Bear for the specific purpose of informing on Chandler. Abrams told this story with pride to Chandler biographer Frank MacShane. The plan worked: Chandler was tossed out on his ear and for a while thought about bringing suit against Abrams for slander. Instead, he gained revenge in a more delicious way, dishing insider dirt on Dabney's operations to his old friend Warren Lloyd, who'd invited Chandler to L.A. in the first place. The Lloyd family was involved in a lawsuit with Dabney over disputed revenues from an oil field in Ventura. Chandler's dope helped the Lloyds win their suit.

The whole episode has a nice heft to it, stopping short of violence but bristling with arrows of human malice and foible. The Lloyds thanked Chandler by giving him an allowance of $100 a month, money without which he and his wife Cissy would never have kept themselves afloat through the very tough coming years. By the end of 1932 Chandler had already changed his listing in the Los Angeles directory, giving his occupation, more than a little hopefully, as "writer." Literary ambition had never left him, and he was determined, more than twenty years after the flop in London, to try again. Unlike Leslie White, however, he had no facile knack for story; and also unlike White, he was no longer young. He was forty-four, angry and despondent, an alcoholic, a self-destructive and divided man thrown on a new course.

"Wandering up and down the Pacific Coast in an automobile, I began to read pulp magazines, because they were cheap enough to throw away," Chandler later wrote. "This was in the great days of the *Black Mask* (if I may call them great days) and it struck me that some of the writing was forceful and honest . . ." He decided this might be a good way to try to learn to write fiction and get paid while he was learning. For Chandler, it proved a long and difficult process. His career, like Los Angeles itself, built slowly and took off with a series of rocket-like explosions. The early and the middle years of the 1930s entailed a torturous grind, but between 1939 and 1943 he would publish four novels: *The Big Sleep*; *Farewell, My Lovely*; *The High Window*; and *The Lady in the Lake*. And then Hollywood ("the golden graveyard" as he named it) came calling, in the dapper and impish form of director Billy Wilder, with whom he cowrote the classic script for *Double Indemnity*. Other screenplays followed, notably for *The Blue Dahlia*, and Chandler was at last flush again. His great success came, as producer John Houseman observed, when his creative days were almost over.

Before the fame and the money Chandler scraped a bare living, often earning less than $1,000 a year. It was a long slog through the 1930s, through the pages of the pulps and the years of the Depression. There were whole days when he and Cissy had nothing to eat but canned soup; they never starved but sometimes came close. He wrote twenty stories until *The Big Sleep*—twenty stories in seven years, a period during which Leslie White published a memoir, three novels, a couple of screenplays, and more than fifty first-person articles for the slicks, in addition to the pulp tales he sold almost monthly. White was a factory; Chandler, by the standards of the time, a trickle—but there was the matter of quality.

To make a beginning, Chandler read a novella by a star in the market: Erle Stanley Gardner, Leslie White's friend. Chandler made a synopsis of the novella and wrote from that, then rewrote, and rewrote again. This first story, which Chandler called "Blackmailers Don't Shoot," took five months to complete. Joseph Shaw bought it for *Black Mask* in 1933 for a fee of $180—nowhere near enough to cover living expenses through the time of composition, but the first tiny miracle in Chandler's writing life had occurred. He wasn't prolific but he sold what he wrote thereafter, and Shaw knew that he'd found a different sort of talent. Much later, Chandler said that his early stories worked because they carried with them "a smell of fear"—his own fear of failure, fear of violence, fear of death. They were about "a world gone wrong, a world in which, long before the atom bomb, civilization had created the machinery for its own destruction, and was learning to use it with all the moronic delight of a gangster trying out his first machine-gun. The law was something to be manipulated for profit and power. The streets were dark with something more than night."

Something more than night: the phrase has become famous, suggesting an inner darkness that might exist during the brilliance of the day. All of Chandler's early stories are cynical about motive and character, and all are set in the same place—a corrupted but still beautiful place, the bright and guilty place: Los Angeles. In "Spanish Blood," which made the cover of *Black Mask* for November 1935, political boss Donegan Marr is found shot dead in his office. "A cigar had gone out in a tray with a bronze greyhound on its rim. His left hand dangled beside the chair and his right hand held a gun loosely on the desk top. The polished nails glittered in sunlight from the big closed window behind him."

The bronze greyhound at the tray's edge, the shiny fingernails of the corpse: these are the clinchers, exact details of the kind that Leslie White and a vast majority of pulp writers had no wish, or talent, to observe. "Spanish Blood" lays out its plot and backstory. "He was a lone wolf," says one of the investigating cops to the other, talking about the gray-haired Donegan Marr. "In a few more years he'd have taken the town over."

The cop notices an appointment book. Somebody called Imlay had been due in Marr's office at twelve-fifteen. The second cop, the hero, Pete Delaguerra, looks at the cheap watch on his wrist and says, "One-thirty. Long gone. Who's Imlay? . . . Say, wait a minute! There's an assistant D.A. named Imlay. He's running for judge . . ." A few pages later, Delaguerra talks to Donegan Marr's widow, Belle. "This Imlay is running for judge with the backing of the Masters-Age group," Delaguerra says. "It seems he's been playing house with a night-club number called Stella LaMotte. Somehow, someway, photos were taken of them together. Very drunk and undressed. Donny got the photos, Belle. They were found in his desk. According to his desk pad he had a date with Imlay at twelve-fifteen. We figure they had a row and Imlay beat him to the punch."

In this early story Chandler recycles details of Charlie Crawford's death at the hand of Dave Clark, an event that had snagged in the writer's mind and surfaced again. Did Chandler suspect that work he'd done while with Joseph Dabney was part of the twisting chain of events that led to Crawford's death? Perhaps. The connection was real, though several links back from the moment when Dave Clark's newly bought Colt spat flame and caused death in the back office of 6665 Sunset Boulevard. What's important is that Chandler was a part of all this, not merely an observer. The history of Los Angeles through the late 1920s and early 1930s sank into his blood and became a part of his writerly DNA because he'd been a minor player in that history. He'd felt its breath. Chance and the loss of his job forced him to turn to the pulps, but L.A. made him the only kind of writer he could have become. Chandler remembered and used one of

Clark's suggested motives, namely that someone had taken compromising photographs somewhere down the line. Chandler's fiction abounds in blackmailers who get what's coming to them (or don't), in crooked D.A.s, violent cops, exhausted cops, disinterested cops, tough cops that can be greased but aren't all bad, shyster lawyers, sinister racketeers, bent doctors, victim chauffeurs, seedy pornographers, gamblers too slick for their own good, and always the ruthless rich who do as they will and expect to buy their way out of whatever jam they land in. Philip Marlowe becomes a private eye after having been an investigator for the D.A.'s office, leaving when he realizes he can no longer live in that compromised world—like Leslie White.

Frequently Marlowe finds himself calling upon wealth. At the end of the 1930s Chandler began to plan full-length books. Like everything else in his career, this happened in an unusual way: he cannibalized his pulp stories, carving great chunks out of them, fusing and adding characters, picking out scenes, themes, sentences, paragraphs, and blending everything, amazingly, into his great early novels. At the beginning of the first of them, *The Big Sleep*, Marlowe is summoned to the Sternwood place, a vast pile with an enormous hothouse at the side, containing a steaming jungle of tropical plants like the famed collection the Dohenys maintained in their own enormous hothouse at Chester Place. The Sternwoods, too, have made their money in oil; and General Sternwood himself, with whom Marlowe has an interview, is an old man with Mexican connections and a sentimental fondness for the IRA. In the second novel, *Farewell, My Lovely*, Chandler has Marlowe visiting a big residence that resembles the other Doheny mansion,

Greystone, making the joke that he owed to Leslie White about the place being smaller than Buckingham Palace and having fewer windows than the Chrysler Building. It's here that Marlowe encounters the special kinds of light and silence that extreme wealth can buy. In the next book, *The High Window*, when confronted by a couple of jaded detectives, Marlowe asks if they remember "the Cassidy case."

One of the cops sighs and, as if knowing what's coming, says: "Murder and suicide during a drinking spree. The secretary went haywire and shot young Cassidy. I read it in the papers or something. Is that what you want me to say?"

Marlowe replies:

You read it in the papers, but it wasn't so. What's more you knew it wasn't so and the D.A. knew it wasn't so and the D.A.'s investigators were pulled off the case within a matter of hours. There was no inquest. But every crime reporter and every cop on every homicide detail knew it was Cassidy that did the shooting, that it was Cassidy that was crazy drunk, that it was the secretary who tried to handle him and couldn't and at last tried to get away from him but wasn't quick enough. Cassidy's was a contact wound and the secretary's was not. The secretary was left-handed and he had a cigarette in his left hand when he was shot. Even if you are right-handed, you don't change a cigarette over to your other hand and shoot a man casually while holding the cigarette. They might do that on "Gang Busters," but rich men's secretaries don't do it. And what were the family and the family doctor doing during the four hours they didn't call the cops? Fixing it so there would only be a superficial investigation. And why were no tests made on the hands for nitrates? Because you didn't want the truth. Cassidy was too big.

Raymond Chandler hated big money and the opportunities for negligence and the abuse of power that big money gives to those who possess it. "Young Cassidy" shot the secretary and then himself, Marlowe believed, just as Chandler believed that Ned Doheny shot Hugh Plunkett then himself, even though the Doheny family made sure that in the official version of the story Hugh Plunkett got the blame. In this, Chandler agreed with Leslie White—indeed, White was the source of his information.

On January 11, 1936, Chandler attended a get-together for *Black Mask* writers living on the West Coast. It was the only time he and Dashiell Hammett were ever in the same room. A photograph of the event was taken by Leslie White, who kept himself out of the shot this time, unlike that earlier occasion by what remained of the St. Francis Dam. But White met Chandler at least this once, and perhaps more often. Chandler read *Me, Detective* and drew on White's account of the Doheny murder/suicide for the words he put in Marlowe's mouth in *The High Window*. There's nothing surprising here. As said, L.A.'s sensational crimes and history of graft were part of the raw material upon which Chandler drew as he imagined the city into life. He became a haunting poet of place—this place, L.A., whose split personality of light and dark mirrored his own. He caught the glaring sun, the glittering swimming pools, the cigar-stinking lobbies of seedy hotels, the improbable mansions, the dismal apartment buildings, the sound of tires on asphalt and gravel, the sparkling air of the city after rain and the smell of fog at the beach at night. The talk, lights, smells, people, streets, and buildings of L.A. cling to and issue from his fiction.

The 1938 story "Red Wind" begins with a famous description of what the city is like when the bad winds blow, when the eyes burn and the scalp screams, and the Pacific turns ominous and glassy, like a sheet of bronze. "There was a desert wind blowing that night. It was one of those hot dry Santa Anas that come down through the mountain passes and curl your hair and make your nerves jump and your skin itch. On nights like that every booze party ends in a fight. Meek little wives feel the edge of the carving knife and study their husbands' necks. Anything can happen."

What's remarkable, though, is the way Chandler seizes this idea in "Red Wind" and runs with it, turning a pulp story into an extended prose poem through which the winds gust with an insane, constantly redoubled ferocity—scorching, swirling dust and torn paper. Chairs creak harshly. The tobacco in Marlowe's cigarette is so dry that it burns like grass. "It was a small house, near a canyon rim out beyond Sawtelle, with a circle of writhing eucalyptus trees in front of it," Marlowe notes, while across the street somebody is having delirium tremens in their front yard. "Everywhere along the way gardens were full of withered and blackened leaves and flowers which the hot wind had burned." The observed details are brilliant and instantly recognizable; Chandler is writing about a city that seems to be in screaming agony.

29

Sad Song

"I think that Dave Clark's head has been turned by adulation and ambition. He has a handsome face and a fine physique but I'm afraid that he has lost his soul," Joe Ford had said, and many had assumed this was rhetoric, a prosecutor laying it on thick in the hope of securing a verdict. How could a jury look into the coolness of Dave Clark's eyes and pronounce that he had lost or killed something inside? A soul is an amorphous concept, and people can rush on without one.

Having been acquitted, Clark left the firm of Wellborn, Wellborn & Wellborn, and set up his own legal practice. His primary client was his friend Guy McAfee, the gambling lord; Clark became a gangland lawyer, and was paid well for it, though he spent whatever he earned. He was reckless with money, as always. Toward the end of March 1933, Nancy Clark was about to board an El Paso-bound train, planning to cross from Texas into Mexico to obtain a quicky divorce from her husband. In the art-deco hall of L.A.'s Union Station, with the ticket in her hand, she changed her mind, turning on her heel to return home to their new and bigger house at 554 Moreno Drive. "I just talked with Dave and we've decided we could never, never separate. We love each other too much," she told a reporter from the *Times*. "There will be no divorce. It was just a little family spat—I have a temper and that is the trouble."

Clark was on the front pages again in January 1937 when he left for San Francisco, telling Nancy that he was involved in a big deal, and disappeared. "Dave Clark vanished as completely as if he had been swallowed up by the earth beneath him," wrote *Liberty* magazine. Days went by, and Nancy was hysterical, afraid that Dave had been kidnapped and killed for the large sum of cash he'd been carrying with him—about $5,000. After several weeks, with no money to pay the bills, Nancy started selling the furniture and placed their latest new home, an even grander residence at 131 S. Rossmore Avenue, up for sale. On March 15 a headline appeared on the front page of the *New York Times:* "MISSING AMERICAN FOUND." Dave Clark was in Nice, France, having checked into an expensive hotel carrying nothing but a cane and "without so much as a five centime piece in his pocket." The American Consul in Nice, Richard Hull, was notified, and word was sent to Nancy.

Clark told the story of his wanderings to a Los Angeles reporter. He'd visited the areas of France where he'd served in WWI, but had found everything changed. "Things aren't the same now," he said. He'd traveled through Italy, following a route that he and Nancy had once taken in happier days, and had left his bags at the Hotel Excelsior in San Remo, where they had stayed together. "I've been here in Nice for about a month. And I am broke," he said. "There was no trouble at home that caused me to leave. At least it wasn't real trouble. I had a lot of debts and too many things to think about and I guess I just went screwy. I guess I have just been plain crazy."

He sent word to Nancy. "She's the only woman in the world I have ever loved. I want her to know that I could never love anyone else," he said.

Richard Hull, the consul, said Clark had told him "he was insane and without the courage to commit suicide."

"I'd sell my last ring and go to him in burlap if necessary," Nancy told a reporter, trying to figure how to bring her husband home. Guy McAfee took care of that, wiring Clark $600 for a ticket, and Clark arrived back in New York aboard the American Export liner *Excalibur* on April 2, 1937, "well-dressed and in an amiable mood," according to the *New York Times*. He left the downtown pier where the liner docked and asked a cabbie the fare to the Commodore Hotel in midtown Manhattan. Not having the money, he took the subway instead.

Five months later, it was Nancy's turn to make the headlines. "WIFE OF D. H. CLARK, EX-PROSECUTOR OF LOS ANGELES, IS RELEASED AFTER NIGHT IN LOCK-UP," said the *New York Times* on November 27, 1937. Nancy, unable to pay her hotel bill, had been arrested; she was forced to sell her mink coat, valued by detectives at $3,000 or more, to raise the money. By then she and Dave were separated, and she was living in an apartment in Hollywood. She'd followed her husband to New York, however, registering at a Lexington Avenue hotel under the name Mrs. Natalie Crane. She secured her release from jail quickly enough, but by now the marriage was over. Nancy finally divorced her husband in Reno on July 10, 1939, on grounds of desertion. Clark's annual income at that time was $52,000. Within days he was remarried, in Tijuana, to a wealthy divorcee and society figure, Mrs. Richmond Edwards, formerly Dorothea Jump, daughter of Jimmy Jump, the millionaire and record-holding sports fisherman who had befriended the Clarks on Catalina Island all those years before. The newlyweds honeymooned on *The Lively Lady*, a yacht that Clark now owned. During the course of the war years, Dave and Dorothea had three children; but she divorced him on February 1, 1946, in Reno, charging that he spent too much on booze and often left her alone. She married him again on March 3, 1946, in Yuma, Arizona, and divorced him for the second and final time on September 17, 1947. This rollercoaster ride of a relationship suggested something of the passion and chaos that the suave Clark created around himself. He had power over women, but never enough control of himself.

Clark's life spiraled downward. His friend and patron Guy McAfee, run out of Los Angeles at last, had decamped to Nevada, where in 1938 he opened a gambling club on Highway 91, a few miles short of Las Vegas. Recalling L.A.'s Sunset Strip, McAfee named the highway in front of his joint "The Strip." "McAfee stumbled into history," notes the writer David Thomson.

Clark's law practice foundered and for a while he lived obscurely as the operator of a small store near Costa Mesa— the days of the yachts long gone—and he often drifted down into Mexico, driving about. Some friends remained loyal, however, and he was taken in by George Blair, another lawyer, a colleague from USC in the early 1920s. Clark stayed with Blair and his wife Rose "Toots" Blair through the summer and fall of 1953. On Armistice Day, November 11, there was a family party. After the guests had departed, George Blair, drunk, passed out on the sofa. "I heard a kind of explosion, like a backfire. I didn't get up, not right at first. I lay there some little time," Blair said later. "Then I kind of sat up and looked around the room. Dave was sitting there in a chair.

"I said to him, 'Where's Toots?' He looked at me then. He said, 'I killed her.'"

Blair found his wife in the kitchen, lying on the step, dead in a pool of blood with her shoulder blown off and the door blown open. Clark had killed her with a shotgun after an argument about him "mooching" on the family. So he went on trial for murder for the third time in his life.

Before the trial began, though, Nancy Clark, going by her maiden name of Nancy Malone, died of a broken heart in her Los Angeles apartment on New Year's Day. She'd never remarried, and was buried in Calvary Cemetery on Whittier Boulevard in East Los Angeles. Dave Clark changed his not-guilty plea to that of guilty of murder in the second degree, and on January 30 was given a sentence of five years to life. He would serve less than three weeks. In Chino Prison he suffered a brain hemorrhage and died on February 20, 1954.

So concluded the story of Dave Clark and Nancy Malone, bound together in death as they had been in life, like characters in a tragic and romantic ballad. She left him and never stopped loving him while each day ruing the fact that they'd ever met. The murder of Rose "Toots" Blair threw a backward light on the shootings of Crawford and Spencer, and though what precisely had happened in the iron-shuttered star chamber of 6665 Sunset Boulevard would still never be established, it was impossible now for anybody to believe in Clark's blamelessness and innocence. Perhaps that's what broke

Nancy in the end. She knew she could no longer pretend to accept the lie. Dave was a killer, a once upright, brave, and hopeful young man who went bad, drawn into the rackets and unable to control the self-destructive sexual drive or murderous rages he was slick enough to cover up only after the event.

30

Lives Go On

Lucien Wheeler, the capable Notre Dame graduate, presidential bodyguard, FBI man, private eye, and short-lived head of the D.A.'s investigative unit, headed up the West Coast office of OSS, forerunner of the CIA, during WWII. He died in 1950 and his grandchildren are active in political life today. Blayney Matthews quit the D.A.'s office and was, for more than twenty years, the head of security at Warner Bros. No doubt he knew where plenty of bodies were buried.

C. C. Julian, the pied piper of Julian Pete, died of a drug overdose presumed a suicide at a Shanghai Hotel in 1934; he received a pauper's funeral. For years people chased Jake Berman (aka Jake Bennett) and the loot he'd stashed in banks around the world, but both money and the "two-name man" contrived to elude pursuers.

E. L. Doheny died on September 8, 1935, never having recovered from the stroke that struck him soon after his final acquittal. His wife Estelle buried him, not with his son Ned and his first wife Carrie in Forest Lawn, but in another family mausoleum at Calvary Cemetery in East L.A. As it happened, Nancy Clark would be laid to rest nearby eighteen years later. Nancy's grandchildren and great-grandchildren, the descendants of the daughter she brought with her when she married Dave Clark, remember her with fondness.

Examiner reporter Morris Lavine wrote a novel while he was in jail, and on his release campaigned for the governor's pardon. He got one, and became a celebrated attorney, fighting cases to the Supreme Court and living into his eighties. When he died, his daughter took over the firm he'd created. "There was a lot more to my dad than the melee over the $75,000," she told me.

Gene Coughlin lived a long life of writing and reporting, a newsman of the old school. The Reverend Bob Shuler lost his radio station and his magazine, lost a tumultuous campaign in which he ran for California senator, lost much of his power and vanished from the big public stage; but he went on pounding away from the pulpit. The Reverend Gustav Briegleb became a private eye for a while, but then he too returned to preaching. W. I. Gilbert died suddenly in 1941, while still one of the city's most sought-after defense attorneys.

In 1937 Buron Fitts was wounded by a volley of shots while leaving his home—another episode in the struggle for control of the Los Angeles underworld. Fitts reached a troubled accommodation with the regime of Mayor Frank Shaw, holding onto his position as D.A. when Shaw was booted out in 1938. In 1940, though, Fitts failed in his bid for yet another term. He rejoined the Army with the rank of major, and in WWII served with distinction in North Africa, Europe, and the Pacific. In 1973, old and infirm, he put a handgun to his head and pulled the trigger, killing himself.

Clara Bow's attempts at a comeback failed. She married her boyfriend Rex Bell and had children with him, but suffered numerous nervous breakdowns. She died in 1965, just as a new generation of critics started looking at silent films and got ready to champion the importance of her career. "It was people like Clara Bow who taught cameras how lucky they were," writes David Thomson in *A Biographical Dictionary of Film.*

Guy McAfee prospered in Las Vegas, where historians tend to ignore him in favor of more glamorous figures like Bugsy Siegel. But then nobody ever shot McAfee in the eye with a rifle. He died, old and rich and apparently happy, in his bed, while still a large shareholder in The Golden Nugget and The Last Frontier, two of the casinos he'd founded.

Raymond Chandler was seventy years old when he died in 1959. By then he'd been living for years in La Jolla, north of San Diego, having finally been exhausted by the city whose bard he remains. His detective Marlowe is always getting drugged or smacked on the head, blackouts and amnesia being standard plot devices in Chandler's work. In a similar way, noir film and fiction have become, for Los Angeles, forms of forgetting, a system of lenses through which the city has chosen to observe—and often distort—its past. People tend to take their water history from *Chinatown,* and the Black Dahlia murder is known primarily through the fictive product of John Gregory Dunne and James Ellroy. The history of the bombing of the *Times* building in 1910, as yet unfilmed and the subject of few books, is scarcely known at all; the Greystone tragedy is seen in fragments, in biographies of E. L. Doheny or studies of Teapot Dome; and Chandler's prose is often recommended as the best source for getting a sense of what L.A. actually feels like, even today.

The external fabric of Los Angeles—its buildings and how they look—is in a constant state of flux and evolution, hence the city's value and reputation as a playground for architects. But while much does feel new—and always somehow temporary and insubstantial in the too-bright light, as Scott Fitzgerald said all those years ago—the barnacles and growing residue of history have become harder to ignore, even here where history tends to mean the history of forgetting and rewriting.

Greystone itself, still situated on Loma Vista Drive in Los Angeles, was far too extravagant a production to be knocked down or monkeyed with in any substantial way. Lucy, Ned Doheny's widow, remarried and raised their five children in the house, choosing to live with the phantoms. When the family was raised and the Dohenys had left, Greystone was bought by the City of Beverly Hills in 1964. The mansion features as a location in many movies, including *The Witches of Eastwick*, *The Big Lebowski*, *Attack from Mars*, and most recently, *There Will Be Blood*, loosely based on Upton Sinclair's 1925 novel *Oil!*, and so remains connected to the Doheny story in more ways than one. The events of the night of February 16–17, 1929, provide one of L.A.'s central mysteries—typical in being only vaguely remembered and a metaphor for power's secret reach and power's ultimate futility. Leslie White had entered the majestic hallway at Greystone with understandable trepidation, daunted by the splendor of the furnishings and the vaulting height of the leaded windows, which today provide the same stunning views, albeit of a transformed city. The silence, when the heavy doors shut in that hallway, is still striking. Greystone is a haunted time capsule, magnificent but mad and melancholy, imbued with the dark past of the city whose destiny E. L. Doheny transformed with a pick and shovel.

Charlie Crawford's lair at 6665 Sunset Boulevard is now a sex shop (he'd have no doubt smiled at that), but his grand Beverly Hills villa stands and is the residence of a successful movie producer. Sunset Boulevard—along which Dave Clark fled in his yellow Ford Roadster—is still a long and curving road, both immensely dangerous and immensely romantic, flanked by swank homes as it sweeps ocean-ward. Downtown, many of the movie theaters and huge numbers of office buildings that shot up in the 1920s are still there, though shabbier now and featuring street-level storefronts with signs in Spanish or Chinese or Korean—fine buildings in their way and surprisingly solid, by no means ghosts. The neighborhood is in the midst of a "revival," a contemporary booster ploy, and some grand structures get new lives as lofts, galleries, restaurants.

The gray granite Hall of Justice has been empty for years. It suffered damage in the Northridge earthquake of 1994, the same tremor that my then bungalow home survived by wafting its flimsy walls in rhythm to the movement of the earth. The Hall of Justice is boarded up and fenced off, dwarfed on two sides by newer and taller buildings, awaiting rehabilitation like a forgotten prisoner.

Leslie White kept going, undaunted and indomitable, an oddball who, once he got into stuff, went all the way. In the late 1930s, inspired by the example of Lincoln Steffens, White started a muckraking magazine, *Focus*, and was soon in trouble for publishing his crime-scene photographs of the corpses at Greystone. He went on selling crime stories to the pulps and to Hollywood, though his writing career fizzled for a time at the outset of WWII. By the end of the war, however, he had met Helen, who would become his third wife, while driving a cab through the streets of Los Angeles. Together they sailed a boat around America to the East Coast where they bought a small farm in Virginia. White raised herds of Aberdeen Angus and became president of the local beef cattle association and of the local farm bureau. Occasionally, on a summer night, he would gather his children on the porch in the dark and tell stories. "It wasn't a nightly or a weekly occurrence, but he was a fabulous vocal storyteller," his daughter told me. "He was quite a reticent man. But even at the end of his life he was bothered by what he'd seen in the flood after the dam burst."

White was also president of the National Model Railroad Association, and his family have kept his original model train layout in the barn where he made it. Through the late 1940s and 1950s he published another string of books, historical novels this time, with titles like *Lord Johnnie*, *Sir Rogue*, *The Highland Hawk*, and *His Majesty's Highlanders*. He wrote about loners and rebels and heroes who went their own way. He never lost his knack for a yarn, and toward the end of his life recalled his pulp days by binding up in leather some of his early stories. On the spine of these self-published volumes, in gilt, are the words: "LESLIE WHITE, DETECTIVE, WRITER."

Leslie White came to L.A. and managed to get away. Dave Clark was born here and never escaped. The stories of both men are emblematic of the city and the fates that touch human aspiration. The one man speaks of hope and luck, the other portrays doom. White worked with the D.A.'s office for a little more than two years, an action-packed period that was never repeated in his life. The events he witnessed neither tortured nor twisted him; rather they changed him and allowed him to grow. Dave Clark, meanwhile, was drawn in deep and became a noir movie before the genre existed; his real-life story, an intense drama of failed promise, seems predictive. He lived for the moment and was killed by his past.

Dave Clark got away with things for years, while a moral and spiritual bleakness slowly possessed him. He didn't look well when he walked into court for that last time, to face the charge of murdering Rose "Toots" Blair. He looked like a shadow of his former self, a broken man, his characteristic swagger that had bordered on arrogance reduced to an apologetic shuffle, his gorgeous clothes replaced by an ill-fitting sportscoat. But reporters noted how he regained himself as proceedings got under way. His back straightened, he drew himself upright, and he changed his plea to "guilty" with composure and dignity. Trials were Dave Clark's stage, theaters where he'd known triumph. Like L.A. itself, even when he was howling inside, he never quite lost his glamor.

31

A Personal Note

On a furnace-hot day late in October 2007, when birds were catching flame in the air above the fires that had been burning for days in Malibu, when houses were exploding and vanishing into ash and the smoke drifting across the city had turned the sun smoggy and yellow, I saw a man waiting for a bus on Ocean Park Boulevard turn his body sideways so he could step into the narrow slot of shadow thrown by a telegraph pole. It was one of those moments when I thought: How can people live here, so close to the edge? More to the point, I thought: Why do I live here, in a place that can be so hellish?

Long before I first came to Los Angeles, or ever dreamed that I would, when I was a teenager in the north of England, I stumbled upon the novels of Raymond Chandler, green-spined Penguins, in a local bookstore. I can't remember which I read first, *The Big Sleep* or *Farewell, My Lovely*. At first, like most readers, I fell in love with the verve of Chandler's language, the show-stopping one-liners. "She was a blonde," said Marlowe, "a blonde to make a bishop kick a hole in a stained glass window." Of another woman, less fortunate in appearance, Marlowe observed: "She was as cute as a washtub." I enjoyed Marlowe himself—the romantic loner, the sad knight with a .38 who treated rich and poor, powerful and weak, with the same cynical and self-protecting detachment. He knew the world but couldn't be bought. He solved the murders even if he missed bringing to justice the bad guy, or more usually, the *very* bad woman who tried to sit in his lap while he was standing up, or gave him a smile he could feel in his hip pocket.

Even then I realized that in Chandler's writing something more than bullets and dames was going on. Marlowe's heroism was noble yet careworn and sad. "I brushed my hair and looked at the gray in it. There was getting to be plenty of gray in it. The face under the hair had a sick look. I didn't like the face at all." And here was Marlowe at night, heading into one of the Santa Monica canyons. "There was loneliness and the smell of kelp and the smell of wild sage from the hills. A yellow window hung here and there, all by itself, like the last orange. Cars passed, spraying the pavement with cold white light, then growled off into the darkness again. Wisps of fog chased the stars down the sky."

This wasn't just action writing. Marlowe lived in a beautiful world that had gone wrong, a paradise that would never be restored and in whose existence he had long since ceased to believe. He lived in Los Angeles.

———

I first came to L.A. in the early 1980s, just before the Olympics were staged here for the second time, when Mayor Tom Bradley claimed that L.A. was becoming "world class." On the freeways it was still sometimes possible, as the grumpy father insists in the movie *Clueless*, to get from "anywhere to anywhere in twenty minutes." The city welcomed me with its polyglot dazzle; people I met seemed energized and friendly, up for "it"—meaning enthusiasm, change, openness, everything that London, where I was then living, no longer represented for me. In the years that followed I returned to L.A. again and again—for work, for romance, for vacations, for whatever reason I could invent— until finally in 1991 I shattered my English life for good and came to live here, permanently I sometimes fear, planning a six-month stay that has turned into seventeen years. Something happened. The city took hold.

In the beginning my wife and I rented an apartment, part of a large Spanish villa that had been built by Cecil B. DeMille in the 1920s. It featured floors of gleaming oak, high timbered ceilings, baronial fireplaces, and a mosaic-tiled fountain in the interior courtyard. On foggy autumn nights, with walnut and pine crackling in the grate, I felt a tingling connection with the city's romantic past. We'd rented a piece of the history that people in L.A. weren't supposed to concern themselves with. I could imagine that Marlowe himself might have visited this very building. I doubt that I'll ever live anywhere more beautiful.

It turned out that the building was two blocks away from Yucca and Wilcox, known as crack alley, one of the worst drug-dealing neighborhoods in the city—a fact the realtor had omitted to mention to two European greenhorns.

Thundering LAPD helicopters woke us at night and the spectral blue beams of their searchlights probed our bedroom. Then in April 1992, the Rodney King riots rolled to our doorstep and we watched looters trash and empty the local stores. We moved to Venice, only for the Northridge earthquake to shake the foundations of our 1921 bungalow, make its flimsy walls waft and wave, but somehow leave it standing. Our children were born here, on the sixteenth floor of the Santa Monica Hospital, delivered by an Armani-clad über-doctor who, while slipping into his scrubs, gazed out of the window and espied an apartment building that he owned, muttering: "I'm looking at my money." For months I reported on the LAPD for the *New York Times Magazine*, speeding around Rampart and South Central in the back of rattling black and whites. In MacArthur Park, beneath a tree that stank as though a hundred horses had pissed on it, a man died in front of my eyes. He had a blade in his hand and a bullet in his eye, prompting a watching cop to adopt a laconic pose and utter a line that perhaps did spring from the streets but had been recycled in a dozen movies and TV shows: "Guy brought a knife to a gunfight." It was a question of life imitating art imitating life, or maybe just life imitating art— this was L.A., after all.

The innocent eyes with which I once viewed the city put on dark glasses and I saw that to get "from anywhere to anywhere" might take a lot longer than twenty minutes— might, in fact, take a lifetime. It occurred to me that a modern version of Kafka's *The Castle* could feature a character, an English writer say, drawn to L.A. for what seem simple reasons, but who finds himself staying and staying and staying, unable to escape while the city eats his soul and he crumbles away. I was overstating the case, but in perceiving myself as lost and adrift in the city was conforming to what the historian Norman Klein calls a "noir imaginary," a ghost version of L.A. that can nonetheless control the patterns of real life that people weave for themselves. So much sun here, so much light, so much boredom and despair. Where had it come from, I wondered, this *anomie*—"a type of blight that answers none of the classical descriptions," said the great Austrian architect Richard Neutra, who came here in the late 1920s—and why did it belong to Los Angeles in particular? This book has been an attempt to explore that question.

In 1933, at the height of the Depression, the now forgotten writer Myron Brinnig, fresh to the city from Montana, closed his novel *The Flutter of an Eyelid* with an earthquake and a fantastic, perhaps prophetic, vision: "Los Angeles tobogganned with one continuous movement into the water, the shoreline going first, followed by the inland communities. The small pink and white blue and orange houses of the shore were blown like colored sands into the tempest." Brinnig seemed to convey that sliding into the Pacific and sinking without trace was an inevitable and desirable result for the city.

The young John Fante, meanwhile, recently arrived from Colorado, was living in a cheap hotel on Bunker Hill and working as a busboy while gathering material for *Wait Until the Spring, Bandini* and *Ask the Dust*, the two Depression-era novels that would make his reputation. Fante saw the "futile palm trees standing like dying prisoners" and the city boosters who, "in spite of all the evidence, whooped it up for the sunny south." He saw the "tens of thousands of vagrants" and "the old folk from Indiana and Iowa and Illinois, from

Boston and Kansas City and Des Moines—they sold their homes and their stores, and they came here by train and by automobile to the land of sunshine, to die in the sun, with just enough money to live until the sin killed them." At the same time, however, Fante found L.A. irresistible and wrote about the city in terms of jubilant sexual desire: "Los Angeles, give me some of you! Los Angeles come to me the way I came to you, my feet over your streets, you pretty town I loved so much, you sad flower in the sand, you pretty town."

Fires, earthquakes, floods, murders, the lofty palms that bend torturously back upon themselves as the gentle ocean beach surrenders to a pitiless Santa Ana: these are part of the local imagination. But they're not the whole story. Unthinking optimism and the blind, unreasonable belief that lives can be remade are forces that drew people to L.A. in the first place, and still do. It's the Great Gatsby of American cities, as historian Kevin Starr has said, magnifying dreams and expectations before it twists and perhaps trashes them; a mood disorder afflicts L.A. like a revolutionary dialectic, swinging through freedom at one end of the cycle to hysteria at the other.

I've tried to evoke the time when these aspects of the city's personality, embedded from early on, came into sudden definition, sharp against the brittle brightness. In the early 1930s innocence was swept away once and for all by a mature yet troubled duality. A personality was fixed, and a plethora of future scenarios would grow as if set in place like bad seeds in the Garden of Eden. The Manson murders could only have happened in Los Angeles, likewise the O. J. Simpson murders, and the Menendez brothers' murder of their parents, and the Night-Stalker murders, and the Phil Spector murder, and so on, and on. The actor Robert Blake, when accused of a murder that happened in his car in the San Fernando Valley, threw up his hands and pleaded that he hadn't been there. At the moment the shooting occurred he'd been heading back into the restaurant where he and the victim had just eaten, to collect a gun he'd left on the table. That was his *alibi*, and when asked about the oddity of this he shrugged, as if murder is merely the price to pay for a life based on ambition and fantasy.

Such cases, and the public glee that greets them, are psychic manifestations, just as the riots of 1965 and 1992 were angry social ones. For sure L.A. will always get great murders; the subconscious of the city demands them like box office. It's guaranteed, too, that these violent cul-de-sac dramas will be counterpointed by the SoCal flipside, playing out against some exhilarating soundtrack, such as the Beach Boys wanting "Fun, Fun, Fun." The Eagles exhort us with such bright brio to check into the dismal confines of the Hotel California. Los Angeles is never just light or dark; it's always both at the same time.

Sources

In researching the book I've conducted interviews and used archive material, trial transcripts, newspaper reports, and books to construct mosaics of the various incidents. When I refer to the *Times*, I mean the *Los Angeles Times*.

Chapter 1: The Mystery Is Announced

I've relied on reports from the *Los Angeles Illustrated Daily News*, generally referred to as simply the *Daily News*, for March 20, 1931, and later. Charlie Crawford's relationship with Kent Parrot is outlined by Tom Sitton in "The Boss Without a Machine: Kent K. Parrot and Los Angeles Politics in the 1920s" (*Southern California History*, Summer 1985). Matt Weinstock's quote is from his book *My L.A.* For information about him, and the history of the *Daily News* in general, I consulted the Matt Weinstock papers held by UCLA Special Collections. Robert Rosenstone's essay on "Manchester Boddy and the L.A. Daily News" (*California Historical Quarterly*, December 1970) was useful; and Rob Leicester Wagner's book *Red Ink, White Lies* is terrific on the L.A. Press and this period generally. The Leslie

White material comes from *Me, Detective;* the D. J. Waldie quote from a conversation with the author. The building figures are drawn from the Federal Writers Project Guide to Los Angeles.

Chapter 2: Dam Disaster

Background is from W. W. Robinson's *History of Ventura*, and *Me, Detective.* I consulted the Ventura City Directories at the Ventura County Museum, where I also examined the bound back copies of the *Santa Paula Chronicle* for the paper's stunning coverage of the St. Francis break. Charles Outland's *Man-Made Disaster* is still the best book on the subject, diligent local history with enormous depth. Marc Reisner's *Cadillac Desert* (the chapter titled "The Red Queen" deals with L.A. and water) was also very useful, likewise the books on William Mulholland by Margaret Leslie Davis and Catherine Mulholland. The "Joint Citizens' Report" on the disaster, in a typewritten document held by the Ventura County Museum, and Leslie White's photographs of the victims form part of that evidence. Bernie Isensee's panoramic photographs are also at the Ventura County Museum.

Chapter 3: A Hero Named Clark

U.S. Census records for 1910, 1920, and 1930 furnished background on Dave Clark's family. The U.S. National Archives provided details of Clark's Annapolis record, and the British National Archives at Kew hold his Royal Flying Corps record. The transcripts of his two trials, *People v. Dave Clark*, buried in the vaults of the Los Angeles County Hall of Records, also gave invaluable personal detail on Clark. Daniel Beecher's pamphlet about the District Attorney's office, essentially a self-boosting device commissioned by Buron Fitts (Beecher was one of Fitts's top deputies), gives great specifics on how things worked down at the Hall of Justice. For information on the Marco trials, I relied on reports from the *Daily News*, the *Los Angeles Examiner*, and the *Los Angeles Evening Express*, for the dates July 6, 1928, and following, and the trial transcripts at the Hall of Records.

Chapter 4: Angel City

White records his arrival in L.A. in *Me, Detective* and in his diaries, lodged at Boston University. Edmund Wilson's remarkable essay first appeared in *New Republic* (December 29, 1931) and was later collected in his book *American Earthquake*. Sarah Comstock's reflections on the city appeared in *Harper's* (May 1928). The Carey McWilliams material is drawn from *The Education of Carey McWilliams* and *Southern California Country: An Island on the Land*, still the best history of the period. Louis Adamic's *Laughing in the Jungle* records his own early impressions.

Chapter 5: The Gangster Goes Down

Here I relied on reports from the *Daily News*, the *Examiner*, the *Express*, and the *Times* for the days August 24, 1928, and following, as well as the trial transcript: *People v. Marco. The Leisure Architecture of Wayne McAllister* by Chris Nichols, a lovely book, details the history of the Agua Caliente resort.

Chapter 6: Oil, Law, and Scandal

The history of the Julian Pete was first told by local reporter and civic activist Guy Finney in *The Great Los Angeles Bubble*, published soon after the event and still invaluable. A few years later Lorin Baker published *That Imperiled Freedom*, an early example of conspiracy theory run amok, from which one gleans how far and wide the scandal did indeed spread. Jules Tygiel's *The Great Los Angeles Swindle* is the definitive study, dense and richly informative—one of the key books on the era. Upton Sinclair's *Oil!* gives a superb on-the-ground sense of the oil craze, a feeling captured best of all in Albert Atwood's pieces for the *Saturday Evening Post*, titled "Money from Everywhere" (*Saturday Evening Post*, May 12, 1923), "When the Oil Flood Is On" (*Saturday Evening Post*, July 7, 1923), and "Mad from Oil" (*Saturday Evening Post*, July 14, 1923).

Chapter 7: Our Detective Learns the Ropes

White's accounts—in his diaries and memoir—were again useful for background on Jake Berman, Tygiel, and Finney; likewise the *Times* and *Examiner* coverage.

Chapter 8: Shots in the Night

The first two-thirds of the story of E. L. Doheny is wonderfully told by journalist James C. Young in a long biographical study entitled "Doheny's Napoleonic Career" (*New York Times*, February 17, 1924). The biographies by Margaret Leslie Davis (now the standard) and Dan La Botz (more abrasive) were very useful here, as were Roger Ansell's book and the obituaries that appeared in the *New York Times* and the *Los Angeles Times* (September 9 and 10, 1935). The story of Teapot Dome is excellently told in the books by Burl Noggle, and more recently by Laton McCartney. Frederick Lewis Allen's classic *Only Yesterday* is great on the oil scandals and gives remarkable period flavor.

Chapter 9: Beverly Hills C.S.I.

White's memoir and his diaries were invaluable again here. The profile of Lucien Wheeler that appeared in the *Los Angeles Times* (May 23, 1911) is great. To study the coverage of the Doheny murder/suicide that appeared in the *Times*, the *Examiner*, the *Express*, and the *Daily News* in the days immediately following the tragedy is to be enthralled. It's like stepping into Agatha Christie, but with motives and a blunt use of power that were beyond her ken. For information on the fascinating life of Miriam Lerner, I started with Hurewitz's *Bohemian Los Angeles* and Lionel Rolfe's *Literary L.A.*

Chapter 10: Cover-Up

I relied on White's accounts as well as the *Times* and *Examiner* reports for the two days after the killings—page after page of coverage. Guy Finney and Jules Tygiel are good in their different ways on Buron Fitts, who painted handsome portraits of himself in *Who's Who in L.A.* (1928, 1929, 1930). In his autobiography Cecil B. DeMille tells the story of how Doheny tried to recruit him as, in effect, a publicist—as if Bill Gates were to try to hire Steven Spielberg to make a biopic.

Chapter 11: Good Time Charlie

The Ned Doheny funeral received novelistic coverage in the *Examiner*, the *Times*, the *News*. The history of the brilliantly named Wellborn, Wellborn & Wellborn is recorded in W. W. Robinson's *Lawyers of Los Angeles*. Robinson, himself an attorney, wrote many books of excellent local history. The report on the LAPD for 1924, commissioned by August Vollmer during his brief tenureship, gives background and interviews. Beverly Davis told her story in the riveting memoir *Call House Madam*.

Chapter 12: Systems Under Siege

Good additional information on Lucien Wheeler came from the F.B.I. and White's diaries. Detail on the Jacobson case is from the *Times* and the *Examiner*. Edmund Wilson is excellent on Bob Shuler.

Chapter 13: Reach for a Typewriter

Alva Johnston's *Saturday Evening Post* profile of Erle Stanley

Gardner (*Saturday Evening Post*, October 5, 12, and 19, 1946) was very useful. The books by William Nolan and Ron Goulart are good on the history of *Black Mask* and the pulps. White's first story, "Phoney Evidence," appeared in *Dragnet* (February 8, 1930).

Chapter 14: Raymond Chandler—Oil Man!

I've drawn on Raymond Chandler's marvelous letters, the Chandler papers held by UCLA Special Collections, and material concerning Joseph Dabney and the Dabney Oil Syndicate at the California Institute of Technology. There's a lot of great writing about Chandler. Frank MacShane's biography still remains the standard, and Judith Freeman's recent book, though much more personal in approach, is a beautiful book. Philip Durham's early study weaves in a lot of original Chandler material.

Chapter 15: Entrapment of a News Hound

Morris Lavine's daughter still runs the law firm that bears his name in Los Angeles. She gave me great background on Lavine and the "melee" concerning the $75,000. The rest of this chapter draws largely on White's various accounts.

Chapter 16: Running with the Foxes

The fallout from the lawsuit brought by Joseph Dabney and others is thoroughly charted in the *L.A. Times.* White recorded his version of the Crawford trial. The trial of Edward L. Doheny was a nationwide event. The *New York Times* colorfully evoked the courtroom scene.

Chapter 17: Zig-Zags of Graft

Buron Fitts released details of Clark's promotion to the *Times.* The *New York Times* obituary gave background on James T. Malone and his family. Nancy Clark's granddaughter gave me an interview—one of those moments when history seemed to reach forward and touch the writer. Herbert Asbury's writings on Chicago are from his book *Gem of the Prairie*. White's story of his trip to Chicago is enthralling. For Charlie Crawford's sudden finding of God: the *Times*, the *Examiner*, the *News*, the *Express* all covered this event with glee.

Chapter 18: Red Hot Bow

Guy Finney's quote is from his muckraking book *Angel City in Turmoil*. For Clara Bow (great fun to write about), I looked to Budd Schulberg, David Stenn's excellent biography of Bow, F. Scott Fitzgerald, David Thomson, and books by Elizabeth Kendall and Jeanine Basinger. Background to the DeVoe/Bow trial is from the *Times* and the *Examiner*. The James Richardson story is recorded in his autobiography *For the Life of Me*. Great background on W. I. Gilbert, the famed attorney, is to be found in Robinson's *Lawyers of Los Angeles*.

Chapter 19: The Gutting of Clara

Details of Dave Clark's various trips to Agua Caliente emerged later, at his own trial. *People v. DeVoe* received exhaustive and colorful coverage in all the L.A. papers for the days following January 12, 1931. Budd Schulberg is incisive on how his father ruthlessly shrugged off the unwanted baggage that Bow had become.

Chapter 20: Hard Times in Lotus-Land

The *Times* and the *Examiner* recorded the premiere of *City Lights*. Charlie Chaplin's autobiography is excellent here, likewise Charles Maland's British Film Institute study. Dorothy Comingore gave her interview to Studs Terkel—it's in his book *Hard Times*. Gene Coughlin writes about meeting Einstein in his memoir—it's funny stuff. The statements about the Depression, and the apparent absence thereof, that were habitually made in the *Times* throughout the early 1930s strike us now as an extreme example of the willful sticking of the corporate head in very soggy sand. Leslie White's son, Skip, remembers how his father told him stories of his L.A. experiences at this time—the almost comical gangland adventures that could have so easily resulted in death.

Chapter 21: Double Death on Sunet

In writing about the deaths of Charlie Crawford and Herbert Spencer, and the subsequent trials of Dave Clark, I constructed a detailed timeline from the trial transcripts of *People v. David Harris Clark* and from all the newspaper coverage I could lay my hands on (about three thousand pages in all) from the *Times*, the *Examiner*, the *Express*, and the *Daily News*. Gene Coughlin, lured back to the *News* by owner Manchester Boddy, wrote wonderfully about these events.

Chapter 22: The Ballad of Dave Clark

Robinson's *Lawyers of Los Angeles* has good detail on prosecutor Joe Ford. Geoffrey Cowan's *"People v. Clarence Darrow"* discussed Ford's earlier career and his involvement in the jury-tampering prosecutions of Clarence Darrow following the bombing of the *Times* building in 1910.

Chapter 23: They Can Hang You

Here I relied on the trial transcript and my newspaper timeline. Interestingly, each of the major papers had, along with their chief reporters (like Coughlin), another reporter who sat in court and made a transcript of what was said during the most important moments of testimony. Human accuracy being what it is, these supposedly exact records differ in terms of nuance and how dialogue is recorded.

There's no real reason to suppose that the court stenographer was necessarily more accurate than these newspaper professionals—but when a discrepancy appears glaring, I've gone with the dialogue as in the trial transcript.

Chapter 24: Telling It All

Bob Shuler's *The Strange Death of Charlie Crawford* is, as they say in the antiquarian trade, "a tough book"—in other words very difficult to find. UCLA's copy has been stolen, likewise that belonging to USC. The Los Angeles Public Library's copy was destroyed in a fire. I consulted the one at the California State Library in Sacramento.

Chapter 25: Verdicts

Again, I've relied here on the trial transcripts and the timeline I made from the press coverage.

Chapter 26: A Hooker's Tale

Much here is drawn from White's diaries and *Me, Detective.* The Love Mart trial received extensive coverage in the *Times*, the *Examiner*, and the other papers. "Brick" Garrigues's swashbuckling pamphlet "So They Indicted Fitts!" was also useful here. George Creel's piece "Unholy City" appeared in *Collier's* (September 2, 1939).

Chapter 27: Music of the City

I first came across the phrase "a bright and guilty place" in *The Cinema of Orson Welles*, a 1961 book by Peter Bogdanovich. I was lucky enough to meet Welles in London back in 1983. When asked about Los Angeles, he merely roared with laughter. More of Leslie White's writing deserves to find its way back into print. Copies of *Me, Detective* are tough to find, and expensive.

Chapter 28: Black Mask Merry-Go-Round

This chapter is indebted to the Chandler sources detailed above. To the best of my knowledge, nobody has ever before spotted the connection between his early story "Spanish Blood" and the Spencer/Crawford killings. In his essay "Cracking the Cassidy Case" (a Chandler fictional case), Robert Moss drew the parallel between *The High Window* and the Doheny affair. The history of *Black Mask* is well recorded by both William F. Nolan and Otto Penzler. Horace McCoy's papers are at UCLA.

Chapter 29: Sad Song

That Dave Clark's wanderings and misbehavings should continue to be the subject of reportage not only in Los Angeles but in New York, too, is a mark of the huge impact those trials made in 1931. His end is haunting, and Nancy Clark's descendants attest that she loved him to the end.

Chapter 30: Lives Go On

In tracing the future histories of my characters, I relied on interviews, newspaper obituaries, and the mentioned biographical sources. The surface of Los Angeles evolves by the moment, and there is something in the flatness of the customary daytime light that dissuades the viewer from contemplating the city's past. But it's there, if you look long enough.

Chapter 31: A Personal Note

Bill Buford, back in the days when he was editing *Granta*, called me when the Rodney King riots kicked off and demanded that I hit the streets and do some reporting. I suggested to him that he wanted me to get myself killed. Bill paused before replying: "No. Injured would be good." The piece I wrote prompted Kyle Crichton, then an editor on the *New York Times Magazine*, to ask me to write about the LAPD and whether, in the wake of everything that had happened, the department could be fixed. A simple magazine assignment turned into months of work and a 40,000-word first draft delivering a simple enough answer: probably not. The photographer, Joe Rodriguez, and I became so obsessed that we just disappeared into the story. We got to know the guys at the Rampart precinct so well we were simply showing up at the bunker-like car park and jumping in the back of squad cars. For the public relations department of the LAPD, this was no doubt a nightmare, but for Joe and me it was a transformative eye-opener. We saw bad cops, dumb cops, violent cops, and great cops too. The city came alive for me, and the story, which appeared on the cover of the *New York Times Magazine*, prompted an ACLU investigation. It was David Ulin who switched me on to Myron Brinnig's extraordinary novel in which, at a moment of ultimate climax, Los Angeles simply slides into the Pacific. It probably won't happen, but then in L.A. you never can tell.

Bibliography

Adamic, Louis. *Laughing in the Jungle.* New York: Harper, 1932.

Adamic, Louis. *My America.* New York: Harper, 1938.

Allen, Frederick Lewis. *Only Yesterday.* New York: Harper, 1931.

Ansell, Martin R. *Oil Baron of the Southwest.* Columbus: Ohio State University Press, 1998.

Asbury, Herbert. *Gem of the Prairie.* New York: Knopf, 1940.

Baker, Carlos. *Ernest Hemingway.* New York: Scribner, 1969.

Baker, Lorin L. *That Imperiled Freedom.* Los Angeles: Graphic Press, 1932.

Banham, Reyner. *Los Angeles: The Architecture of Four Ecologies.* New York: Harper, 1971.

Basinger, Jeanine. *Silent Stars.* New York: Knopf, 1999.

Beecher, Daniel. *A Study of the Office and Problems of the District Attorney of the County of Los Angeles.* Los Angeles: Law Library of L.A. County, 1931.

Bessie, Simon Michael. *Jazz Journalism.* New York: Dutton, 1938.

Birmingham, Stephen. *California Rich.* New York: Simon and Schuster, 1980.

Bogdanovich, Peter. *The Cinema of Orson Welles.* New York:

Museum of Modern Art, 1961.

Bonelli, William G. *Billion Dollar Blackjack.* Beverly Hills: Civic Research Press, 1954.

Brooks, Louise. *Lulu in Hollywood.* New York: Knopf, 1982.

Brownlow, Kevin. *The Parade's Gone By.* New York: Knopf, 1968.

Caughey, John, and Laree Caughey, eds. *Los Angeles— Biography of a City.* Berkeley: University of California Press, 1977.

Chaplin, Charles. *My Autobiography.* London: The Bodley Head, 1964.

Cooper, Stephen. *Full of Life: A Biography of John Fante.* New York: North Point, 2000.

Coughlin, Gene. *How to Be One Yourself.* New York: A. S. Barnes, 1961.

Davis, Beverly, as told to Serge G. Wolsey. *Call House Madam.* San Francisco and New York: Martin Tudordale, 1954.

Davis, Margaret Leslie. *Dark Side of Fortune: Triumph and Scandal in the Life of Oil Tycoon Edward L. Doheny.* Berkeley: University of California Press, 1998.

———. *Rivers in the Desert: William Mulholland and the Inventing of Los Angeles.* New York: HarperCollins, 1993.

Davis, Mike. *City of Quartz.* London, New York: Verso, 1990.

DeMille, Cecil B. *The Autobiography of Cecil B. DeMille.* New Jersey: Prentice Hall, 1959.

Domanick, Joe. *To Protect and to Serve.* New York: Pocket Books, 1994.

Durham, Philip. *Down These Mean Streets a Man Must Go: Raymond Chandler's Knight.* Chapel Hill: University of North Carolina Press, 1963.

Federal Writers Project. *The WPA Guide to California.* Introduction by Federal Writers Project. *The WPA Guide to Los Angeles.* New York: Hastings House, 1941.

Finney, Guy. *Angel City in Turmoil.* Los Angeles: American Press, 1945.

———. *The Great Los Angeles Bubble.* Los Angeles: Forbes, 1929.

Freeman, Judith. *The Long Embrace*. New York: Pantheon, 2007.

Friedrich, Otto. *City of Nets*. New York: Harper & Row, 1986.

Gardiner, Dorothy, and Kathrine Sorley Walker. *Raymond Chandler Speaking*. Boston: Houghton Mifflin, 1962.

Garrigues, Charles Harris. *So They Indicted Fitts!* Los Angeles: C. H. Garrigues, 1936.

———. *You're Paying for It! A Guide to Graft*. New York: Funk & Wagnalls, 1936.

Garrigues, George L. *He Usually Lived with a Female: The Story of California Newspaperman Charles Harris (Brick) Garrigues*. Austin, Texas: Quail Creek Press, 2006.

Gebhard, David, and Harriette Von Breton. *L.A. in the Thirties: 1931–1941*. Salt Lake City: Peregrine Smith, 1975.

Giesler, Jerry. *The Jerry Giesler Story*. New York: Simon and Schuster, 1960.

Gottlieb, Robert, and Irene Wolt. *Thinking Big: The Story of the Los Angeles Times*. New York: Putnam, 1977.

Goulart, Ron. *Cheap Thrills: An Informal History of the Pulp Magazines*. New York: Arlington House, 1972.

Gregory, James N. *American Exodus: Dust Bowl Migration*. New York: Oxford University Press, 1989.

Gross, Miriam, ed. *The World of Raymond Chandler*. New York: A & W Publishers, 1977.

Gwendolyn Wright. *Building the Dream: A Social History of Housing in America*. New York: Pantheon, 1984.

Hecht, Ben. *A Child of the Century*. New York: Donald I. Fine, 1985.

Henstell, Bruce. *Sunshine and Wealth*. San Francisco: Chronicle, 1984.

Hiney, Tom. *Raymond Chandler*. New York: Atlantic Monthly Press, 1997.

Hiney, Tom, and Frank MacShane, eds. *The Raymond Chandler Papers*. New York: Atlantic Monthly Press, 2000.

Hoopes, Roy. *Cain*. New York: Holt Rinehart Winston, 1982.

Horne, Gerald. *Class Struggle in Hollywood, 1930–1950*. Austin: University of Texas Press, 2001.

Hundley, Norris. *The Great Thirst*. Berkeley: University of California Press, 1992.

Hurewitz, Daniel. *Bohemian Los Angeles and the Making of Modern Politics*. Berkeley: University of California Press, 2008.

Jennings, Dean. *We Only Kill Each Other*. New York: Prentice Hall, 1967.

Johnson, Diane. *Dashiell Hammett*. New York: Random House, 1983.

Kahrl, William L. *Water and Power*. Berkeley: University of California Press, 1982.

Kaplan, Justin. *Lincoln Steffens*. New York: Simon & Schuster, 1974.

Kendall, Elizabeth. *The Runaway Bride*. New York: Knopf, 1990.

Klein, Norman. *The History of Forgetting*. London, New York: Verso, 1997.

La Botz, Dan. *Edward L. Doheny*. New York: Praeger, 1991.

Lambert, Gavin. *The Dangerous Edge*. New York: Grossman/Viking, 1976.

Layman, Richard, ed. with Julie M. Rivett. *Selected Letters of Dashiell Hammett, 1921–1960*. New York: Counterpoint, 2001.

Layman, Richard. *Shadow Man: The Life of Dashiell Hammett*. New York: Harcourt, Brace, 1981.

MacShane, Frank, ed. *Selected Letters of Raymond Chandler*. New York: Columbia University Press, 1981.

MacShane, Frank. *The Life of Raymond Chandler*. New York: Dutton, 1976.

McCann, Sean. *Gumshoe America*. Durham, N.C.: Duke University Press, 2000.

McCartney, Laton. *The Teapot Dome Scandal*. New York: Random House, 2008.

McDougal, Dennis. *Privileged Son: Otis Chandler and the Rise and Fall of the L.A. Times Dynasty*. Cambridge, Mass: Perseus, 2001.

McWilliams, Carey. *The Education of Carey McWilliams*. New

York: Simon and Schuster, 1979.

———. *Louis Adamic & Shadow America*. Los Angeles: Whipple, 1935.

———. *Southern California: An Island on the Land*. Salt Lake City: Peregrine Smith, 1973.

Maland, Charles. *City Lights*. London: British Film Institute, 2007.

Messick, Hank. *The Beauties & the Beasts*. New York: McKay, 1973.

Moore, Charles, Peter Becker, and Regula Campbell. *Los Angeles: The City Observed*. New York: Vintage, 1984.

Moss, Robert, ed. *Raymond Chandler: A Literary Reference*. New York: Carroll & Graf, 2003.

Mulholland, Catherine. *William Mulholland and the Rise of Los Angeles*. Berkeley: University of California, 2000.

Nichols, Chris. *The Leisure Architecture of Wayne McAllister*. Salt Lake City: Gibbs Smith, 2007.

Noggle, Burl. *Teapot Dome: Oil and Politics in the 1920s*. Baton Rouge: Louisiana State University Press, 1962.

Nolan, William F. *The Black Mask Boys*. New York: Morrow, 1985.

O'Brien, Geoffrey. *Hardboiled America*. New York: Da Capo, 1997.

Outland, Charles. *Man-Made Disaster: The Story of the St. Francis Dam*. Spokane, Wash.: A. H. Clark, 2002.

Parrish, Michael. *For the People*. Los Angeles: Angel City Press, 2001.

Pinkerton, Roy. *The County Star: My Buena Ventura*. Ventura, Calif.: Pinkerton, 1962.

Pitt, Leonard, and Dale Pitt. *Los Angeles A to Z*. Berkeley: University of California Press, 1997.

Rappleye, Charles, and Ed Becker. *All American Mafioso: The Johnny Roselli Story*. New York: Doubleday, 1991.

Reisner, Marc. *Cadillac Desert*. New York: Viking, 1986.

Robinson, W. W. *Lawyers of Los Angeles*. Los Angeles Bar Association, Los Angeles, 1959.

Reid, Ed, and Ovid Demaris. *The Green Felt Jungle*. New York:

Pocket Books, 1964.

Rice, Craig. *Los Angeles Murders*. New York: Duell, Sloan and Pearce, 1947.

Richardson, James. *For the Life of Me*. New York: Putnam, 1954.

Robinson, W. W. *The Story of Ventura County*. Los Angeles: Title Insurance and Trust Company, 1955.

Rolfe, Lionel. *Literary L.A.* Los Angeles: California Classic Books, 2002.

Russo, Gus. *Supermob*. New York: Bloomsbury, 2006.

St. Johns, Adela Rogers. *Final Verdict*. New York: Doubleday, 1962.

———. *The Honeycomb*. New York: Doubleday, 1969.

Sante, Luc. *New York Noir*. New York: Rizzoli International Publications, 1999.

Sante, Luc, and others. *Unknown Weegee*. New York: ICP/Steidl, 2006.

Schulberg, Budd. *Moving Pictures: Memories of a Hollywood Prince*. New York: Stein and Day, 1981.

Server, Lee, and others. *The Big Book of Noir*. New York: Carroll & Graf, 1998.

Server, Lee. *Encyclopedia of Pulp Fiction Writers*. New York: Facts on File, 2002.

Shippey, Lee. *The Luckiest Man Alive*. Los Angeles: Westernlore Press, 1959.

Sitton, Tom. *Los Angeles Transformed*. Albuquerque: University of New Mexico Press, 2005.

Starr, Kevin. *Endangered Dreams: The Great Depression in California*. New York: Oxford University Press, 1996.

———. *Material Dreams: Southern California Through the 1920s*. New York: Oxford University Press, 1990.

Steffens, Lincoln. *The Autobiography of Lincoln Steffens*. New York: Harcourt, Brace, 1931.

———. *The Shame of the Cities*. New York: Hill and Wang, 1992.

Stenn, David. *Clara Bow: Runnin' Wild*. New York: Doubleday, 1988.

Stoker, Charles. *Thicker'n Thieves*. Santa Monica, Calif.: Sidereal, 1951.

Terkel, Studs. *Hard Times*. New York: Pantheon, 1970.

Thomson, David. *The Big Sleep*. London: British Film Institute, 1997.

———. *In Nevada*. New York: Knopf, 1999.

———. *A New Biographical Dictionary of Film*. New York: Knopf, 2002.

Trope, Michael Lance. *Once upon a Time in Los Angeles: The Trials of Earl Rogers*. Spokane, Wash.: Arthur H. Clark, 2001.

Tygiel, Jules. *The Great Los Angeles Swindle*. New York: Oxford University Press, 1994.

Tyler, Gus. *Organized Crime in America*. Ann Arbor: University of Michigan Press, 1962.

Ulin, David, ed. *Writing Los Angeles*. New York: Library of America, 2002.

Vollmer, August. *Law Enforcement in Los Angeles: A Report on the LAPD*. Los Angeles: LAPD, 1924; reprinted in New York: Arno Press, 1974.

Wagner, Rob Leicester. *Red Ink, White Lies*. Upland, Calif.: Dragon-flyer Press, 2000.

Weinstock, Matt. *My L.A.* New York: Current Books, 1947.

Werner, M. R., and John Starr. *Teapot Dome*. New York: Viking, 1959.

White, Leslie. *Me, Detective*. New York: Harcourt, Brace, 1936.

Wilkman, Jon, and Nancy Wilkman. *Picturing Los Angeles*. Layton, Utah: Gibbs Smith, 2006.

Wilson, Edmund. *The American Earthquake*. Garden City, N.Y.: Doubleday, 1958.

Wilson, Robert, ed. *The Film Criticism of Otis Ferguson*. Philadelphia: Temple University Press, 1971.

Wolf, Marvin J., and Katherine Mader. *Fallen Angels: Chronicles of L.A. Crime and Mystery*. New York: Facts on File, 1986.

Wyatt, Will. *The Secret of the Sierra Madre: The Man Who Was B. Traven*. New York: Doubleday, 1980.